Jane Austen and the Province of Womanhood

Jane Austen and the Province of Womanhood

ALISON G. SULLOWAY

upp

University of Pennsylvania Press • Philadelphia

Printed in the United States of America

Library of Congress Cataloging-in-Publication Data

Sulloway, Alison G.
Jane Austen and the province of womanhood / Alison G. Sulloway.
p. cm.
Bibliography: p.
Includes index.
ISBN 0-8122-1338-6
1. Austen, Jane, 1775–1817—Criticism and interpretation. 2. Satire, English—History and criticism. 3. Sex role in literature. 4. Women in literature. I. Title.
PR4037.S85 1989
823′.7—dc19 88-38889
CIP

First paperback printing 1990.

To my sister, Georgina G. Martin,
and to my colleagues
Mary C. Carras, Anthony Colaianne, Ruth Salvaggio, and
Jane Vargo,
and above all
to the mother of this book,
my acquisitions editor, Patricia Smith

Contents

Abbreviations

E	*Emma*
Facts and Problems	*Jane Austen: Facts and Problems*, R. W. Chapman, ed. (London: Oxford University Press, 1948; rpt. 1970)
Letters	*Jane Austen's Letters to her Sister Cassandra and Others*
LL	*Jane Austen: Her Life and Letters, a Family Record*, William Austen-Leigh Richard Arthur Austen-Leigh, 2nd ed. (New York: Russell & Russell, 1965)
Memoir	*Memoir of Jane Austen by her Nephew James Edward Austen-Leigh* (London: Oxford University Press, 1926; rpt. 1967)
Monaghan	*Jane Austen in a Social Context*, David Monaghan, ed. (Totowa, N.J.: Barnes & Noble, 1981)
MP	*Mansfield Park*

MW	*Minor Works*
My Aunt	*My Aunt, Jane Austen: A Memoir*, Caroline Austen (London: Spottiswoode, Ballantyne, 1952)
NA	*Northanger Abbey*
Only a Novel	*Only a Novel: The Double Life of Jane Austen*, Jane Aiken Hodge (New York: Coward, McCann & Geoghegan, 1972)
P	*Persuasion*
PP	*Pride and Prejudice*
SS	*Sense and Sensibility*

Primary Sources

Letters: *Jane Austen's Letters to her Sister Cassandra and Others*, collected and edited by R. W. Chapman, 2nd ed. (London: Oxford University Press, 1969)

Minor Works: *The Works of Jane Austen*: Vol. VI, *Minor Works*, R. W. Chapman, ed. (London: Oxford University Press, 1954)

The Novels of Jane Austen, R. W. Chapman, ed., 5 vols., 3rd ed. (London: Oxford University Press, 1932–1934)

Preface and Acknowledgments

Jane Austen's satire is the product of two conflicting satirical sources. One source has its origin in classical and English neoclassical satire, to which Austen responded ambiguously, even while she zestfully acknowledged her debts to it. The other source exemplifies a satirical mode that as yet has no official name or terminology, nor does it yet appear in standard academic discussion of satire as one type among several. The first source is the satire of the insider, or of those who have been taught from birth that something intrinsic about themselves entitles them to struggle for the role of insider. The second source, for which Austen had far more precursors than literary history usually records, and which she helped to shape for future generations, is the satire of the outsider—those required by social myths or by received opinions deeply encrusted among insiders to remain for life in the outsider's marginal province.

The university model for the study of satire is descended almost entirely from Greek and Roman comedy and from those two dichotomous types, the genial Horatian and the irascible Juvenalian. In a dozen or so institutions of higher learning that I have recently investigated, or where I taught or studied, the material offered scholars studying this subgenre is almost entirely written by ancient or modern men, the courses are largely staffed by men, the secondary sources are written almost entirely by men, and the perspective is understandably predominantly male.

The two traditionally approved types of English and American satire originated largely in men who had access to a solid education, and who were expected to live successful public lives. Even Horace, the son of a freed slave, was probably better educated for his time than all but the most fortunate or rebellious Englishwomen until the period between the two great wars. For this reason, most practitioners of satire think of it as a male art,[1] and many students and faculty still harbor a vague suspicion, which Freud and Jung and their successors fostered, that it is not an altogether appropriate art for women. For instance, instructors will assign snippets from Fielding, Swift, Pope, Smollett, or Sterne to represent the great English age of satire, while ignoring Behn, Burney, Edgeworth, or Austen.

From a historical perspective, the privilege of writing satire has indeed customarily belonged to men—at least, as far as the records thought worth preserving can tell us. Those who resorted to satire often exploited it as one of many techniques to keep outsiders in a marginal place, when they were not engaged in a fierce struggle to validate their own right to a primary place with others of their type.

The group of outsiders to which Austen and other women satirists belong is a heterogeneous collection of the rejected and the devalued members of society. This group includes the poor, slaves, servants, foreigners, immigrants, the sick, the elderly, and various other peripheral types whose legal, social, or economic disenfranchisement has archetypally placed them among the acceptable ranks of satirical targets, rather than among the ranks of the successful attackers and counter-attackers. Yet when these outsiders resort to satire, as our fresh perspectives on literature and society now suggest, their satirical mode is quite rich and various. Whether it is fierce and vengeful, sly and cutting, or gentle and overtly accommodating, or whether it adopts all these types of rhetoric, and others, it originates in marginal places. One finds it among the terminally ill, in prisons, in concentration camps, on the gallows, in the back of the bus, in the underground press, over the back fence, in the women's pages, or in the servants' quarters. It always seeks its satirical voice under mild or fierce threats of retaliation, often under siege, and sometimes at very grave risk to its perpetrators. No wonder that from Mary Astell to Jane Austen and well beyond, women's satire is often anonymous, and no wonder that it is an anathema to totalitarian governments.

In a distinct yet covert way, Austen perceived the struggle of the satirists to rise out of the battle of the sexes. Just as male satire is understandably male-centered, and just as it assumes that men may vary tremendously in their talents and temperaments, their sins and their follies, and therefore their appropriate availability as satirical targets for each other, so women's satire is equally understandably centered in the experiences and the idiosyncratic predicaments of their sex. Women's satire usually includes vicious and ridiculous people of both sexes, all ages, and as many classes and professions as the satirists' experience permits, as Austen's writing does. Women satirists thus tend to pay other women the compliment of assuming that the female sex is as various as the male in its sensibilities, values, talents, and achievements, or lack of them, and therefore as varied as the male sex in its indictable sins and follies, which women satirists do not consider to be innate in their sex.

The Augustan wits tended to make women as an entire sex a target for their wit. The noun *women* was then all too often synonymous with nouns and adjectives such as "fools," "vain peacocks," "vapid chatterers," or creatures who were either "sly, wily, and seductive" or "cold and pretentiously studious," or who clung frantically to the very same males to whom they were predictably "inconstant." In Austen's *Persuasion*, Captain Harville casually hurls the conventional myth of "women's inconstancy" at the despondent Anne Elliot, who after eight years is still grieving over Frederick Wentworth, while she watches Frederick flirt with two women at once (*P*, 232–236).

Enlightenment and post-Enlightenment women were offered a satirical vision of themselves, which was itself an appropriate target for their own satire. When they were not publicly charged with innate intellectual and moral failures, they were accused of ugly and blasphemous attempts to educate themselves beyond their proper province and, even worse, with attempting to remedy conditions that were often considered neither unjust nor remediable. Although the male impulse to discipline the monstrous regimen of women has been with us almost since the first written records, typical male models of satire before and during Austen's life offered a communal vision of women as inconsequential lumps of clay, at best, or swarms of pestilential creatures, at worst.

The generic topics of eighteenth-century women satirists, such as Austen and her favorite fictional predecessors, Frances Burney and Maria Edgeworth, included not only the abusers of women and other underdogs but also the very patriarchal systems that granted men absolute legal and social power over them. Austen's satirical purposes may have been so oblique that they have not been recognized for close to two centuries, but when she satirized male privileges and female disenfranchisements, her purposes were as insurrectionary as those of Mary Wollstonecraft and Wollstonecraft's feminist colleagues of the 1790s and later. When the authorial voice in *Northanger Abbey* ironically insists that "the [male] Reviewers" write nothing but "common cant" about the fiction of such "geniuses" as Burney and Edgeworth, not only is she adopting a favorite phrase of her favorite Dr. Johnson for purposes that he would have condemned, but she is also offering a microcosmic judgment of the century's "common cant" about women in general. When she asks rhetorically, "Alas, if the heroine of one novel be not patronized by the heroine of another, from whom can she expect protection and regard?" she is ironically reminding women, as readers and writers alike, that they were constantly under attack; they "must not desert one another"; they "are an injured body." This barbed but playful counterattack upon the Augustan wits and the whole tribe of male conduct-book writers and unctuous woman-watchers is a classical example of feminine satire in a genial Horatian mood (*NA*, 37).

Austen and her fictional predecessors, Burney and Edgeworth, were shaped eventually by the French Revolution and the feminist revolt of the 1790s, which Gina Luria has brought to readers' attention with her 1974 reprints called *The Feminist Controversy in England 1788–1810*. There are almost a hundred volumes that constitute fresh evidence of a woman's movement—its passions, its satire—and the predictable backlash against it. Luria's reprints include conduct books for women written by radical women such as Wollstonecraft, and those written by the more moderate women who now faced the male wrath that the radicals had engendered. There are also the conduct books of Anglican churchmen and other orthodox males who represented the patriarchy in a form that they conceived to be more persuasive than the harsh or condescending caricatures of the Augustan wits and their followers.

This is the fertile controversial material that shaped the fiction of Jane Austen, a provincial Christian gentlewoman whose contempt for the overt and hidden ethical disjunctions at the heart of all satire politely but obsessively pierces destructive myths and assumptions about her own sex. It is a credit, both to her social and to her artistic discretion, that only now have a few readers begun to recognize the explosive qualities embedded in her fiction. To be sure, she now mediates the battle of the sexes all over the world, even for those readers who know nothing about the conduct-book literature. Yet most readers, professionally trained or otherwise, still ignore Austen's "commitment to a woman's point of view," because, as Leroy Smith suggests, in *Jane Austen and the Drama of Women*, they are still "unprepared to identify its source."[2] Although David Monaghan's collection of Austenian essays does identify that "woman's point of view" on almost every page of its various contributors' essays, the critical reception of this splendid anthology barely recognized its contribution to Austen, the proto-feminist. As an example of this point of view, Nina Auerbach's essay describes "the radical ambivalence which remains at the heart of Jane Austen's finished art," as Auerbach does in all her Austenian work. Leroy Smith associates Austen's "drama of woman's subjugation and depersonalization" as part of the " 'feminist' element" in Austen's novels, and "her main subjects" as "the abuse of the patriarchal system, not the transgressions of individuals." Tony Tanner describes the frequent silences of Austen's heroines, "sometimes from necessity, from suffering," or from "sheer lowliness of social or familial position." Monaghan, the editor, reluctantly admits that Austen "often appears to be closer to Mary Wollstonecraft" than to the male conduct-book writers whom she read. Yet the opening sentence of Monaghan's essay sets the tone for the anthology: "women can rarely have been held in lower esteem than they were at the end of the eighteenth century."[3] Half a decade later, Mary Evans's *Jane Austen and the State* addresses the "radicalism" in Austen's fiction, which quietly denounces the "greed and strength of the rich and powerful" members of a "self-serving patriarchy. . . . whose concerns are frequently legitimated as the common sense of the age."[4] These dozen or so authors and others of equal interests now represent an increasing body of Austenian scholars who recognize the principal source of Austen's satire and the grief and anger beneath it.

Because this book has undergone several drafts, I have accumulated many debts to foundations and individuals. I was the grateful recipient of a summer grant from The American Council of Learned Societies, so that I could cull a few great research libraries to see what they had on Austen as a post-Enlightenment novelist conscious of herself as a member of "an injured body" of people. In 1979, the National Endowment for the Humanities awarded me a year-long grant to collate my work with the fresh material that was beginning to emerge, little by little, on women as writers and as the subject of other women writers. I want here to offer Dr. Kathleen Mitchel, of the National Endowment for Humanities, my most ardent thanks for her kind reassurances during my labors on this book.

I wish also to acknowledge the generous support of innumerable librarians, both faculty and staff, at Virginia Polytechnic's Newman Library. When fresh materials on Austen as a woman-centered novelist were scarce, or later when they were less so, these librarians, from senior faculty to student shelvers, entered into my search for materials with a zest comparable to my own and a professionalism that requires respectful acknowledgment. Merely for instance, I need to thank Donald Kenney, head of Reference; Anita Malabranche; Dorothy MaCombs; Paul Metz; Alice Moody; Lynne Cochrane, head of Interlibrary Loan; M. K. Lane; and a particularly kind student shelver, Victor Dillard. With a team like this, scholars are only a librarian away from the great research centers or from that elusive information tucked away at one's home library.

Professors David Meredith and Henry Way of Cedar Crest College read my first draft with respectful yet scrutinizing eyes. Nancy Clausen had the rare gift of accepting my governing arguments and of functioning as the facilitator rather than as the destroyer of them. I have been immensely lucky with my three readers whom the University of Pennsylvania Press assigned to this book. Margaret Doody, Carolyn Heilbrun, and an anonymous reader disagreed only in manageable minutiae as to what should stay, what should go, and what should be added, but all three confirmed the legitimacy of my Austenian vision and assisted me beyond what I can describe in pruning, qualifying, enriching, and thus in justifying it. Professor Heilbrun's readership particularly touched me because it combined great kindness with the unsparing and specific advice that every complex book in progress requires.

I have also benefited from the readings of two young colleagues, Ruth Salvaggio and Jane Vargo, both of whom offered sophisticated advice and the sustained belief in this book that writers in isolation need. But my most profound debt should be offered here to Patricia Smith, my acquisitions editor at the University of Pennsylvania Press, whose tenacity on her authors' behalf and whose patience with them is exemplary. She is known for acquiring admirers as she acquires books, which improve accordingly. It is a healthy outcome of women's colleagueship that the original disciples become the mentors, or the daughters the mothers, and the young scholars and professionals assume the roles of wise and seasoned benevolences.

I am also grateful for permission to allude to my two published essays on Austen. Marilyn Gaul, then the editor of *The Wordsworth Circle*, gave me free permission to allude to my essay, "Emma Woodhouse and a *Vindication of the Rights of Woman*." Professor Rhoda Nathan was equally happy to have me paraphrase from my essay that I read at the Hofstra University Conference on nineteenth-century women writers, which examined well-known and little-known women writers from two continents, four centuries, and innumerable perspectives (fall 1981). This essay, "Jane Austen's Mediative Voice," was published in the conference *Proceedings*. Its title indicates where I place Austen in the 1790s battle of the sexes. She was too devout an Anglican and too astute a social observer of possibilities and impossibilities to have become a radical feminist. Yet she was too intelligent and too ironic an observer, even a ruthless observer, of social patterns that she considered destructive to family peace and to women's moral life, to have become the mere conduit for the *status quo*, which many readers still assume she is. And so her fiction mediates between the traditional forces of hostility and inertia toward women and the counterforces of radical disruption, without denying the tragic sources of that disruption.

Because Austen wrote as though hostile relationships between adults and children, rich and poor, socially established or obscure—that is, between the empowered and the disempowered—are paradigms for the feminine predicament, to say nothing of the human predicament, as indeed they are, she has now become a woman for all seasons. Even her conventional closures, sometimes so difficult to accept in modern women's terms, are themselves mute emblems of her own internal struggle with feminine conditions that she could neither change nor wholeheartedly respect, but that she could record in her novels with anger and yet with perfectly believable tenderness and affection. In these ways, as a sometime rebel and a sometime accommodator, reluctant or otherwise, she now speaks to us out of her local time and her feminine province, and in transcendent time and space.

Blacksburg, Virginia
June 1988

Part I

The Rights of Man and the Duties of Woman

1

"Pride" and "Prejudice" and the Compensatory Equation

I

One of the most urgent and haunting preoccupations that shaped Jane Austen's satire was the harsh and irrational treatment of women during the Age of Reason and its aftermath. The 1790s, when Austen began to write for publication, were years of upheaval and violence in France, and according to the historian, G. M. Trevelyan, "of repression of Reform and all discussion of Reform at home." The "repressive spirit of the times" provided material for women satirists: the repressions exemplified "a hardness of heart toward the victims of the Industrial Revolution,"—including women of all classes, although they were hardly ever mentioned in traditional histories—"and to the poor generally, as potential Jacobins. . . . Loyalist Associations were formed all over the country, usually headed by Churchmen against their local enemies, the Dissenting Reformers; these Associations organized opinion behind the government" in the pursuit of the most Draconian measures. Publishers, editors, "Non-conformist preachers," and "speculative persons of a propagandist disposition" were prosecuted and jailed, and in a few cases faced capital punishment before they were finally deported for high treason.[1]

The decade of the 1790s was characterized by a legacy of the Enlightenment, which for a brief few decades was almost as volatile as the international debates over "the Rights of Man." All over Europe, and especially in England, France, and Germany, pre-Revolutionary women had already begun to think that the injustices imposed upon women of all classes were as legitimate a subject for rational debate as the wrongs of any other disenfranchised groups. But when Austen began her mature work, champions of women's rights were considered as insurrectionary as those other restless reformers whom Trevelyan described. As a member of a clerical family, she was anxious to spare herself and her family any ugly notoriety, and so she adopted policies of thematic and rhetorical caution and hid behind anonymity of authorship. Even the possibilities of finding a publisher at all depended not only on what she said but how she said what she said.

Fanny Burney and Maria Edgeworth, whose novels Austen praises in *Northanger Abbey*, also faced this need for calculated ambiguity. And just as Austen does, they too obliquely addressed a problem peculiar to the Age of Reason, which equally distressed Catherine Macaulay, Mary Wollstonecraft, and Mary Hays, the most eloquent and theoretical of the 1790s feminists addressing women's predicament and its causes and cures. This particular version of women's oppression occurred in the form of a bizarre compensatory equation: the more "the Rights of Man" came in time to seem legitimate questions to some enlightened men, the more men of almost all persuasions demanded restrictions upon women even beyond the customary hardships. In this search for balance between freedom and order, the masculine craving for new and enlightened liberties under laws was ironically counterbalanced by a renewed and vehement public insistance upon woman's confinement in her limited province. In some unspecified way, woman's segregated domesticity was supposed to compensate for man's expanding universes and to forestall revolution both at home and overseas.

The social necessity—or the pathology—of this compensatory equation formed an extended debate between male and female theorists about women's nature, which flourished throughout the eighteenth century and most passionately during the 1790s. The implications of "the woman question," as it was often called, shape the plots, invigorate the satire, inform the emblems, and reverberate in the dialogues and the authorial voices throughout Austen's fiction. It is therefore very useful to look at some characteristic attitudes about women and their predicament, as well as Austen's responses to them.

As rationally educated women struggled by various means in public and private to be permitted to apply the fruits of the Enlightenment even marginally to themselves, a predictable hostility emerged toward women in general and women writers in particular, and they were subjected to fierce criticism by orthodox churchmen as well as laymen of all faiths and almost none. The vituperation that greeted the famous or infamous trio, Macaulay, Wollstonecraft, and Hays, was even more mean-spirited in the 1790s and afterward than that which had earlier attempted to discredit the achievements of Mary Astell's *Serious Proposal to the Ladies for the Advantage of their True and Greatest Interest*, after its publication in 1694 and throughout the reign of *The Spectator* and *The Tatler*. The popularity of Astell's incisive essay, as judged by its appearance in four editions over ten years, did nothing to grant it a fair reading or to protect Astell's reputation. The mindless drubbing that Astell received and the rage or the condescension that assaulted the works of Macaulay, Wollstonecraft, and Hays a century later, as well as the works of most writing women throughout the eighteenth century, represent one of the saddest and most unenlightened characteristics of an otherwise distinguished age.

The epithets that greeted Macaulay, Wollstonecraft, and Hays as feminist theorists about women's predicament were often directed at some unorthodox conduct: Macaulay's entire canon was later condemned because as a widow she married a man twenty-six years younger than she, which was particularly galling to the customary vision of the husband as father and tutor of his wife. Mary Hays was quite aware that Macaulay's unconventional marriage only provided an excuse to attach her theories: "A female historian by its singularity, could not fail to excite attention: she seemed to have stepped out of the province of her sex. . . . The author was attacked by petty and personal scurrilities. . . . Her talents and powers could not be denied; her beauty was therefore called into question." Boswell and others felt justified in calling any feminist a mere woman "whining about liberty,"[2] "a thing, ugly and petticoated, who seeks to 'ex-syllogize a God with cold-blooded Precision . . . and run Religion thro' with an Icicle,' "[3] or "a hyena in petticoats." Writing women were sneered at as imitative "philosophers," "Politicians," "Gallic fanciers," or French Revolutionaries, "Deists!" or women vaunting "the imperious mien," the legitimate target of the "genuine" male-poet's "genuine rage," "The Amazonian band," "the Unsex'd Females," sporters of "The bronze of impudence,"[4] and "the blasphemous band," and generically, "Wollstonecraftians."[5]

One of the fiercest pieces of misogyny, which nonetheless has characteristics to be found in most 1790s literature against women, emerged from the Reverend Richard Polwhele, who published a thirty-two-page diatribe with copious explanatory footnotes, which fulminated against any women whose writing betrayed them as "Wollstonecraftian" creatures because they dared to "vindicate *The Rights of womankind.*" He gloated over Wollstonecraft's love affairs, her marriage to Godwin late in her pregnancy, and, above all, her agonizing death in childbirth (Polwhele, "The Unsex'd Females," 15–16, 23–25, 28). His final malediction could not have been improved by any Dantean or Thomistic dismissal of sinners to an everlasting inferno: "I cannot but think, that the Hand of Providence is visible, in her life, her death and in [Godwin's] Memoirs themselves." Wollstonecraft was "let to follow her own imaginations" and "her heart's lusts" so "that the fallacy of her doctrines and the effect of an irreligious conduct, might be manifest to the world" (Polwhele, 29–30).

Polwhele exemplified an unnerving habit of discourse, which pragmatic philosophers from Bacon to John Stuart Mill repeatedly identified as slip-shod logic that was intellectually and morally dishonest. Polwhele would announce one questionable or outrageous premise as God's truth, and then unconsciously slide from that unverifiable premise to another equally unverifiable, and so on, creating a chain of myths, hopes, and suppositions, syntactically linked in an apparent logical procession, but in fact and in logic profoundly flawed. Austen was thoroughly familiar with this polemical process in men who wrote conduct books that described women's marginal capacities and functions, and it formed a significant part of her satire.

Not only did Polwhele assume that God had designed Wollstonecraft's misconduct as a warning to women of similar persuasions, and that her grim death, also designed by God, resulted from her treasonable ideas and conduct, but he also preached that Macaulay, Hays, and other "Wollstonecraftians" deserved an equally horrible death and eternal damnation as well. His arguments became even less logical and less like Christ's utterances when he claimed that "the distinction of sexes" is "so strongly marked" as to exemplify Wollstonecraft's death in archetypal ways: it "points out the destiny of women" (Polwhele, "The Unsex'd Females," 25). This assertion contains another lapse in logic: although a shocking number of women did die in childbirth,[6] including two and probably three of Austen's sisters-in-laws, nevertheless for Polwhele to describe maternal mortality as the potential destiny of all women was to destroy his priestly argument that Wollstonecraft's death was no more than she deserved.

One of the Wollstonecraftians' greatest crimes, according to Polwhele and other masculine advisors to women, was their "impudent" habit of practicing "philosophism," by which he meant that they adopted syllogisms and accretionary arguments and that they discussed the logical, theological, social, and scientific absurdities in women's predicament. Although he was sickened by any woman's capacity for abstract arguments, nonetheless he mocked Wollstonecraft as a lovesick creature who was ruled more by her feelings than her mind (Polwhele, 25). One need not deny Wollstonecraft's poor judgment, in the context of the double standard, and even in the context of her own intellectual standards of sturdy feminine independence, to see the frightened and defensive rage in Polwhele's diatribe.

Since each feminine attempt at reasonable legal and personal autonomy and reasonably civil treatment in the presses had been greeted with more and more mockery throughout the Age of Reason, it is not surprising that both radical and moderate feminists sometimes despaired of English justice and that they alluded to "the woman question" as "the man and woman question," and sometimes, in satirical desperation, as "the man question." Macaulay's *Letters on Education*, Wollstonecraft's *Vindication of the Rights of Woman*, and Hays's *Letters and Essays, Moral and Miscellaneous* and her *Appeal to the Men of Great Britain in Behalf of Women* all insisted that women's life-long custody to masculine requirements was neither divinely nor genetically ordained, but largely man-made. They saw, as their moderate feminist successors later saw, despite considerable theoretical differences, that women's predicament was in shocking disjunction with sophisticated men's delight in post-Renaissance empiricism and ever-increasing intellectual autonomy, which even the upheavals caused by the French Revolution could not entirely eradicate.

For feminists of all persuasions, the greatest paradox during and after the Age of Reason was the difficulty of reconciling themselves to the prevalent indecision as to whether "the female is included in the species," as the moderate feminist Priscilla Wakefield sadly described masculine difficulties.[7] In their conduct books for other women, radical and moderate feminists alike questioned whether this age could be called enlightened, if "half the human race" had been excluded from the fruits of a profound social evolution considered so beneficial to the other half. What was rational or enlightened, they asked, about a social climate that tempted so many masculine beneficiaries of the Enlightenment to reassert their ancient rights to the bodies, minds, and services of women? It was an unproven assumption that all women had been divinely robbed of the reasoning faculty, and it resulted not only in bad public policy but in private marital and parental disasters.

The radical feminists of Wollstonecraft's persuasion and their moderate successors all adopted two code-nouns, *pride* and *prejudice*, to describe in terse shorthand their rage and grief over the feminine predicament. *Pride* indicated the contemporary male's habit of boasting to women about his achievements, his privileges, and above all his divine right to dominate women. The noun *prejudice* encompassed masculine contempt for everything feminine, including not only the obvious sins and follies that many women's traditional deprivations drove them to commit, but even the very archetypal virtues of women, which men often shamelessly exploited even while they cited these virtues as reasons to keep women ignorant and confined.

Although in the short time that the Reign of Terror lasted it could not obliterate the Renaissance and post-Renaissance language of rationalism and empiricism now in common parlance among educated churchmen and laymen alike, yet when men took to the pulpits and the presses to instruct women upon the rights of man and the duties of women, their pride in their dominion and their prejudice against every manifestation of feminism induced some of them to try to expunge or condemn a most illustrious period in English history. They decried the noxious influence of Queen Elizabeth, the learned ladies of the Renaissance, and even much of the literature between the death of Henry VIII and the ascension of James I. In satires or sermons, they hoped to stem the infection unwittingly spread to women by Locke, Hume, Hartley, and *The Royal Society*, and deliberately by that noisome quartet, the late seventeenth-century feminist Mary Astell and her late eighteenth-century successors, Macaulay, Wollstonecraft, and Hays.

The Scottish clergyman William Duff merely echoed the national mood of masculine anxiety when he reminded his feminine readers "that there are many of our sex, who though sound Whigs in their political principles, retain a little tincture of Jacobitism in their principles of domestic government; and how much soever they detest those exploded doctrines of passive obedience and nonresistance in the government of the state, they are not for excluding them altogether in the government of their households."[8]

Duff's *Letters on the Intellectual and Moral Character of Women* was published in 1807, thirty years after the Declaration of Independence, almost two decades after the fall of the Bastille, and fifteen years after Wollstonecraft's *Vindication of the Rights of Woman*. These three shots and others heard round the world may have caused Duff to modify his language, so that he did not feel free to harangue women in a manner more characteristic of his older colleague, Polwhele, or some of the Augustan wits. In fact, the male conduct-book tracts for women usually heaped praise upon women who functioned according to the compensatory equation. The Reverend Thomas Gisborne, the only ecclesiastical monitor of women's conduct, and the only male conduct-book writer of any profession for whom Austen expressed some respect, also apparently felt compelled to appease his feminine readers, as though he, too, unconsciously feared that he was reasoning unhistorically and in bad faith. Still, without any awareness of a logical discrepancy, he argued that women needed to accept both more traditional discipline and less, in these troubled times: "In the cultivation of the female understanding, essential improvements have taken place in the present age. Both in schools and in private families there prevails a desire to call forth the reasoning powers of girls into action, and to enrich the mind with useful and interesting knowledge suitable to their sex."

But Gisborne's ultimate mission was to reinstate more firmly than ever the concept of women's divinely ordained subjection to men. Throughout his *Enquiry into the Duties of the Female Sex*, he summoned the support of St. Paul and other apostles, *Paradise Lost*, and Mediterranean history, both classical and Judeo-Christian, in order to argue that "a point not left among Christians to be decided by speculative arguments" as to "whether marriage established between the husband and the wife a perfect equality of rights, or conveys to the former a certain degree of superiority over the latter." For the stain of Eve, "communicated to the first woman after the fall, is corroborated by various injunctions delivered in the New Testament," and this stain descends to Eve's daughters in perpetuity, establishing that ineradicable inferiority to men that required women's subjection.[9]

In order to benefit from the spirit of empiricism abroad, Gisborne exploited a popular form of pseudoscience that radical feminists contemptuously labeled the "doctrine of innate feminine inferiority," and they condemned this original patriarchal premise, which supported women's disenfranchisement as scientifically undemonstrable, morally self-serving, and socially destructive. According to Gisborne, "The Power who called the human race into being, has with infinite wisdom, regarded in the structure of the corporeal frame, the tasks which the different sexes were to perform." To men, God "has imparted the strength of limb, and the robustness of constitution, requisite for the preserving endurance of toil," as though no underfed Englishwomen had ever been or were now condemned to crushing toil in the home and in the fields, the shop, or the new primitive factories. In England, and in other "countries where the progress of civilization is far advanced," and where the "female form" is "not commonly doomed . . . to labours more severe than the offices of domestic life," women have been divinely "cast in a smaller mold, and bound together in a looser texture" (*Duties of the Female Sex*, 19–20).

In the first sentence, Gisborne has created false causalities between the will of a divine anthropomorphic being, the soft bodies of English gentlewomen (often, in fact, ennervated by unwholesome diets and enforced idleness indoors), and the inflexible decisions of destiny—in England. Gisborne is actually describing social conditions that shape nature without any divine intervention. When women's lives are rugged, they become tougher than their pampered counterparts: the divine rule, then, is not ubiquitous, it would appear, since it fails to function in countries where civilization has not progressed as it had, at least among the English gentry.

One is bound to wonder how a rational ironist such as Austen would have responded to this specific instruction to women, and whether she thought it was as useful to "the cultivation of the female understanding," and as happy an example of the modern "desire to call for the reasoning powers of girls into action," as Gisborne had assumed.

In a chapter entitled "On the Peculiar Features by Which the Character of the Female Mind is Naturally Discriminated From That of the Other Sex," Gisborne once again resorted to circular reasoning and false syllogisms, each dependent upon the will of God as manifested in the male treatment of women and in the sexual and emotional needs of men. Gisborne described "the female mind" as though the mind of each woman was like that of another woman. All of them are born with a "natural tenderness" for husbands and children. But "the mind" of woman "is particularly exposed by its native structure and dispositions" to "failings and temptations" unknown to the other sex. Yet since "the hand of God has impressed" the female mind with just this very post-Edenic propensity for sin and bodily weakness, the male sex should not try to "efface" the "natural peculiarities of the female character," since to do so would thus "deprive women of their distinguishing excellences" not here described (*Duties of the Female Sex*, 30, 33, 79–80, 39).

One of Gisborne's most horrifying examples of self-serving circular reasoning is his pronouncement that women

> in consequence of the slighter texture of their frame do not undergo in the amputation of a limb and other cases of corporal suffering, the same degree of anguish which is endured by the rigid muscles and stubborn sinews of persons of the other sex under similar circumstances; and that a smaller portion of fortitude is sufficient to enable the former to bear the trial equally well with the latter. (*Duties of the Female Sex*, 28–29)

Once again, Gisborne deceived himself that God's plan for women equips them to bear with equanimity anything destiny or men require of them. Thus, the providentially arranged "natural peculiarity of the female character" is socially serviceable according to divinely planned genetics. Providence itself had initially designed that a woman's life "ultimately depends" not on her "own deliberate choice, as on the determination, or at least the interest of the parent, or the husband," and that same divine wisdom has "implanted" in women "a remarkable tendency to conform to the wishes and examples" of those whom they love and even those with whom they frequently associate. In order to facilitate women's divinely implanted capacity to yield to men's needs, providence has created them all essentially from the same fluid materials. "The sphere of domestic life . . . in which female excellence is best displayed," drastically diminishes "female diversity of action, and consequently of temptation," compared with the various types of men, who enter those "widely differing professions and employments which private advantage and public good require." But men's wives and daughters "are scarcely distinguished" from one another "by any peculiarities of moral obligations."

Gisborne even claimed that class differences between aristocratic women, gentlewomen, lower middle-class, and plebian women tended to disappear in "the general similarity" of women's "situation" (*Duties of the Female Sex*, 116, 2–4). Gisborne inherited his false sexual dichotomies directly from John Locke, the Enlightenment saint and educator of young men. Locke was convinced that if a boy's tutor combined rigor with a playfulness that indicates both affection and respect for each boy's idiosyncratic talents and temperament, the boy was almost bound to become a cultivated Christian gentleman. As a mature young man and a public figure, he would delight his father with his quiet self-confidence, which was based on his thorough knowledge of who he was, what he did well, what he deserved and what he owed other men. One need only compare this delightful post-Renaissance idea of a gentleman's training with Locke's insistence upon preserving the young woman's anatomical and psychological "delicacy," or John Bennett's stoutly self-confident pronouncement that "Confidence" in women " 'is a horrid bore,' " to appreciate how aptly Austen's satirical shafts pierced tired archetypes of this sort.[10]

Pope's dismissal of women's predicament was far less polite than Locke's or Gisborne's, and it was a model for Bennett's. But Bennett, like other conduct-book males, loved to quote just those lines in Pope that were most obviously designed to accomplish women's discomfort, and especially so when Pope placed his rejection of any female possibilities in the mouth of the archetypally feminine Martha Blount:

> Nothing so true as what you once let fall,
> Most women have no Characters at all:
> Matter too soft a lasting mark to bear
> And best distinguish'd by black, brown, or fair.

It was something of a puzzle to radical and moderate feminists alike that so bland and characterless a creature as Pope's woman could "create" such hostile "passion" in men "As When she touch'd the brink of all [they] hate" ("Epistle to a Lady"). Yet when feminists considered the literature of the conduct-book men, they could see that for all this masculine posturing as the didactic friends of women, the men's superficially charming yet actually degrading images of the female sex were just as thoroughly designed to keep women in their province as the lethal satirical barbs of Pope. But just in case the male authority in these conduct books failed to silence the sex that was becoming ever more intelligently articulate, the male tutors to women all exploited adjectives such as "disgusting," "terrifying," "repellant," "loathesome," and so on, in the repressive rhetoric that Austen borrowed for her cold patriarchal tyrant, Sir Thomas Bertram.

The moderate feminist, Jane West, responded to this masculine dismissal of women's human dignity, whether from the Augustan wits or the ponderous preachers, with a devastating description of the new terms now governing the ancient "contest between the sexes." The "privations of submission" demanded of women some "excruciating" and "exquisitely painful" constraints, full of "mortifications" and "peculiar" sufferings, which rendered them all the more wretched because they had rationally hoped that the Age of Reason might have ameliorated their predicament.[11] Ellen Pollak, a twentieth-century literary historian, observed the same post-Renaissance phenomenon as West had described:

> The late seventeenth and early eighteenth centuries mark a critical point in the codification of modern strategies for conceptualizing women. As patriarchal notions of divine right monarchy were rejected by political theorists, and benevolist attitudes began to infiltrate religious thought, as empiricist philosophy increasingly designated the human subject as the focus of both psychic and referential truth, new terms in keeping with those individualistic traditions gradually evolved to accommodate the ongoing subordination of women to men in social, political, economic, intellectual, and domestic life.[12]

Pollak has neatly identified the profound irony that characterized the Enlightenment for thinking women. John Locke's treatises on understanding, education, government, and toleration represent some of the most significant contributions to the Age of Reason as it benefited men. Repeatedly throughout his writing life, Locke identified subtle but crucial distinctions between axioms, clearly demonstrable proofs, means and ends, causes and effects, on the one hand, and beliefs, opinions, myths, and faith on the other. Myths are important because they encode the moral history of the race, but they are suspect as automatic guides for contemporary conduct. Beliefs are important because they are often true, although not demonstrable. But neither magistrates nor priests have the right to force one religious or social practice upon other groups of people. Even in private discourse, whenever we wish to discuss abstract subjects, particularly with an eye toward formulating laws and customs for ourselves and other people, we ought "to examine our own abilities, and see what *objects* our understandings were, or were not, fit to deal with." Locke urged his readers, whom he assumed to be male, always "to use their own thoughts in reading . . . if they are taken upon trust from others, it is no great matter what they are; they are not following the truth, but some meaner consideration."

Among the "meaner considerations" that Locke discusses in his various treatises are party politics that exclude ethics; punitive enforcement of religious or political conformity; casuistic arguments; various chains of delusions, each falsely associated with another for self-serving purposes; the seductions of power and control; and a craven acceptance of "received opinion." Yet in his *Two Treatises on Government*, Locke unthinkingly resurrects the familiar Edenic myth to justify the subjection of the wife to the husband, and he combines it with the pseudo-scientific doctrine of innate feminine inferiority in mind and body. The masculine right of government over women is a "Punishment laid on Eve . . . in her, as their representative, to all other Women." And furthermore, since men and women have "different understandings, [they] will unavoidably sometimes have different wills too, it therefore being necessary, that . . . the Rule should be placed somewhere, it naturally falls to the Man's share as the abler and stronger."[13]

Locke's unconscious archetype masquerading as enlightened reasoning is important because it thereafter helped to set the quasi-logical ground rules by which the male conduct-book writers quelled women's desire for rational self-determination. Locke also shifts from a logical mental process when he discusses all public affairs and the education of boys to false and circular reasoning and the adoption of repressive archetypes when he discusses the province of women. As Pollak demonstrates, this archetype represents one of "the stock codes" of "a bourgeois myth of women that was not self-evidently more benevolent than earlier attitudes simply because it presented itself that way." In fact, according to Pollak, its "mask of sentiment and liberal benevolism" merely characterizes one of the "fuller and more complex strategies" which "began to emerge for resolving the inconsistency between the increasing autonomy of the masculine subject, in a culture which increasingly affirmed the prerogatives of individual desire, and the systematic denial of either desire or autonomy in women" (Pollak, *The Poetics of Sexual Myth*, 26, 2).

It is a critical commonplace that Austen ignored the American, French and feminine rebellions during which she lived. But her very irony, so often praised but so seldom scrutinized for what it reveals, is itself an acknowledgment of social upheaval. Austen's fiction imitates Wollstonecraft's polemics in that it dared to turn "the woman question" into "the man and woman question," and to imply in fiction what Wollstonecraft overtly explained: that to dismiss the evolutionary needs of "one half the human race" was dangerous for the whole race.[14]

There is a profound responsive connection between Austen's satire and the satire of Pope, Swift, and the periodical essayists when they indulged in the national sport of chastising women. As the eighteenth century progressed, the successes of Burney, Edgeworth, Radcliffe, and a whole new tribe of Gothic novelists created even greater fears of women's insubordination, more masculine sermons and satires of the Polwhele kind, and ever more woman writers, until, according to some recent literary historians, more women were publishing novels than men.[15] It is not accidental that Polwhele's diatribe was published in the 1790s, in the middle of the feminist upheaval, just when Austen was beginning the early drafts of her mature fiction. Polwhele himself deplored the astonishing numbers of publishing women, and he condemned their "smile of complacency" and their "glow of self-congratulation," which could not hide these shameless public examples of "comparative imbecility" ("The Unsex'd Females," 16).

What else in Austen but an abiding fear of such vicious public rejection can explain the worlds of pain behind such fictional moments as her descriptions of Miss Bates, a woman like her contemporary self, "neither young, handsome, rich nor married"? What constant humiliations, encountered either through reading or personal experience, must have become translated into Austen's grimly ironic comment that

Miss Bates had "no intellectual superiority to make atonement to herself, or frighten those who might hate her into outward respect" (*E*, 21)?

It is no wonder, then, that all during Austen's life, "to become an author," particularly an ironist whose principle topic was that of the moderate feminist, Priscilla Wakefield, the author of *Reflections on the Present Condition of the Female Sex*, "was itself a feminist act."[16] Nor is it any wonder that one of Austen's many identifying voices, as she attempted to make a place for herself in a society that had no place for her, should have been the utterances of an exasperated satirist for whom the world, as she was officially ordered to see it, often made no sense.

But for all the difficulties Austen encountered as a writer, her family's cheerful eclecticism about what young women could read and write clearly counterbalanced the prevailing hostility to women writers, in a way that might have been less likely had she been born to working-class parents. Nevertheless, she was poor all her life, and thus unable to provide herself with the dowry that would have doubled her chances of marrying. Her post-Enlightenment predicament was therefore simultaneously more frustrating, and less so, than that of women born into higher or lower classes. As a writer, she had been granted the very best kind of education then permitted to women, but as a spinster, her feminine humiliations were doubled. One of the results of the new compensatory equation, he for his new rights and she for a redoubled training in her duties to him, was a renewed hostility toward spinsters. There was an obsessive restatement of the doctrine that for women "a dignified marriage" followed by the birth of sons was the only "grand promotion of which *they* are capable," according to the post-Wollstonecraftian clergyman, John Bennett (Bennett, 107). And Austen, that laughing, dancing, sociable, gently teasing young woman who loved to exchange badinage with young men and who had been trained at an early age to relieve her mother of domestic management, had cheerfully assumed that she would marry.

Any easy route to "the grand promotion" was barred to her because her father had neglected to provide a dowry for his daughters, and neither his disposition of funds nor his domestic inclinations permitted him to arrange a season in London for her. She was poignantly aware of the extent to which feminine poverty or provincial isolation were women's issues that frequently made marriage almost impossible for them. In her letters to her niece Fanny Knight, she cautioned the flighty

Fanny against expecting perfection in a suitor. After describing the "one in a Thousand" ideal male, "the Creature" in whom "Grace and Spirit are united to Worth," and "where the Manners are equal to the Heart & Understanding," Austen warned Fanny that such a "person may not come" her "way, or if he does," he may not be able to afford to marry her, or live close enough to her to be able to court her.

If Fanny had a delicate sense of ethics about marriage, finding a husband would present an even more difficult task: "Anything is to be preferred or endured rather than marrying without affection. . . . and nothing can be compared to the misery of being bound without love . . . to one, and preferring another." Yet the sad fact was that "single Women have a dreadful propensity for being poor—which is one very strong argument in favor of Matrimony." Austen's valediction to one of these letters is sad indeed: "Think of all this Fanny" (*sic*; *Letters*, 409–410, 483).

Had Austen been born to the aristocracy or to wealthy landowners, instead of to the minor gentry, or had her family provided her with a patron, she would have been sent to London to find a suitor, as Catherine Morland was sent to Bath with wealthy neighbors. On the other hand, if she had been born of yeoman stock, she might have been allowed to provide her own dowry: she might have raised chickens or tended cows, and the funds from the sale of eggs and the milk would partly have been hers to save toward her marriage. If she had been a shopkeeper's daughter, she might have been permitted to accrue a modest dowry by selling goods, printing bills, or keeping the books, and all this useful work, so frequently advocated by both the radical and the moderate women who wrote conduct books for their own sex, would have taken place while she learned the archetypal feminine lessons of social utility under her parents' eyes.

To be sure, Austen's sister Cassandra did succeed in becoming engaged. But even here, custom intervened and prevented the outcome for which Cassandra longed. Austen and her sister, who were each given £20 a year during their lifetime, were hampered in providing for their own marriages not only by their father's slender means and their mother's small dowry but also by the assumption that although a man should support his sons through his own talents and initiative, yet it was not right to "provide for daughters by *dividing* an estate" (*SS*, n. to p. 4).

Cassandra's suitor, Thomas Fowle, a third son of an Anglican clergyman, who had just recently been ordained himself, was also the inadvertent victim of custom. Apparently primogeniture functioned even in modest clerical circles. Fowle's eldest brother was the incumbent of several livings, whereas he was forced to accept a year-long appointment as a regimental chaplain in the West Indies. Just before he was scheduled to return, having made enough money on which to marry until his titled kinsman could find him a rector's living, he died of yellow fever.[17] The whole sad ending of Cassandra's hopes that she was about to achieve her own "grand promotion" was made even sadder by Lord Craven's shocked comment that had he known his cousin Thomas was engaged to be married, he would never have proposed this money-making journey to so dangerous a part of the world.[18]

If Austen had not been a "young female scribbler," her own case would have been as sad as her sister's. But her father was neither a prude nor a misogynist. He considered that active wit contributed to domestic felicity and to the development of all the children's talents, including even those of the two young girls. Austen's family obviously refused to impose the most rigid female constraints upon her, and her family's delighted approval of her scribbling propensities was almost a miracle for a post-Enlightenment Tory family.

Even the refusal of Austen's father to provide a dowry for her was a paradoxical blessing. Her spinsterhood spared her a husband's customary disapproval of writing wives as well as the sheer exhaustion of constant pregnancies. It is frightening to think that she might have suffered the same fate as her sisters-in-law and half-a-dozen neighbors, who died in childbirth. Although "the one grand promotion of which *she* was capable" had been denied her, and although she was traditionally bidden almost everywhere except at home to bury the one great talent that is death to hide, she ignored all taboos, ancient and recent, and quietly wrote and improved her mature fiction for almost a quarter of a century.

Nonetheless, as a daughter of the age of satire who had been practicing satirical fiction since she was twelve (*MW*, 1), her counter-satire itself announces that she resented the insults to which spinsters were increasingly subjected during the eighteenth century. Her "dear Dr. Johnson" (*Letters*, 181) enjoyed his wit at impoverished spinsters' expense as much as the next man: "When a man sees one of the inferior creatures perched upon a tree, or basking in the sunshine, without any apparent endeavor or pursuit, he often asks himself, or his companion, 'on what that animal can be supposed to be thinking?' "

The Augustan wits' frequent association of women with animals might now have alerted Austen that her dear Dr. Johnson was about to enjoy himself at women's expense:

> To every act a subject is required. He that thinks must think about something. But tell me, ye that pierce deepest into nature, ye that take the widest surveys of life, inform me, kind shades of Malabranche and of Locke, what that something can be, which excites and continues thought in maiden aunts with small fortunes; in younger brothers that live upon annuities; in traders retired from business; in soldiers absent from their regiments, or in widows that have no children. (*Idler*, No. 24)

In *The Rambler* No. 112, Johnson described typical celibates as "morose, fretful, and captious, tenacious of their own practices and maxims, soon offended by contradiction or negligence," since they have lived too long "without the necessity of consulting any inclination but their own." Spinsters, he thought, were peculiarly likely to be distempered by a "peevishness" that is "generally the vice of narrow minds." For when "female minds are imbittered [*sic*] by age or solitude, their malignity is generally exerted in a rigorous and spiteful superintendence of domestic trifles."

Mockery of spinsters constituted one of the satirical staples of the periodical essayists. Social "Fawners," says the contributor to *Spectator* 305, "are forced to strain and relax the Muscles of their Faces," while distinguishing between "a Spinster in a coloured Scarf and a Hand Maid in a Straw Hat," whereas those who wish to behave according to acceptable custom simply "use the same Roughness to both." Yet the spinster's proverbial neglect of her appearance was also a handy satirical weapon against women. In *Tatler* 210, one of the beleaguered sisterhood of single women claimed that her own sex giggles over her future disgrace in the hereafter, which is to be even more humiliating than her disgrace on earth. She will be placed in a Dantean circle of hell, where she will be an ape leading bands of other female apes.

The Spectator was the most offensive of all the periodicals because it was so obsessed with the varieties of methods, types, and topics by which it could humiliate women as an entire sex. Every type and condition of woman—old or young, married or single, rich or poor, gentle or plebian, plain or pretty, husband-seeking or passively waiting, intelligent or even scholarly, or illiterate and frivolous—would soon find herself as a figure of ridicule. One is reminded of Anne Elliot's sad comment to Captain Harville: "Men have had every advantage of us in telling their own story. Education has been theirs in so much higher degree; the pen has been in their hands. I will not allow books to prove anything" (*P*, 234).

The most frequent periodical advice that contributors offered to bored and lonely women was to employ their hours rationally and improve their minds by "the long-neglected Art of Needlework," adorning their clothes with imitation "Fruits and Flowers," and applying "themselves rather to Tapestry than Rhime" or solid reading. Of course, persistent reading of *The Spectator* was considered beneficial to women, since its contributors were obviously women's most trustworthy friends (*Spectator*, 10, 265, 296, 271, 366, 242). But the prevalent opinion of *Spectator* contributors was that "The Lump" of the female sex are "thoughtless creatures," yet any attempt of "these lovely pieces of human nature" to improve their minds by serious reading brought another scornful essay from the friends of women (*Spectator*, 4, 53).

Over a half-century later, Austen offered a mocking request to another member of "the fair sex," as women were invariably called when they were not enduring ridicule, by demanding that Cassandra should advise her about the latest styles in hats: "I cannot help thinking that it is more natural to have flowers growing out of the head than fruit. What do you think on that subject?" (*Letters*, 67).

Austen's letters bear painful witness to the frequent occasions as an impoverished spinster, when she was "the proper sport"—in Emma Woodhouse's scornful terms—of healthier, richer, and more socially acceptable neighbors and relatives, and when she feared to go into company because her clothes were so shabby and she had been "an ape-leader" for so many years. Austen's ironic heroine, Emma Woodhouse, dismisses impoverished spinsters with an acerbity worthy of an Augustan wit at his most rancorous: "Never mind, Harriet," she says, "I shall not be a poor old maid; and it is poverty only which makes celibacy contemptuous to a generous public! a single woman, with very little income, must be a ridiculous disagreeable, old maid!" These comments and those to follow represent some of Austen's most convoluted satire, during which she simultaneously fires off shafts at several clichés, some self-mocking, some satirizing others, and some occasionally conflicting with others. For instance, Emma's comment that "a very narrow income has a tendency to contract the mind, and sour the temper" of single women performs two functions: it recalls the easy Johnsonian assumption that celibacy demeans women more than men, and it also may well have functioned as a warning to Emma's creator.

Austen loved to exploit the literary device of the court fool or the villain who tells a variety of unpleasant truths that conventional people would rather not hear. Emma is ungenerously indulging herself in the national sport of spinster-baiting, partly to distance herself from economically and socially deprived spinsters such as Jane Fairfax, Harriet Smith, Miss Bates, and the little crowd of lonely female hangers-on who keep Mr. Woodhouse amused. But Emma is a ruthless truth-teller: she has identified poverty and social humiliation as a feminist issue, as it was for her creator, but not for her.

After Emma's provocative speech about the mistreatment of spinsters, Harriet Smith begs Emma to find a husband in order to escape just the threat of gratuitous insults typified by *The Spectator*: "You will be an old maid! and that is so dreadful!" wails Harriet, in response to Emma's insistence—which several Austenian heroines stress—that many women refuse the unattractive role of pining spinster, which the periodical essayist had assigned to them (*E*, 85).

Miss Bates, one of the objects of Emma's scornful rejection, is indeed a ridiculous old maid, and from an ironic truth-teller's perspective, cruel though it may be, she is the proper sport of both the heroine and her author. Miss Bates's life and her social expectations are as empty as her sycophantic chatter, and as exasperating. The attentions heaped upon her are painfully patronizing, and she serves as a grim example of what happened to women who were mortified by forlorn social and economic conditions, and who had been permitted no training or education for the opportunities a single life afforded. Austen is suggesting in her covert way that Emma, whose unchanneled active mind created fictions at other people's expense, and Miss Bates, whose passive mind was intellectually and imaginatively empty, might both have been happier if they had dared to take to the pen.

It is not accidental that *Emma*, which features a heroine's discussion of the plight of spinsters—and indeed, of women—should also feature four trapped spinsters of various social and economic conditions. Emma, the most fortunate as to money and social position, is bored and restless because the few amusements that her hypochondriacal father will allow her are "contrived" for her, "rather as she is 'a woman' than as she is a reasonable creature," and they are indeed "more adapted to the Sex, then to the Species," as the contributor to *Spectator* 10 remarks. And Knightley, for all his genuine kindness to her and to everybody, is himself guilty of a masculine conflict of interest, because he wants her to read only those unsubversive texts that will fit her to survive in hermetic Highbury where he rules, rather than trouble herself with those problematical feminist ideas that exemplify where her mind is going. The other three spinsters, Harriet Smith, Jane Fairfax, and Hetty Bates, are all feminine allegories of abandoned or scantily supported spinsters who must somehow survive with pitiful support.

Austen's disparaging comments on *The Spectator* and her preoccupation with the predicament of spinsters exemplifies again her capacity to encapsulate "the woman question" from a woman writer's perspective. In *Northanger Abbey*, she accuses this periodical of publishing essays "in which either the matter or the manner" is bound to "disgust a young person of taste: the substance of its papers so often consisting in the statement of improbable circumstances, unnatural characters, and topics of conversation, which no longer concern any one living; and their language, too, frequently so coarse as to give no favourable idea of the age that could endure it." These comments are immediately followed by praise of Burney's *Cecilia* and *Camilla* and Edgeworth's *Belinda*, all of them novels, says Austen "in which the greatest powers of the mind are displayed," and "the liveliest effusions of wit and humour are conveyed to the world in the best chosen language" (*NA*, 38).

II

The male conduct-book writers so popular during Austen's writing life served women as a sex, and spinsters as socially marginal embarrassments, no better that the periodical essays had done. While deploring the Augustan wits' treatment of women, these male tutors to the female sex cheerfully exploited the characteristic misogyny of many Augustan wits. Throughout the pages of these conduct books for women stalk several familiar feminine stereotypes. If young gentlewomen wished to appeal to courting men, they must master the fine art of not appearing to need or want what they were forced to hope for, and to hope for alone. Yet the churches, the law, the customs, and the satirists and sermonizers all told women, regardless of their class or economic condition, that marriage was their only permissible profession and their only socially acceptable form of support. Spinsters were often condemned as aberrant creatures who had deliberately flouted the codes of female conduct and who therefore deserved their marginal position. On the other hand, the conduct books written by women to solace and encourage their own sex almost invariably described the spinster's condition as altogether "so dreadful!" as Austen's Harriet Smith feared it would be, but they refused to place the blame entirely upon women. Instead, they cited the custom of money marrying money, the inability of women to command or to earn a dowry or to get an education appropriate to their class, and the relative scarcity of marrying males whom England's various imperial wars and colonial ventures had not yet removed from local circulation. Male tutors to women continued to describe the marriageable woman as a beautiful but reformed and penitent Eve, while the propaganda against the spinster often described her as "hag-ridden" if she was "impenitent," or contemptible if her spirits had been crushed by neglect and female poverty.

The Reverend James Fordyce, for example, was one of the earliest male conduct-book writers to earn the contempt of the radicals Wollstonecraft and Hays as well as the moderate Austen, whose Fordycean clergyman, Mr. Collins, read Fordyce's *Sermons to Young Women* to a bored audience of Bennet sisters. Fordyce's language helped to perpetuate the post-Augustan mawkish attitude toward women's sexual functions, which precluded the idea of an older single woman as feminine, or even altogether human.

Spinsters, Fordyce assumed, were usually responsible for their forlorn condition, since they must have refused to leave the thinking and the acting to men: "our first Mother Eve was betrayed by the pride of knowing," and "knowing" disfigures women's faces, bodies, and spirits. An "agreeable tincture of Intelligence" and "Intellectual Accomplishments" of a minor sort, particularly cheerful family letters, were acceptable ways for a young woman to endure the emptiness of virginal waiting. Fordyce even timidly sanctioned "any other composition which may fall from her pen," as long as it did so in an unambitious and unpremeditated way.[19] Fordyce's marriageable woman was modeled, as he said, upon Milton's Eve before the fall. She was all sweet, sexually titillating compliance and artfully appealing graces. No wit, no scrutinizing intelligence was allowed her, and benevolent silence became her more than any discourse of which she was capable.

It is no wonder that the scrutinizing spinster Austen declared a satirical war upon Fordyce and his kind. But the Fordycean woman elicited her deep compassion as well. In a letter to Cassandra, written two months after her father's death, when the full extent of her own economic hardships had been brought home to her, she described a painfully shy Miss Seymore who was out walking with her fiancé: "I have not yet seen her face, but neither her dress nor air have anything of the Dash nor Stilishness [*sic*] which the Browns talk of; quite the contrary indeed, her dress is not even smart, and her appearance very quiet. Miss Irvine says she is never speaking a word. Poor Wretch. I am afraid she is *en Penitence*" (*Letters*, 149).

The 1790s had culminated in a century of women writers, advancing fresh ideas about the actual nature "of half the human species," which decried the penitential role enjoined upon women and the consequential horror of older spinsters not under a husband's discipline. But these women writers exercised only a modifying influence upon the typical ecclesiastical conduct-book writer of the 1790s and afterward. The Reverend John Burton, for example, admitted that "a certain degree of knowledge is both ornamental and useful," and he made his bow to "the Wollstonecraftians" by acknowledging that it was "an illiberal prejudice to say, that Women should be kept in ignorance in order to render them more docile."[20] But he and his colleagues coupled each specific encouragement to women with endless warnings calculated to summon up the horrid specter of the spinster who had challenged the female code of intellectual feebleness, and praising articulate or intelligent women with faint damns. Only geniuses ought to take to the pen, they said, and genius in women was providentially very rare.

If all these frightening visions of despised and lonely single impoverishment failed to deter any woman from attempting more than an "agreeable tincture of Intelligence," the alarmist masculine murmur of "reputation, reputation," must have fatally discouraged many a potential woman writer. The fierce condemnation that male critics often felt compelled to inflict upon women writers thus became a weapon for relatives to brandish against any "scribbling" woman.

Such unfeminine misbehavior, women were often told, would not only place an unfair burden on their fathers, who must support them in useless spinsterhood, but it would materially injure the marital chances of their sisters.

But persistent condemnation could not arrest the unleashed energies of newly articulate women, who were bound to have discovered satire as a useful tool "to be revenged on their constrainers," as Robert Polhemus suggests:

> If we substitute "women" for "man" in the following excerpt from Shaftesbury's essay "The Freedom of Wit and Humour" (1790), we can understand, partly at least, how and why Austen's ingenious comic sense was generated: "The natural free spirits of ingenious man, if imprisoned or controlled, will find out other ways of motions to relieve themselves in their constraint; and whether it be in burlesque, mimicry or buffoonery, they will be glad at any rate to vent themselves, and be revenged on their constrainers. . . . 'Tis the persecuting spirit has raised the bantering one."[21]

There was much to be "revenged" by the bantering spirit. Austen was legally classified with a category of noncitizens that included the mad, the indentured servant, the untutored (Kirkham, *Jane Austen, Feminism and Fiction*, 5), and even infants under maternal care, but women's primitive moral and intellectual condition was counterbalanced, said Locke, by their fragile beauty and their innate "innocence" and "bashfulness,"[22] all traits that confirmed spinsters were said to have lost. No matter that women's beauty was as fleeting as the butterfly's, which they resembled; their instructors warned them against seeking any intellectual recompense for their ordained mental emptiness. The Reverend John Bennett, writing specifically to correct the errors of Macaulay, Wollstonecraft, and Hays, reminded women that those who "meddled" in masculine occupations, such as writing or serious reading, could never achieve anything beyond vulgar pendantry. Those who attempted intellectual improvement created a "total putrefaction of the moral air" and they were the objects of masculine horror because God's "sentence of subordination" had forbidden them to "aspire" to any "sacred greatness," or even to seek "literary refinement." In "distending" their minds, with impermissible ideas, they were sinning against nature, which intended that their imaginations—and implicitly their wombs—be filled only with distensions that their husbands had created.

Bennett thought of studious women as gas balloons, swelling with noxious toxics during the ascent, and shriveling during their descent into "a race of pigmies." He was clearly frightened by the spectacle of "female literature," which "in this country" had "swelled beyond its *natural* dimensions." A husband was entitled to "a sound and undistended state of the female understanding" that consisted solely in "the tenderness" and "the sincerity" a woman felt for him. By "sincerity," Bennett meant the woman's total preoccupation with her husband's needs. He repeated the same false dichotomies as his predecessors and his successors, between a reading, thinking, writing woman—or merely an articulate one—and domestic "vexation" of one kind or another: a noticeably intelligent woman was bound to be a sloppy housekeeper and a poor mother. But worst of all, she could no longer continuously reassure the husband that she flourished under his dominion, and the male ego, badly damaged by decades of marauding women, now required more feminine reassurance than ever before.

Bennett's theories typify eighteenth-century male strictures about women. Books that provided any woman with "the charms of knowledge" also provided her with "incentives for a speedier seduction," if she were married, as though intellectual liberty led to sexual licentiousness. But if she were single, she probably exemplified a shrunken thing, or perhaps "the cold, *forbidding* pride of a studious virginity." Pride in one's intellectual capacities, he said, was appropriate, and therefore permissible, to the male sex alone (Bennett, *Female Education*, 44, 108, 94–95).

Bennett laid himself open to considerable female "bantering" with his contorted wisdom that thinking and reading women were simultaneously levitating gaseous giants, shriveled pygmies, titillating sirens, or cold and under-sexed virgins. Austen's Mary Bennet is an ironic imitation of that conduct-book monstrosity, a vulgar, unmarried female pedant, whereas those self-effacing heroines, Catherine Morland and Fanny Price, represent ironic versions of the marriageable feminine model.

John Gregory, a Scottish physician, also offered contorted advice to his motherless daughters. On the one hand, he warned them that "nothing renders a woman more despicable, then her thinking it essential to her happiness to be married. Besides the gross indelicacy of the sentiment, it is a false one, as thousands of women have experienced." But on the other hand, Gregory's descriptions of "the forlorn and unprotected situation of an old maid," and "the chagrin" customarily "infecting" the "tempers" of spinsters, as well as "the great difficulty of making a transition with dignity and chearfulness [*sic*], from the period of youth, beauty, admiration and respect, into the calm, silent unnoticed retreat of declining years" suggest that to him "the situation of an old maid" also "renders a woman so despicable" as to make her a spectacle of "gross indelicacy."

For Gregory, spinsters come in various types: those who risk "degrading themselves" in dissipation; those who intrude "into the private life of acquaintances," and those who spread "scandal and defamation." These types of spinsters were all "women of active vigorous minds, and great vivacity of spirits" needing a husband's discipline to curb them. But the archetypally "bashful and timid" conduct-book women who somehow failed to capture a husband, those "gentle modest" women "blessed with . . . every milder feminine virtue of the heart," even these women atrophied morally, and they were likely to "sink into obscurity and insignificance . . . gradually losing every elegant accomplishment."

To forestall the horrors of spinsterhood surely awaiting assertive women, Gregory advised his daughters to "be even cautious in displaying your good sense. It will be thought you assume superiority over the rest of the company."[23] Yet Gregory listed the men whom his daughters should avoid, even at the risk of spinsterhood: there is the egotistical seducer, who looks and behaves tenderly, but who promises nothing. Austen's George Wickham, Henry Crawford, John Willoughby, and Frank Churchill exemplify this type. There is the man who assumes that any woman whom he decides to honor with his attentions will immediately reciprocate. Fitzwilliam Darcy, John Thorpe, Henry Crawford, Mr. Collins, and Mr. Elton demonstrate this type. There are the flirts, the Willoughbys and Crawfords who move easily from one woman to another. These men are in the minority: "Very few men will give themselves the trouble to gain or retain any woman's affections," except perhaps during courtship or during an attempted seduction (*Legacy to his Daughters*, 100).

Gregory was in a precarious state of health when he offered this advice to his motherless daughters, and sealed it with a very tender valediction (*Legacy to his Daughters*, VII, 131). But just as Austen, who was beginning her own long insidious slide toward death,[24] felt morally obligated to warn her niece Fanny Knight about how unlikely it was that a truly admirable potential husband would ever "come [her] way," the greatest kindness that Gregory could perform for his daughters was to warn them that in accepting a husband, they must also accept some harsh facts not usually considered wise or suitable to discuss with young unmarried women: not only were their husbands unlikely to think enough of them to love them, but "not one" out "of a million" Englishwomen was likely to "marry with any degree of love." In fact, they were unlikely to marry at all, unless they did so primarily for "gratitude." Gregory then sketched the common process of marital choice open to women, which Austen's tender irony recreated in the early stages of Elizabeth Bennet's engagement to Darcy: most women marry for reasons of "gratitude, and a partiality to the man who prefers [them] to the rest of [their] sex." The man "contracts a partiality" for a woman which "excites" her gratitude; this "gratitude rises into preference, and this preference perhaps at last advances to some degree of attachment, especially if it meets with crosses and difficulties" (*Legacy to his Daughters*, 80–84). That strong sexual attraction, coupled with growing mutual respect and affection, could bind a couple most appropriately, as it did in Elizabeth's and Darcy's case, did not seem an appropriate enough or perhaps even likely enough a prospect for Gregory to suggest.

Despite Dr. Gregory's obvious love for his daughters, Wollstonecraft specifically condemned his advice, because it placed the burden of accommodation upon women and forced them to appear silly rather than rational, in order to appease "the warped reason of man," and to "gain the applause of gaping tasteless fools" (*Vindication*, 46, 98). Mary Hays, Wollstonecraft's immediate successor, was as exasperated with such counsels as Wollstonecraft. Hays called them a series of "absurdities" that characterized men's "system of contradications" in their assumptions about women, that flouted reason, religion, justice and sound social policy alike (*Appeal to the Men of Great Britain*, 49). Two of Austen's favorite novelists, Burney and Edgeworth, implicitly repeated the same charges from novel to novel. And Austen's ironic compliment to Henry Tilney, during which she alludes to Burney's *Camilla*, that most men want actual "imbecility" in women, whereas Henry merely requires "ignorance," arose out of the same baffled exasperation (*NA*, 111).

When faced with a constant dose of advice such as this, whether offered in covert hostility to women, or as in Gregory's case, in caring and prophetic if bleak concern, it is not surprising that Austen, whose intelligence and dowerless poverty had already imposed a mandatory spinsterhood upon her, should have been guardedly pleased to encounter the Reverend Thomas Gisborne. Gisborne had apparently moved enough with the times to accept the mildest examples of female autonomy with some equanimity: "I am glad to recommend Gisborne," Austen wrote to Cassandra, "for having begun [*An Enquiry into the Duties of The Female Sex*], I am quite pleased with [it] and I had quite determined not to read it" (*Letters*, 169).

One of the Christian duties of the female sex, in Gisborne's controversial moral vision, is the duty to develop one's talents, even if one is married, and especially if one is a spinster. Gisborne had obviously been reading Wollstonecraft or he had somewhere encountered an echo of her rhetoric: "Is [female] folly to be pretended because sense may displease [a husband]? Because a man is absurd," he asked, "is a woman to be a hypocrite?" Such conduct, he warned, is morally offensive, not only in the man who demands it but in the women who fulfill these degrading demands; it is "dissimulation, it is deliberate imposition," and it is not consistent with the ethics of Christian marriage.

If this one remark was not enough kindness to elicit Austen's commendation, the uncommon respect with which Gisborne discusses the plight of spinsters, during a century in which women increasingly encountered a scarcity of marriageable males, the moral outrage he felt toward the isolated and impoverished condition in which they were often left and the "unjust" and "ungenerous contempt" systematically heaped upon them was bound to soothe Austen's heart (*Duties of the Female Sex*, 263–264, 404–408).

Despite Gisborne's kindness to spinsters, and his occasional appeasing remarks about women writers, he was not free of some distinctive rhetorical excrescences, which he shared with other conduct-book clergy. These men tended to relish allusions to young unmarried women of the aristocracy and the gentry not only as fruit and flowers but also as providers, according to the Reverend John Burton, of "the milk of human kindness" (*Female Education*, II, 54). They also loved pastoral metaphors of women as cattle or sheep and men as shepherds, or women as mute and decorative foliage on the "fringe" of the central places tilled by male gardeners. Imagery of this sort, so popular with Fordyce and his successors, and so appealing to Austen's Mr. Elton, was a distorted product of the chivalric code and Renaissance pastoral poetry. But the relatively prominent role of women in these earlier pastoral forms, subsidiary as it was, still proved too visible, too articulate to reassure eighteenth-century conduct-book males. They therefore shifted their didactic imagery so that it reassigned women to the functions of attracting and serving men in an even more diffident and selfless manner, and bearing and nourishing their children.[25]

Since "the women question" was centered largely in the educated classes, insofar as women of these classes were educated, the masculine conduct-book literature scarcely took account of a typical double feminine jeopardy: women with many servants were left without either active domestic or intellectual functions, whereas women with a dozen children and one domestic assistant, or none, would have howled with satirical laughter to consider themselves flowers.

Gisborne, Austen's qualified favorite, admitted that he exploited these pastoral metaphors of women in a moist, prelapsarian Eden as a form of persuasion intended to save women's souls. He compared male influence to the periodic inundation of a river, which "overspreads once a year a desert with transient plenty." Women's influence is more "like the dew of heaven which descends at all seasons, returns after short intervals, and permanently nourishes every herb in the field." These metaphors represent some contorted preaching, since Gisborne imagines women both as a parched "desert" requiring the male's nourishment from above and as a constant benevolent supply of gentle, unassertive dew constantly nourishing all domestic things and creatures below it (*Duties of the Female Sex*, 12).

The Reverend William Duff described women's domestic influence as a series of gentle "rivulets that run through and diversify the field of female manners." Her "temper" should imitate "the effulgence of the sun, ever mild and serene," and all attempts at "persuasion" must be "like the silent and salutory dews of heaven upon the tender plant which spreads its leaves and raises its head upon their benign and genial influence." Again, the illogicality of similes that simultaneously compared women to tender plants, to the dews which nourish them, to wetting agents such as soft little brooks and unobtrusive dew, and finally to the sun, a benign drying and heating agent usually associated with the male, apparently escaped Duff. And one of Duff's similes compared women to the dew nourishing the male plant and its offspring, whereas another symbolized the archetypal female as the plant itself, dangerously luxuriant before the male gardener "pruned" it, "but which when . . . bent and trained in a proper direction, might be rendered an useful and ornamental shrub in the garden of beauty, pleasing to the eye, and no way noxious in its flavour or its fruit" (*Character of Women*, 25, 305, 279, 112).

Fordyce compared women not only to the soft and appeasing prelapsarian Eve, to benign atomizers spraying soft rain over their domestic provinces, or to useful or decorative plants but also to "the smiling form of Peace, robed in white, and bearing a branch of olive" (*Sermons to Young Women*, II, 160, 162). Fordyce's woman is first her human and utilitarian self in Edenic form, then a plant, then the rain that nourishes the plant, and then a silent statue bearing a plant. Maria Edgeworth's satirical imitation of these sermons described a typical conduct-book man's woman as a loose, fragile piece of ivory sturdily supporting a massive but collapsing edifice.[26] Bennett's woman was simultaneously a plant "too delicate . . . to bear the scorching method of exposure" that public life would inflict upon her, and "untilled soil" needing her husband's discipline; after his tillage, she becomes another oxymoronic figure: she is now a "rich, *spontaneous* harvest," responding dutifully to his precise horticultural plan.

Another clerical confusion arose between woman as a flexible creature, able to "multiply and varigate herself as exigencies require" (Bennett, *Female Education*, 14, 112–114), and woman as a creature with but one character innately imposed upon her, as Duff's full title—*Letters on the Intellectual and Moral Character of Women*—signifies. But after these clergymen had described women as similar to one another, they often congratulated themselves that they at least recognized women's one character, since Pope had insisted that the female sex had no character at all.

Despite the polemical and intentional similarities in most conduct-book literature, the rhetoric and stress on one myth or dogma about women rather than another created two overlapping subtypes of conduct-book literature, the ecclesiastical and the secular. It is important to distinguish between them, because both types were ironical targets for Austen. Dr. Gregory was one example of the layman describing women's province to them, but his model was clearly Lord Halifax, whose late seventeenth-century *Advice to a Daughter* was still immensely popular in Austen's day and well into the nineteenth century. Both of these men exhorted women largely with secular rhetoric, which stressed law, tradition, pseudoscience, and the masculine idea of sound social policy to a far greater extent than it stressed any divine plan. Their arguments supporting the superiority and dominion of their own sex possessed the surface appearance of logic. The rare woman who could identify the clerical arguments as emanating from human, fallible prophets and apostles, since Christ's sayings rarely appear in this literature, were urged by the secular conduct-book literature to seek natural and secular reasons, but still immutable ones, for their predicament.

Halifax provided one of the earliest models for the circular and presumably inevitable associations between women as "the weaker sex" and "*Masculine Dominion*," "*Law and Custom*," man's "*Right*" and "*Privilege*" over women, and that comforting "Establishment," domestic and public, "upon which the Order of Humane society doth so much depend."[27] The arguments that men's bigger and hardier bodies created bigger and hardier brains, and that women's soft curves were predictably analogous to their soft, small brains, were as useful to Halifax and Locke in the 1690s as they were to Gregory and his colleagues, lay and clerical, in the late eighteenth century. Anne Elliot's gentle objection to Captain Harville's similar clichés indicates how thoroughly Austen was aware of their prevalence in literature addressing the "woman question." Harville says that he thoroughly accepts "the true analogy between" the "bodily" and the "mental frames" of the two sexes. Anne replies with "the same spirit of analogy" that men may be "more robust" than women, but that just as women are "longer-lived" than men, so their thoughts, their "feelings" and their "attachments" tend to be "the most tender" and last the longest (*P*, 233).

Anne apparently accepted that women were formed for "Compliance," as Halifax of course believed. But neither she nor her creator could have accepted Halifax's humiliating assumption that "*Men*" have "the larger share of Reason," because they have larger bodies and are permitted more aggressive temperaments than women. Halifax reasoned from tradition and law to men's needs, instead of beginning with men's needs and seeing the whole patriarchal edifice as a superstructure built upon anthropomorphic considerations, rather than divine or "Humane Order." On the contrary, Halifax assumed, "*Religion*" and "Reason" are so in accord with masculine needs, which both religion and reason dictate, that both bid women submit to men with that acquiescence which "cleanseth" feminine "*Understanding*" of vain rebellions. Halifax admitted, as Gregory was later to do, that "bitterness in mere Obedience" is bound to pain all women; for it is always male "*Power*" and not "*Choice* maketh [women] move" (*Advice to a Daughter*, 26, 16–17, 3–4).

Halifax expressed no greater hopes for his daughter's happiness than Gregory had been able to imagine for his daughters, or Austen had been able to imagine for her niece, a century and a quarter after Halifax's paternal advice. He warned his daughter of the various masculine types who were bound to make "the *Lawes* of *Marriage*, rune in a harsher stile toward [the female] *Sex*" than for men. There was the philanderer, whose conduct the wife must not imitate, in fear of the "Blemish" to his hereditary line of descent; there is the drunkard, the irrascible husband, the greedy man, the spendthrift, the niggard, or the weak administrator of estates and of patriarchal discipline (*Advice to a Daughter*, 35–49). But she must bear with all male sins and injustices, because the honor of the marriage was always in her hands, not his.

Another subtype of conduct-book literature that appealed more to clerics than to laymen, and that ponderously dwelt upon the metaphor of the passive woman as a national heroine in times of England's peril, understandably increased after the fall of the Bastille and the loss of the American colonies, and even more so with the Napoleonic threats. When the English monarch had lost his American property and the French monarch had lost his head, that monarch in the house, the post-Enlightenment English husband, to whom Halifax and most theorists about women's subordination had earlier granted the rights of a reigning "Prince" over a subject accepting "*rational Subjection*," remembered uneasily the civil wars in the body politic less than a century and a half ago, when those stern Puritan disciplinarians had felt compelled to depose and decapitate a monarch who did not know how to compel the awed respect of his subjects. The rebellious wife was often said to create as much private havoc as the public chaos created by rebellious subjects of a weak king (Halifax, *Advice to a Daughter*, 60–61).

Oddly enough, the most ardent advocate of the *passive* woman as *vigorous* patriot was not a man, but a woman. Hannah More, Polwhele's favorite, who was hardly a friend to her own sex, exploited this argument throughout the two volumes of her *Strictures on the Modern System of Female Education*. Public policy, so went the popular argument that More elaborates, now requires women's submission to men more than ever. Napoleon—or some other wild and unprincipled foreigner—was bound to interpret women's insubordination as signifying men's lack of masculine resolve, and he would be much more likely to attack England than he would be if Englishmen were seen to be controlling their women as they ought to be controlling them and defending any other property, including England itself. Thus the anxiety about national defense becomes a metaphor for the defense of all men's privileges. More sounds a melodramatic trumpet "call to women to come forward," and to announce to the world their wholehearted pleasure in moving backward as a sex. "In this moment of peril," she cries out to them "with a 'warning voice,' which should stir up every latent principle in their minds, and kindle every slumbering energy in their hearts," so that they can "contribute their full and fair proportion toward the saving of their country." Constant prayers for England's safety and constant attention to men's needs will protect England from the infection of foreign ideas as nothing else can do. Yet women are to perform this miracle "without departing from the refinement of their character" and "without blemishing the dignity of their sex" with that pernicious concept called "*the rights of woman*."[28]

Austen, who cast an ironic eye upon More, must have had such illogical passages in mind, as well as More's novels, which she did not particularly admire. In a letter to Cassandra describing her "disinclination" for More's novel, *Caelebs In Search of a Wife*, she explains her distaste with the comment, "I do not like the 'Evangelicals' " (*Letters*, 256). As Austen's "dear Dr. Johnson" had advised Boswell:

> Clear your mind of cant. You may talk as other people do; you may say to a man, "Sir, I am your most humble servant." You are *not* his humble servant. You may say, "these are bad times". . . . You don't mind the times. You tell a man, "I am sorry you had such bad weather the last day of your journey and were so much wet." You don't care a six-pence whether he is wet or dry. You may *talk* in this manner; it is a mode of talking in Society; but don't *think* foolishly.[29]

Appeals to women's patriotism contain some of the most obvious cant designed to depress feminine aspirations following the insurrections of the French disenfranchised classes and the English disenfranchised sex. Anne Elliot's long debate with Captain Harville establishes Anne, among its other multiple functions, as a woman capable of an unassertive patriotism, a yearning anxiety over the fighting man, which tended to prevail over any active consideration for herself, and which Hannah More and the male conduct-book writers would have admired, "in these anxious days," as More called them. But it also pleads the case of devalued spinsters, of young women considered unmarriageable, and of women traditionally forbidden to speak to men on subjects of national importance, even in the unthreatening way that Anne allows herself.

Another technique for feminine containment, exploited by clerics and lay writers alike, was the choice of severely biased and truncated portions of history, a study which purists had previously tended to withhold altogether from young girl's schoolrooms. Post-Wollstonecraftian male writers, perhaps stirred by the violence abroad, now began to describe various violent classical and medieval practices against women that duplicated contemporary customs in Asia and Africa, in order to demonstrate that male control over women's minds and reproductive functions, whether of the "enlightened" English sort or the barbaric, was universal in time and place. The pagan sale or execution of women past child-bearing; female infanticide; earlier European customs of witch burnings, drownings, or hangings, the ducking stool, the tongue bridles; the contemporary European right of wife-beating; the mutilation of Chinese women's feet; and female genital surgery throughout Africa all figured as covert warnings to modern rebellious Englishwomen. These descriptions of violent feminine containment often appeared in the conduct books of men whose distortions of English history also eliminated the splendors of Elizabeth's reign. Nor was biblical history exempt from distortion: Old Testament warrior women such as Jael or Judith were either ignored or chastised for their unfeminine behavior in killing an enemy of their people during a period of utmost national peril. What wisps of masculine history women did find in their primers and male conduct books celebrated the great male rulers and warriors, while withholding descriptions of common men—to say nothing of women, common or uncommon.

Bennett and other selective historians for women cheerfully admitted that other ages and other societies had "bound [women] with the fetters of an illiberal oppression." Contemporary Europe, on the other hand, was a feminine "Paradise" for women, and Britain was "the choicest spot" in this prelapsarian Eden, where women ought to be grateful that men did not often treat their wives violently, an assumption that history does not altogether confirm.

Bennett's descriptions of the extraordinary "blessings of liberty" sanctioned by a church free of bias and bigotry, which contemporary Englishmen have conferred on women, were repeated by all his conduct-book colleagues. Although they could not bring themselves to say so explicitly, their arguments and their syntax informed women that the female sex was now merely to be "bound . . . with the fetters" of a "liberal" rather than an "illiberal oppression." For in the franchise, which was legally denied to women; in the management of estates and the control of funds, which in the landed classes were customarily left to men; in formal education, still relatively rarely permitted to women and never in universities; "in the riches of commerce," which gentlewomen could hardly ever create or share, and which working women could seldom keep if they created it; and, of most importance to women writers, "in the improvement of the arts," which Bennett and all his colleagues declared to be a male privilege alone, women, he claimed, "are doubtless equal partakers with ourselves" (*Female Education*, 19, 38).

Bennett and his contemporaries must have known the general contents of Sir William Blackstone's *Commentaries on the Laws of England* (1756), which codified the status of married women: "the husband and wife are one person in law"; in fact, "the very being or legal existence of women is suspended during the marriage, and consolidated into that of the husband, under whose . . . *cover* she performs everything." This principle of *coverture* customarily functioned in actual practice not only for married women but throughout the lives of all women. When the law of femine *coverture* was repealed in 1857 and the *Married Women's Property Acts* of 1879 and 1882 eased the lot of married and divorced women, it was no longer quite as acceptable for a man to assume that he "cannot grant anything to his wife" or to any woman, "or enter into covenant with her" or with any woman, because women, married or single, have no "separate existence" apart from men.[30]

Austen was as capable of "a horse laugh" as Wollstonecraft (*Vindication*, 57), especially in her letters to Cassandra. Her fiction tended to be less harshly satirical than that of the Wollstonecraftians, but

Catherine Morland's description of male history and customs, and masculine assumptions about women, is another example of that lightly "bantering revenge" that Polhemus delightedly attributes to Austen. "The quarrels of popes and kings, with wars or pestilences, in every page, the men so good for nothing, and hardly any women at all," neatly summarizes Catherine's assessment of European male history, which encodes masculine dominion and women's lifelong suspension of separate existence. Catherine might well have found her own predicament "all very tiresome." Yet her comment that the "speeches . . . put in the heroes' mouths" and "their thoughts and designs . . . must be invention" is chilling. Catherine was naively imitating the feminists of the 1790s, yet she was unaware, as her creator was not, of the sinister implications behind her innocent speech.

Feminists of all persuasions considered their innate inferiority to be a masculine "invention," and their predicament to have been created almost entirely by the "thoughts and the designs" of men. The nouns *invention* and *design* appear in most feminist conduct books to describe male myths about the nature and province of women (*NA*, 108).

III

One of the most obvious rebuttals of masculine thoughts, designs, and inventions was Maria Edgeworth's "Letter from a Gentleman to his Friend, Upon the Birth of a Daughter." This semi-autobiographical letter appeared with two other feminist satires in Edgeworth's *Letters for Literary Ladies*. The "friend" was a thinly veiled portrait of Edgeworth's father; the "gentleman" was Thomas Day, whose novel, *The History of Sandforth and Merton*, grounds its plot and characters on Rousseau's false dichotomy between male culture and female nature.[31]

Edgeworth's satire is brilliant because she reassembles in so short a space the circular chain of arguments, presumed to be tightly linked, that characterizes the male conduct-book literature and that usually consumes at least one volume. In the gentleman's epistolary discussion as to why his friend should mourn the birth of a girl, he slides imperceptibly from what women are, that is, delicate creatures in "mind and body who must always see things through a veil or cease to be women" ("Letter Upon the Birth of a Daughter," 34, 7), to what men want in women, that is, creatures who allow themselves to be "quietly conducted to their own good," to the good English law and the solid English custom that makes women's province permanent, whatever the changes in masculine social customs may bring. He summons up the familiar associations between thinking women and "disgusting" "deformed" "monsters" of "unnatural size." "Literary ladies," he claims, are first intoxicated and then sickened "by the pride of knowing," demoralized as wives, mothers or housekeepers, adulterous if they are married or soon shriveled into moribund spinsterhood if they are still single. Intellectual emptiness in women "is friendly to female grace," but when lawless female minds enjoy books and study, the slippery way is prepared for lawless female bodies enjoying other illicit pleasures.

The "gentleman" of the title creates the same unconscious oxymoronic metaphors as Fordyce, Gisborne, Bennett, and other masculine tutors to women. The male sex is simultaneously symbolized as a strong wall without which the frail, feminine ivy cannot take root, and then as a wall loosened by the ivy and finally as "Cupid," a "timid, playful child," quaking at the sight of any intellectual woman ("Letter Upon the Birth of a Daughter," 18, 3–5, 39, 22, 34).

The full title of Edgeworth's three mock correspondences, which includes the gentleman's letter to his disgraced friend, is *Letters for Literary Ladies*. The alliterative title defiantly announces that literary women can still be "ladies," which the gentleman vehemently denies. In this collection of letters, Edgeworth included the fictional correspondence called "Julia and Caroline." These two women represent variations of the traditional feminine dualism between whore and saint, but Edgeworth turns this stereotype on its head. The male conduct-book woman who is ripe for marriage is all "heart" and no head. The spinster is all head and no heart. But in "Julia and Caroline," it is Julia, all "heart" and all hyperbolic pastoral language, who marries without consulting either her head or her heart, and who suffers disaster in the sexual wars. Caroline, who has balanced the claims of the head with the claims of the heart, cautions Julia against potential dishonor and danger to her happiness if she accepts this most passive and irresponsible model of feminine perfection.

Edgeworth's "Julia and Caroline" is one of the models for Austen's *Sense and Sensibility*. This example of the woman endangered by the very advice she receives from most orthodox literature in the school of matrimony appears in all feminist conduct books and in other Austenian fiction, as well as novels by Edgeworth and Burney. This mock correspondence in Edgeworth's *Letters for Literary Ladies* was published in 1795, and according to Cassandra Austen's notes, Austen began *Sense and Sensibility* in 1796 (*SS*, xiii).

Julia is the Marianne Dashwood in this mock correspondence, who is shocked by her sister's advice that she should "*think*" as well as feel, since she prefers "*only to feel.*" She urges Caroline to forgo philosophy as a "rigid mistress" and to embrace the "enchanting enthusiasm" that is not only woman's innate response but the one most appealing to men: "a woman's part in life is to please, and Providence has assigned to her *success* all the pleasure of her being" ("Julia and Caroline," 3–4, 8).

In turn, Caroline is shocked at Julia's "favorite doctrine of 'amiable defects,' " which deliberately imitates Wollstonecraft's paraphrase of Pope's "Epistle to a Lady" ("Julia and Caroline," 12). Wollstonecraft's paraphrase, "fair defects, amiable weaknesses, &c., &c.," which paraphrases Pope's "fine by defect and delicately weak," now finds its echo in Caroline's rebuke to Julia (*Vindication*, 34). It was later to appear in the debates between the attitudinizing Marianne Dashwood and her more mature sister Elinor and in the pedagogical Knightley's final praise of Emma Woodhouse, whom he has disciplined to his satisfaction and who is now all conduct-book contrition: "she is faultless in spite of her faults," he says to himself, and to her, "I would not think about you so much without doating on you, faults and all" (*E*, 433, 462).

"Julia and Caroline" concludes with a paraphrase of Gregory and Halifax: Julia excuses her decision to marry for money and a title with some bleak facts, which nevertheless cannot excuse her solution: "She runs a risk . . . of never meeting her equal—Hearts and understandings of a superior order are seldom met with in the world; or when met with, it may not be her particular good fortune to win them" ("Julia and Caroline," 23). Austen's sad description of the rare husband who could make marriage tolerable—a man with "Grace & Spirit," "Worth" and "Manners" to match his "Heart & Understanding"—also expresses women's sense that they face here, as elsewhere, a double jeopardy between a miserable marriage on the one hand and the inconsequential isolation of spinsterhood on the other (*Letters*, 409).

Austen's appreciation of Edgeworth may well have originated partly in her sympathy for another spinster, who had also undergone a long struggle to establish herself as a professional novelist. In any case,

Edgeworth exemplifies the radical and moderate feminists' satires of patriarchal attitudes.

Austen's famous comment to Cassandra that she thought *Pride and Prejudice* "rather too light, and bright, and sparkling" contains several jokes at the expense of masculine orthodoxy, and most pointedly at Gisborne's condescending classifications of women's minds: providence had designed their intellectual equipment "in sprightliness and vivacity, in quickness of perception, in versatility of invention, in powers adapted to unbend the brow of the learned, to refresh the overlaboured faculties of the wise," and to produce on demand "the enlivening and endearing smile of cheerfulness." Women's writing should approximate the epistolary style of intimate family correspondence, untinctured by anything resembling "the discussion of a board of philosophers" (*Duties of the Female Sex*, 22, 110).

Austen's ironic comments to Cassandra are delightfully convoluted: they ricochet from target to target, gently teasing herself, her sister, Gisborne and the conduct-book males, and even those masculine targets, pedantic women. "The work," she said, "wants to be stretched out here and there with a long chapter of sense," or perhaps "of solemn, specious nonsense about something unconnected with the story," containing just the sort of pompous "philosophisms," in Polwhele's term, that offended Gisborne in women and that Mary Bennet inflicted upon her victims. Perhaps "an essay on writing," no doubt of the Johnsonian kind, or "a critique on Scott, or the history of Buonaparte" would have made her novels "By a Lady" subject to just the drubbing that writing women had all been taught to fear.

Austen knew as well as Cassandra that women had been forbidden to indulge themselves in history, in criticism of male literature, or in anything as theoretical as "an essay on writing." But Austen's teasing valedictory comment suggests that she and her sister differed radically in their acquiescence in male strictures: "I doubt you quite agree with me here. I know your starched notions." In the year of her death, Austen expressed herself even more forcefully on this subject: "He & I should not in the least agree of course, in our ideas of Novels and Heroines; pictures of perfection as you know make me sick & wicked" (*Letters*, 300, 486–487). Austen's ideas of fictional courage were much closer to Wollstonecraft's than to Cassandra's and those of the male conduct books. Wollstonecraft might almost have been prescribing for

Austen's style: "A cultivated understanding and an affectionate heart, will never want starched rules of decorum," but "the behavior here recommended" is "rank affection" (*Vindication*, 98).

IV

Austen's fiction and her correspondence from her earliest writing days ironically reflects the restricted province in which her sex had placed her. The hitherto unrecognized savagery of her juvenilia, the plight of her heroines and the varied responses of each one to conduct-book wisdom, clerical or lay, patriarchal or radical or moderate feminist, all indicate how much Austen had absorbed "the woman question." For example, Fanny Price was probably based on severely diffident and vulnerable neighbors such as the pathologically shy Miss Seymore who apparently lived in permanent "Penitence." Catherine Morland satisfied readers who thought that ignorance is charming in women, and as a daughter, she would have especially pleased Lord Halifax and Dr. Gregory. She and Marianne Dashwood exemplify that intellectual distortion that afflicted women without any formal education. They both exaggerate feelings and avoid sustained thinking or serious reading, for fear, no doubt, of the philosophism that conduct-book males from Halifax through the pre-Victorian Duff had warned them about without recommending the obvious remedy. Elizabeth Bennet, Emma Woodhouse, Anne Elliot, and Elinor Dashwood all think for themselves; and approval or disapproval from readers, then and now, usually depends on the individual reader's sexual politics.

Just as clerical preachers to women differed from their lay counterparts in this or that argument for male dominion and in the rhetoric that advanced their arguments, so Austen's clerical advisors to women, such as Mr. Collins, Mr. Elton, and Edmund Bertram, differ in their euphemistic conduct-book rhetoric, but not in their purposes, from two of Austen's secular heroes, Frederick Wentworth and Mr. Knightley. These two men both exploit the crisp, clear, and authoritative style of Halifax and Gregory, and they also base their arguments upon lay considerations rather than the primary consideration of the divine plan, from which source, to be sure, their assumptions of male superiority originated.

It is an intelligent critical commonplace that the young clergyman,

Henry Tilney, does not sound like an ordained Anglican priest, and these critics who are quite unaware of the eighteenth-century war of the conduct books nonetheless unconsciously respond to something uncharacteristic of Austen's typical priests—and therefore of the historical conduct-book clergy—in Tilney's didactic speech. When he is not ironically imitating the anti-female satire of the Augustan wits, he instructs Catherine Morland as though he were a member of the Inns of Court, rather than a rector of a parish. His role is to induce readers to laugh at Catherine's Gothic sensibilities, and thus he is free of the unctuous pastoral metaphors so comfortable to most of Austen's fictional priests. Yet Henry in turn is an authorial target, for his creator understands as he does not that Catherine's fantasies are the predictable outcome of a society that devalues her and leaves her uneducated. Nor is he troubled because he "consider[s] a certain degree of weakness, both of mind and body, as friendly to female grace" (Edgeworth, "Letter Upon the Birth of a Daughter," 34). As his creator slyly remarks, although to most men, "imbecility in females is a great enhancement of their personal charms," *he* is "too reasonable and too well informed . . . to desire any thing [*sic*] more in woman than ignorance" (*NA*, 111).

Austen's judiciousness prevented her from creating heroines who exemplify the conduct-book "pictures of perfection," nor were her heroes, except for Darcy through Volumes I and II, quite as obsessed with their masculine privileges and as indifferent to the humiliations they inflicted upon the heroines as the heroes of Burney and Edgeworth. Austen's satirical techniques are particularly useful in preserving her judiciousness: they function as ricochets, or as boomerangs, in which her satirical characters themselves become the targets of their targets or, fully as often, of the understated authorial voice. For instance, when Knightley satirizes the clergyman, Mr. Elton, as a man who cannot speak to women without nauseating euphemisms, Austen and her heroine approve. But Knightley himself denied all the evidences of Emma's predicament almost as resolutely as Elton; surrounded as he was with impoverished, exploited, or lonely women, most of them scantily educated spinsters, he could see no generic connections between Emma's case and theirs—that she has been as exploited in other ways to become what she is as they have been to become what they are. Yet his analysis of Emma's moral offenses is legitimate, his syntax on the whole is sensible, and he possesses the reassuring attractions of a squire's authority, which commands most readers' respect, despite his ponderous didactic methods with Emma, and, in many cases, because of them. But Emma's mockery of his heavy male authority possesses a moral resonance that is rarely recognized as the revolt of an outsider who has been placated with some of the insiders' comforts and securities, without their autonomy of mind or movement.

Readers often offer Frederick Wentworth the same forbearance as they offer Knightley, and for the same reason. He is fundamentally a very decent man, and his pride in his talents and achievements is quite legitimate. But because he is free of Anne Elliot's feminine constraints, he has the free person's typical blindness toward other people's fetters, and his proud assumption that he has a right to her prevents him from fighting for her. In fact, he eventually takes his revenge upon her in an ugly way, reminiscent of Henry Crawford. He flirts publicly with two women in front of Anne, thus discomforting three women whose code of feminine decorum prevents them from challenging his duplicity.

Readers do well to feel comfortable when they respond to the appeals of these two heroes, as long as they do not confuse their responses with absolute acceptance of the way the heroes treat women. Frederick Wentworth and Mr. Knightley do both possess a rueful wit with which they are almost never credited, and especially when they admit their own blindness about the heroines. Both of them fully accept their professional responsibilities; and as Alistair Duckworth has pointed out, Knightley's respect for his land is associated with his feudal courtesies toward others (*The Improvement of the Estate*). Austen's own affectionate respect for responsible laymen is one of her most judicious kindnesses toward the male sex.

There are two exceptions to Austen's monitoring of her heroes' rhetoric by profession—lay or clerical—that may seem odd, at first. Edward Ferrars, who is eventually ordained, avoids unctuous rhetoric with women, whereas Colonel Brandon, the layman, does not. Their relative male empowerment during their young manhood was the same, for they were both treated like younger sons, which Brandon was and Edward was not, and both suffered from tyrannical parents. But Edward had not yet emerged into the authority of manhood, with its assumptions of possessive and didactic privileges over women, whereas Colonel Brandon's military service in the colonies had already prepared him for unquestioned authority over disempowered peoples, unobtrusively as he would wish to administer it. Edward, the clergyman in the making, sounds more like an Augustan wit in an uncommonly relaxed and genial mood, in those rare moments when he smiles and lightly teases the attitudinizing Marianne. Brandon, the layman, does not share Edward's occasional Johnsonian wit and pith. He has chosen to establish his masculine authority with rhetoric far closer to Fordyce than is common in Austen's secular males.

The Augustan wits in their misogynist moods were feminist targets as often as the male conduct books, and mocking Pope's mockery of women was one of the feminists' favorite didactic weapons. But they hardly ever mention Swift's poetry, and perhaps for that reason there are no "bantering" allusions to it in Austen's fiction. Swift's slightly condescending attitude toward Stella would not have appealed to her ideal of robust conversational exchange between the sexes. And a woman who found *The Spectator* vulgar and insulting to women would have been disgusted with Swift's excretory poems and his Phillises, Corinnas, and Chloes, drowsy in their moist nakedness, not quite harlots and not quite grunting sows. Austen must have been quite as aware as Swift that "Celia shits!" But she would have encountered no literature that would have suggested so grave a suspension of anatomical probability as to preach that women only create such a "sinking Ooze" as part of their postlapsarian punishment.

Austen's respect for Pope is distinctly guarded. One of her objections must have been his shallow, vain women, his goddesses of spleen and boredom, and his description of them as typifying generic womanhood. She was as capable as he of creating ugly creatures, but her irony is almost always forgiving, or at least understanding. One of the most admirable traits is her habit of explaining the origins of ugly behavior, both in its private and public causes, so that the blame falls upon faulty parentage and hostile social conditions as often as it does on her ugly characters. Pope must have seemed to Austen to lack this Christian and Enlightenment charity toward the fallible human species; above all, to Austen, a member of "an injured body" of people, daily conscious of those injuries, both petty and grave, Pope must have seemed to lack charity toward women (*NA*, 37).

There are two ironic references to Pope in *Sense and Sensibility*. Elinor Dashwood, the oldest of three penniless young women, combines both the "affectionate heart" so dear to traditional moralists, and the analytical "understanding" that feminist literature of both persuasions stressed as imperative for women's survival. Elinor ironically congratulates Marianne, the second sister, because Marianne's suitor pretends, as a seductive ploy, to feel exactly as she does about literature. He values "the beauties" of Cowper and Scott, and he has reassured Marianne that he admires "Pope no more than is proper" (*SS*, 47).

Another ironic scene in *Sense and Sensibility* reduces Pope's *The Rape of the Lock* and all its mocking neoclassical apparatus, to Willoughby's squalid attempt to soften Marianne for seduction. This version of the rape of a lock is reported through the eyes of Marianne's gaping thirteen-year-old sister, who describes how Willoughby waited until there were no adults in the room and then "cut off a long lock of [Marianne's] hair, for it was all tumbled down her back; and he kissed it . . . and put it in his pocket-book" (*SS*, 60).

The oblique contrast between Marianne, a genuinely tender if foolish and solipsistic virgin of seventeen, and Pope's painted Belinda, who knows all the arts of avoiding actual seduction while enjoying its preludes, cannot be accidental. Belinda's "two locks, which graceful hung behind," did so, "to the Destruction of Mankind," whereas Marianne's "long lock," which "tumbled down her back," did so only to her own near destruction. In Pope's mock epic, Belinda's locks are "hairy Sprindges," which "conspir'd" to "insnare Man's Imperial Race." Yet Pope's epic leaves matters open as to which sex was the more ensnared by the other:

> Th' Adventrous *Baron* the bright Locks admir'd,
> He saw, he wish'd, and to the Prize aspir'd
> By Force to ravish, or by Fraud betray.[32]

But Marianne is not at all conscious that she is sexually appealing, although she finds Willoughby so. Austen, who knew the difference between a heartless flirt and a sexually naive young woman in love for the first time, creates in Willoughby the conduct-book warning first to be found in Gregory and Halifax and later in all the feminist writing: Marianne was lucky to have mere fraud practiced on her, as her friends later remind her. Willoughby was summoned elsewhere, and he left the Dashwoods suddenly without explanation, before he could try "Force" or "Fraud" on a young woman he did not intend to marry.

Elinor's mild irony at Pope's expense implicitly includes Willoughby, whom she already distrusts.

Austen was too professional a novelist to ignore the examples of witty syntax that the Augustan wits supplied her. Her own infectious pleasure in *Pride and Prejudice*, especially the "epigrammatism of the general style," indicates that she acknowledged her male predecessors in the arts of satire (*Letters*, 300). She adopted their skills with epigrammatical irony, their aphoristic barbs and wise sayings, their zeugmas and syllepses, their balanced cadences, and above all, their gusty pleasure in verbal virtuosities. Her earliest juvenilia called *Volume the First* is Austen's own version of "A Modest Proposal"; it contains an astonishing demonstration of deliberately unredeemed satire.[33]

Here is an example of Austen's syntax when she was twelve. A duke whose wife has died, "mourned her loss with unshaken constancy for the next fortnight." He then "gratified the ambitions of Caroline Simpson by raising her to the rank of a Duchess." Caroline's sister Sukey, equally ambitious but anxious to achieve her goals through her own efforts, including unmaidenly violence, "was likewise shortly after elevated in a manner she . . . deserved. She was speedily raised to the Gallows" (*MW*, 28–29).

Austen's juvenilia contains one verbal felicity after the other. There is Lady Williams, "in whom every virtue met. She was a widow with a handsome Jointure & the remains of a handsome face." There is "cruel Charles," who "wound[s] the hearts & legs of all the fair" young women for whom he sets steel traps. And there is "the worthless Louisa," who left her husband, "her Child & reputation . . . in company with Danvers &+ [*sic*] dishonour" (*MW*, 13, 22, 110). There is a delightfully ebullient moment when Austen, already the author of two novels, and now at work upon a third, writes to Cassandra: "In a few hours, you will be transported to Manydown & then for Candour & Comfort & Coffee & Cribbage." And there is an unforgettable "Adm. Stanhope," who was "a gentlemanlike Man, but then his legs are too short, & his tail too long" (*Letters*, 302, 129).

What a fine rehearsal this verbal dexterity is for that alliterative moment in *Pride and Prejudice*, when Elizabeth Bennet is leaving Charlotte Lucas, who has disgraced herself by marrying Mr. Collins. Elizabeth is musing to herself about "Poor Charlotte!" and how "melancholy" it was for Charlotte's friends "to leave her to such society" as her husband's: "But she had chosen it with her eyes open; and . . . she did not seem to ask for companions. Her *home*, her *housekeeping*, her *parish* and her *poultry* . . . had not yet lost their charms" (*PP*, 216; emphasis mine).

Elizabeth's sorrow for her friend Charlotte's marital debacle is as genuine as her capacity to refuse to think in cant. Her own bleak future, trapped at home with two outrageous parents and three silly sisters, still seems preferable to marriage with either of the two condescending suitors who had just proposed to her. But Charlotte had been driven to marry for just those motives of feminine desperation against which Halifax, Gregory, and Edgeworth had warned single women, and Austen had warned her niece, Fanny.

Austen's juvenilia is both violent and mournful in ways that anticipate her mature fiction. She learned to modify the violence so that it is almost unrecognizable in her novels, but in "Volume the First" there are numerous descriptions of executions, amputations, female starvation, suicides, and attempted and successful murders of all kinds: matricide, fratricide, sororicide, and the attempted infanticide of an unwelcome new born girl, who takes her revenge far more violently than indulging in some "bantering." She grows up to raise and command an army with which she slaughters her enemies.

In "Volume the Second" and "Volume the Third," there is increased sadness and more open explorations of the themes first discussed by the radical and the moderate feminists. There are scenes of feminine deprivation, such as the abandonment of hungry and threadbare spinsters while male relatives dump their children on the trapped women, and amuse themselves spending the women's marriage portions. While one or another male relative "is fluttering about the streets of London," young and indifferent to the welfare of his abandoned wife and child, or "gay, dissipated, and Thoughtless at the age of 57," the women "continue secluded from mankind in [their] old and Mouldering Castle," often obsessed with food, clothing, and loneliness (*MW*, 111).

In "Volume The Third," the theme of women as outsiders, vulnerable to every contingency of malice, neglect, or mere custom, is more pronounced. Two young women, marriageable but impoverished orphans, are in "great distress" because they "had been reduced to a state of absolute dependence on some relatives, who though very opulent and very nearly connected with them, had with difficulty been prevailed on to contribute anything towards their Support." The solution of the eldest was one with which Austen was familiar, since her father's dowerless sister was forced to go to India to find a husband. This is Austen's fictional version of the same sad solution, written thirty-five years after her aunt's desperate emigration. Already at sixteen, Austen was subliminally aware of what happened to dowerless spinsters. Her fictional spinster "had been necessitated to embrace the only possibility that was offered her, of a Maintenance." This polite sale of herself to an elderly and bad-tempered man was "so opposite to all her ideas of Propriety, so contrary to her Wishes, so repugnant to her feelings, that she would almost have preferred Servitude . . . had Choice been allowed her."

For Mary, another and younger dowerless sister, "There was not indeed that hopelessness of sorrow . . . she was not yet married and could yet look forward to a change in her circumstances." But this unfinished story called "Catherine" leaves Mary still abandoned to the charms of a companion's post, and both hopeless and "depressed" (*MW*, 194–195).

Achievements of Austen's magnitude are always something of a mystery, and in Austen's case, the mystery is even greater than it is for her male colleagues. How did she learn to temper her hyperbolically witty yet bleak child's vision, which could imagine only a world of sycophants and of hostile, competing groups? Where did she learn that buoyancy that she attributes to one of her minor women characters, "that elasticity of mind, that disposition to be comforted, that power of turning from evil to good, and of finding employment which carried her out of herself, which was from Nature alone"? The quietly witty but depressed Anne Elliot asks herself these questions about Mrs. Smith, an ill and penniless widow, betrayed by her husband and now abandoned by society in a back street of Bath. Anne compares Mrs. Smith's buoyant courage, which allows this utterly bereft woman "moments only of languor and depression," to her own permanent state of grieving with far less provocation, she thinks. "A submissive spirit might be patient, a strong understanding would supply resolution, but here was something more. . . . It was the choicest gift from heaven," and, Anne muses, "by a merciful appointment, it seems designed to counterbalance almost every other want" (*P*, 154).

If we assume that there are portions of Austen's own hidden self in all heroines, whether transcended or not, we need to examine some of the subversive attitudes of these heroines. We need to watch the way Austen absorbed many feminist theories and transmuted them into the less contentious, more discreet, and sometimes more light-hearted medium of fiction, even while she retained an abiding contempt for those "meaner considerations" that Locke had identified in his *Essay Concerning Human Understanding*. Her favorite women novelists taught her that women could take as one of their most obvious fictional preoccupations the subject of Priscilla Wakefield's *Reflections on the Present Condition of the Female Sex*, and all the "meaner considerations" upon which traditional wisdom about women was so often based, and find themselves not only a publisher but a public. But Austen's other primary and secret sources were clearly the explosive 1790s battles of the sexes. By October of 1796, when Austen began "First Impressions," *A Vindication of the Rights of Woman* had been flourishing as a "provocative and popular treatise" for four years (Wollstonecraft, *Vindication*, vii).

Nina Auerbach argues convincingly that "Wollstonecraft may help us to read Jane Austen, by defining a similar condition" to Anne Elliot's trapped dependence. Auerbach is one of the rare Austenian scholars to "hear echoes of voices like Mary Wollstonecraft's" and to study them "as an undercurrent throughout Jane Austen's novels." Merely to mention one debt that Austen owed to the feminist conduct-book writers in general, and Wollstonecraft in particular, as the most famous of them all at that time, is to acknowledge just how much Austen's "emphasis upon unequal education rather than inherent inequality once again recalls Mary Wollstonecraft's central thesis in *Vindication of the Rights of Woman*."[34]

The title of Auerbach's essay, "O Brave New World: Evolution and Revolution in *Persuasion*," suggests the nature of my investigation. Austen's canon contains not only themes of women's potential evolution, as she found them in her life and in the novels of her women predecessors, but also themes of the Wollstonecraftian revolution. If we study these two Austenian impulses, the revolutionary and the evolutionary, as they appear first in her feminine models, both theoretical and fictional, and then in her novels, we can partially describe Austen's own fictional alchemy, although we can never satisfactorily explain it. Nor can we ever ultimately explain how she could create so gallant a version of her own "brave new world," qualified as it understandably was by anger and many "moments of languor and depression." We should look further at a few of her letters, which grieve over cases of elderly women, often spinsters, who are left homeless or starving as a public charge nobody wishes to assume. Even Austen's very great fictional skills and her "gifts from nature alone," "her elasticity of mind," and her own "power of turning from evil to good," which Anne Elliot had attributed to the abandoned, impoverished, and severely crippled Mrs. Smith, can never be fully acknowledged until we also acknowledge the extent of so much discreet pain in the Austenian vision as well as its social and sexual genesis. Thus we may learn a fresh respect for Austen's courage and understand why so much courage was necessary. Only then can we clearly see just how gallant, how witty, how morally clear-eyed, and yet how compassionate that vision was.

2

Four "Unsex'd Females," Five Moderately Sexed, and Two Women Novelists with "the Greatest Powers of the Mind"

I

Margaret Kirkham calls Austen's concern with the predicament of her own sex an extension of "rational feminism," or "English Enlightenment feminism." "Burke has often been brought in to elucidate Austen's 'conservatism,' " but "it is now clear that Wollstonecraft and the ethical attitudes of Enlightenment feminists must be brought in as well." Kirkham denies that there was any "well-defined school of eighteenth-century feminist thought in England," an assessment that is accurate in modern terms, but that she qualifies in the context of post-Enlightenment women's writing. She sees a distinct connection between Austen's private emergence as "a novelist in the 1790s, when the feminist/antifeminist controversy was strong," and "a clear and consistent" Austenian "commitment to the rational principles on which women of the Enlightenment based their case."

Kirkham makes a convincing argument for her assumptions that Austen adapted the Wollstonecraftian ethical attitudes of Enlightenment feminism to the conventions and symbolic structures of fiction, since "the novel itself was of particular importance to the debate" on women's province. Wollstonecraft's "*Vindication* draws on an English feminist tradition in which women of orthodox religion, not associated with revolutionary politics, have their place, as Wollstonecraft acknowledges."

According to Kirkham, there is a "central feminist position on morals and education," with an understandable stress on that neglected subject, a vigorous classical education for women. This position includes not only the late Restoration feminist, "Mary Astell, 'a true daughter of the Church of England,' " but it also as clearly embraces Austen herself, another true daughter of the same church.[1]

It is an accurate commonplace that Austen shared the public preoccupation with young women's feeble education, and Astell's *Serious Proposal to the Ladies for the Advancement of their True and Greatest Interest* (1694) was an early archetype of this preoccupation. It is indeed a "modest proposal," which urges the creation of the first women's university. Ruth Perry calls Astell "the first widely read, expressly feminist polemicist," whose "ideas—and often her language" were widely satirized, yet imitated and even plagiarized at length.[2] Although Astell's "life was blameless," and although one of Austen's favorite novels, Richardson's *Sir Charles Grandison*, treats her quite gently, the usual misogynist satire inflicted upon her accused her of lechery, thus pandering to one of the current myths that thinking women were more apt than others to be fornicating women.[3]

Astell's bitter essay, *Some Reflections Upon Marriage*, written several years after *Serious Proposal*, clearly responded not only to attacks that she had already suffered, but it anticipated those to follow throughout the eighteenth century. In her advertisement to her readers, she described why she wrote anonymously: she did not wish to "pull . . . a Hornet's Nest" upon herself; it is a shallow habit of critics, she said, "to regard rather who . . . speaks, than what is spoken." The satire at her expense had taught her a great deal about the politics of readers and reviewers: paraphrasing Locke's *Essay Concerning Human Under-*

standing, she mocked the popular journalistic habit of submitting uncritically "to authority" and to habitual opinions, rather than "to Reason; or, if Reason press too hard, to think to ward it off by Personal Objections." There are "few Minds . . . strong enough to bear what contradicts their Principles, without recrimination when they can."[4]

Astell's attack on the characteristic mockery of writing women is reminiscent of Austen's charges against the same prejudice: "Leave it to the Reviewers," says Austen's ironic authorial voice, to "abuse" such women novelists as Frances Burney and Maria Edgeworth, and of course, by polite implication, the anonymous author of *Northanger Abbey* herself. But from "Reviewers" of this sort, motivated as they all are by "pride, ignorance, and fashion," what else can one expect but "talk in threadbare strains" of the feminine "trash" that fiction-writing women produce? These reviewers prefer republished snippets from "Milton, Pope, and Prior," *The Spectator* or Sterne, or their own patriarchal "History of England," to fiction, one genre in which women were beginning to prevail, even if their novels had "genius, wit, and taste to recommend them" (*NA*, 37).

In *Sense and Sensibility*, Austen's Colonel Brandon makes a remark that is highly uncharacteristic of this naive, sentimental, and benignly conventional soldier: "Where the mind is unwilling to be convinced, it will always find something to support its doubts" (*SS*, 173). These crisp rhetorical cadences are merely sensible on the surface, but they are actually quite subversive and they are more typical of Astell, Locke, or Dr. Johnson, or of Austen herself. Austen's entire canon, the juvenilia, the correspondence, and the mature fiction, represents one long attack upon opinions, and above all, opinions about women, which are glibly received without intellectual and moral examination.

Austen's contempt for the periodical essayists who specialized in attacks upon women writers would be particularly justified if she had had *Tatler* 32 in mind, in which Mary Astell appears as the duped "Madonella," the founder of an enclosed women's college. A group of roisterers force their way in, and led by "a famous rake of that time," flatter Madonella and her colleagues by agreeing with everything the women think. After the verbal seduction has proceeded to the men's satisfaction, each man seizes a woman's hand, and the whole group takes a joyful tour of the college, conversing as they go, as though they were all Cambridge Platonists, following the arguments of reason and justice as recognizable pathways to God: "The conference was continued in this celestial strain, and carried on so well by the managers on both sides, that it created a second and third interview; and without entering into further particulars, there was hardly one of them but was a mother or father day twelve-month" (*Tatler*, 32).

The rakes' behavior anticipates Willoughby's conduct toward Marianne Dashwood in *Sense and Sensibility*. Just as these exploiters feigned intellectual pleasure in the minds of the women dons, as a prelude to the sexual seduction that they assumed would follow their flattering verbal foreplay, so Willoughby "acquiesced in all [Marianne's] decisions" and "caught all her enthusiasms" as a sham prelude to the dishonorable capitulation that he intended to arrange. He "had already done that, which no man who *can* feel for another, would do," and "after such dishonourable usage" toward one fatherless woman, nobody had much doubt as to "his designs on" Marianne (*SS*, 47, 210–211). But Austen's mournful version of the particular sexual myth, that women with active minds have uncontrollable or malleable sexual urges, is as different from the casual and opportunistic assumptions of *The Tatler* as the victim's experience of rape is from her abuser's arrogant myth of successful seduction.

Astell's best known work and her *Areopagitica* is *A Serious Proposal to the Ladies for the Advancement of their True and Greatest Interest*, which overtly expresses the same outrage at the starved lives of most young unmarried women as her radical feminist successors of the 1790s were to describe a century later. Austen and her two favorite women novelists, Burney and Edgeworth, also express the same outrage, although it is muffled according to the dictates of feminine reverence toward the male and the requirements of aesthetic restraint. Astell was as shocked as all her feminist successors, radical or moderate, by theories of female education that prepared young women neither for marriage and motherhood nor for the serious thinking about the afterlife, for which all earthly life was but a preparation. But she was also profoundly aware of the hardships that awaited women who had no dowry to make marriage possible, and nothing in their heads to make spinsterhood tolerable. She hoped that her college could become both a nursery for female souls seeking salvation through enlightened reasoning, and a practical internship in the paradoxical uses and advantages of feminine hardships.

Astell's description of a typical unenlightened young woman on the prowl for a husband foreshadows the Austenian gallery of empty young women such as Isabella Thorpe, the Steele sisters, Lydia and Catherine Bennet, the Bertram sisters, and Elizabeth Elliot. In each case, the historical and the fictional, the husband-hunter has "spread all her Nets and us'd all her Arts for Conquest," only to find that "the Bait fails." During this unprofitable pursuit, "she had no time to improve her Mind, which therefore affords her no safe retreat." In all too many cases, this "poor Lady" then "flies to some dishonourable Match as her last, tho' much mistaken Refuge, to the disgrace of her Family and her own irreparable ruin."[5]

This observation anticipates the persistent campaign of the 1790s radical and moderate feminists to persuade young women to become something more than prowlers after elusive husbands. Mrs. Dashwood's polite rebuke to Sir John Middleton in *Sense and Sensibility* that "*catching*" husbands was "not an employment to which [*her* daughters] had been brought up" might well prepare readers of Austen's fiction for her sad valedictory cadences in *Mansfield Park.* The authorial voice dwells upon Maria Bertram's "guilt and misery," the "shocking" disgrace, and the "grief and horror" that gross parental "mismanagement" had brought down upon a family hitherto completely indifferent to Maria's welfare or her conduct (*SS*, 44; *MP*, 461–463, 440–441). But Austen knew, from experience as bitter as Astell's, why women should be so "terrified with the dreadful name of Old Maid . . . and the scoffs that are thrown on superannuated Virgins." Her letters and her subplots describe one young woman after another who believes, as Astell's pathetic female models do, that "irreparable ruin" would be no more terrifying than "the disgrace to her family" of prolonged spinsterhood (*Serious Proposal*, 39–40).

In *Some Reflections Upon Marriage*, Astell creates many grim vignettes of the requirements that fashionable men seek in wives. The first "Enquiry" is "What will she bring" in "Acres" or "Coin"? The next "Quality" a man looks for is "Beauty," but whether he marries for a woman's money or her looks, he "does not act according to Reason in either Case, but is govern'd by irregular Appetites" (*Some Reflections Upon Marriage*, 20, 25). This frightening assessment of the marriage estate appears again and again in almost all the woman-centered literature to follow, including Austen's, as writing women's thoughts moved around and around the circular subjects of the low esteem in which women were held, and their pitifully few options for survival. In studying this generic sickness at large, writing women provided one exemplary figure after the other, in allegorical essays or in fiction, of ignorant or restless spinsters or married women atrociously mismated and equally ignorant or restless.

In other ways as well, Astell's preoccupations are Austen's and those of many eighteenth-century woman-centered writers. Although they refused to exonerate the shallow recklessness of women denied parental attention and serious education, they considered that the primary sinners were the women's parents: "One would . . . think," said Astell, "that Parents shou'd take all possible care of the Children's Education, not only for *their* sake," but for the sake of the parents themselves. For although "the Son convey the Name to Posterity, yet certainly a great part of the Honour of their Families depends on their Daughters." Yet "the Beasts are better natur'd, for they take care of their off-spring until they are capable of caring for themselves," and custom, women's greatest enemy of all, had rendered them unable to support themselves in spinsterhood, and unable to find men who would marry them for reasons of genuine affection. Even men who are induced to marry by the "irregular Appetites" they call "Love" are one among "thousands" (*Some Reflections Upon Marriage*, 6–7, 25).

Astell knew all too well that most women would be driven to marry by sheer economic necessity, since marrying off dowerless daughters was one way that callous fathers preserved the patrimony of their male heirs. But even when there was no dire poverty to make marriage necessary, women's lives were often deliberately left so empty that without heroic private efforts at self-teaching, often thwarted by parents and by social assumptions, there was nothing else for women to expect, and even worse, Astell thought, nothing else for them to think about. And so her *Serious Proposal* offered the subversive idea of a college that would teach women self-respect and train them to become self-sufficient—as Austen's Jane Fairfax had been trained—and to become serious and vigorous tutors of children while they waited to be married. Those who could not marry would not eventually be so utterly dependent upon brothers, who appear in the conduct books of all three persuasions as very uncertain sources of feminine support.

Astell's *Serious Proposal*, which was to become such a *cause célèbre*, began as all feminists' arguments begin, with the assumption that "the incapacity" with which it pleased men to charge women, "if there be any, is acquired, not natural." Women, said Astell, "are from their very Infancy debar'd those Advantages, with the want of which they are afterward reproached, and nursed up in those Vices which will hereafter be upbraided to them." In this argument as well, Astell foreshadows eighteenth-century feminists and para-feminists: men are blasphemous when they contend that "*Women have no Souls*" and thus cannot achieve eternal life, and when they then deliberately create those conditions that warp women's souls and unfit them for salvation (*Serious Proposal*, 6, 19).

Astell's essay is nicely orchestrated between two themes and their variations. The primary theme is that women are human and therefore born with the divine spark of human understanding in them, but that it benefits from pious cultivation, as it does in men. Such clauses as "Women are Rational Creatures," "God made women Rational Creatures in his Image," "Women are not Brutes, but Rational Creatures," "God gave Women Minds with which to seek him, as any Rational Creature must," echo throughout Astell's *Serious Proposal*, as well as the essays of Macaulay, Wollstonecraft, Hays, and those of their moderate feminist successors. This motif is poignant, in view of the horror it often invoked in women's guardians, and it anticipates all the common sense and the anguish in Elizabeth Bennet's cry to her misogynist suitor Collins, when she is forced into the humiliation of having to beg him to treat her "as a rational creature speaking the truth from her heart" (*PP*, 109).

Astell's second intellectual and moral imperative—that women reject all "receiv'd Opinions," "*judge no further than*" they "*Perceive*," and refuse to "*take anything as Truth*" that they "*do not evidently Know to be so*," which means true according to rational and experiential evidence—is equally a product of the Enlightenment and equally tailored to fit women's condition, which men of the Enlightenment had refused to address. Men harbored the same "Passions" as women, and should be "credited" only "on the score of . . . Reason," and never of that of "Authority." Women must "disengage" themselves "from all sinister and little Designs" upon their integrity, their own or those of anybody else (*Serious Proposal*, 71, 107, 70). The multiple and circular arguments against allowing women to think, study, and pray by and for themselves all issue from those "meaner considerations" that Locke had condemned in petty minds bent on ennobling their desire to rule others.

Astell's visionary quality is never more illuminating than when she describes the processes of thinking and the delights of this civilizing achievement. An exhilarating chapter, subtitled "Of the Capacity of the Humane Mind in General," must have startled its readers with the spectacle of a closely reasoning female mind, trained in "philosophy, logic and mathematics," according to Janet Todd's *Dictionary of Women*. Astell explains in clear yet complex details how the mind works, that is, how it achieves all the complicated processes of idea-making. She traces the progress of its first infant attempts, its stumbles, its gathering self-confidence, and even its charming and quintessentially human capacity for sheer intellectual play. Twelve decades later, Austen was to call this human quality "a lovely display of what Imagination does" and a "delicious play of Mind," a combination of memory, reflection, study, and imagination, and she mourns that her niece, Fanny Austen-Knight, is destined to lose it, as soon as Fanny is "all settled down in conjugal and maternal affections" (*Letters*, 478–479). Wollstonecraft also asked how women could "discover that true beauty and grace must always arise from the play of mind," or how without minds permitted to play or to see the moral and intellectual virtues of such play, they could be expected to relish in a lover "what they do not, or very imperfectly, possess themselves" (*Vindication*, 118–119).

Just as Locke described earlier, Astell explains how the mind starts to learn by an artless imitation of ideas. For this process, the mind needs not only ideas suitable to its stage of development, but tutors, or what we now call "role models." These crucial figures in young scholars' lives not only suggest what ideas to look for and how to look, but they demonstrate by example how felicitous the whole process of thinking can be and, at the same time, how essential it is for one's personal salvation as well as for the enlightenment of whole classes of submerged peoples. Astell discusses the different functions of "the Will," "the Mind," "Intuition"; types of perspectives and ways to correct and extend them; the uses of the past, the present, and of books and public and private experience; the difference between science and faith, "received Notions" and reasoned hypotheses and premises; and all those tools and processes that she perceives as indispensable for the "perfection of the Understanding" and the "clearness and Largeness of its view" (*Serious Proposal*, 70, 76–80, 38). Although women must be taught to value this supremely human achievement for its own sake, Astell insisted as forcefully as "The Unsex'd Females" of the 1790s and their successors, that each woman must exert her mind as fully as her education permitted, in order to protect herself and to serve the community in which she had been placed.

It is not accidental that the heroines of Burney, Edgeworth, and Austen are none the worse when they read, think, and judge for themselves as naturally as they talk and love. One of the obvious pleasures for traditional readers is to watch the spectacle of these heroines gradually accepting the feminine roles still considered appropriate for women. But other readers can experience equal pleasure in the spectacle of the same heroines weighing and comparing the evidence of their ears and eyes and judging their judges for themselves, with varying degrees of success, as partial escapes from their feminine province gives them greater confidence in their autonomous opinions of events and people. Many of the heroines' judgments shock their suitors and acquaintances; and this moral isolation places them in conditions of stress and loneliness quite similar to the plight of the historical feminists whose subversive ideas had reached the creators of these heroines by devious routes.

Even Catherine Morland and Fanny Price, Austen's two models of the male conduct-book woman, are both ignorant as preadolescents, and they are meant to be kept that way. But they both learn some autonomy of judgment—Catherine from experience and Fanny through reading. As Astell stressed to all her readers, even those women who "may not have leisure to Learn languages and pore on books, nor opportunities to converse with the Learned," meaning almost all women, may nonetheless exercise their own judgments. For "all may *Think*, may use their own Faculties rightly and consult the master who is within them" (*Serious Proposal*, 98). And that, by implication, is exactly what Austen and her two favorite women novelists, Burney and Edgeworth, somehow found themselves permitted and empowered to do.

Throughout this generative essay, Astell repeatedly refers her readers to the "Shadow," in the form of myths and "illusions," which permanently darkened women's vision, as opposed to the radiant "Substance" of life, thought, and worship now denied them (*Serious Proposal*, 2, 9, and *passim*). In fact, one of the most attractive Enlightenment characteristics of Astell's mind, which she bequeathed to many of her successors, was her capacity to achieve a balance between theoretical extremes. Men are not classifiable merely as fops shamming love for women or as ascetic misogynists. Women should also refuse to fulfill either of the two stereotypes offered them, the illiterate fool or the learned crank. Although Astell "wou'd by no means encourage pride," yet women who were "content with Ignorance" as an innate female disability were indulging in dishonesty for opportunistic reasons, and those who confused "a mean and groveling spirit" with "true Humility" were endangering their very souls, since humility is due only to God and not to men (*Serious Proposal*, 158).

Astell refused to tolerate rationally and genetically unconnected ideas of women, which were chained together for reasons of sexual politics—such as the myth that to be born female is automatically to be born physically feeble and *thus* incapable of moral and intellectual capacities. She also condemned the irrational separation of ideas and capacities that were assumed to be appropriately joined in men, and that ought to function together in any full human being. She vigorously denounced the popular sentimental celebration of women's hearts at the expense of their minds, and she rejected the demeaning assumption that women with minds lacked hearts, which she knew to contradict the equally fallacious assumption that women with minds had volatile hearts and insatiable sexual drives. Since she specifically ignored the "received opinion" that women's bodies should be kept as quiet and passive as their minds, so that their sexual urges should remain as dormant as such urges were in properly conducted women, she advised a vigorous program that exercised the body as well as the mind; and lest the training for the human imagination be neglected, she recommended music and the plastic arts.

Astell refused to countenance the separation of women's hearts from their total selves, at the expense of their minds and bodies, precisely because she refused to separate nature from grace. Before women could function well, they had to discover what selves they were made of, in short, what natural gifts God had bestowed upon them at birth: "Nature and Grace will never disagree, provided we mistake not the one, nor indulge the petulancy of the other; there being no Displacements in Religion but what we ourselves have unhappily made" (*Serious Proposal*, 22).

One of Astell's most poignant characteristics was her anguish over the thwarted minds and souls of women she encountered all around her, and her tenderness toward those students of her imagination who struggled to overcome the almost insurmountable private and public obstacles placed in the way of their self-teaching. Austen's Fanny Price is a deprived and disenfranchised young women who would have warmed Astell's heart, for Fanny is no more a creature of fiction than the imaginary students in Astell's utopian college for women. Fanny created her own private college of one in her cold attic schoolroom, which afforded her a "safe retreat" from the world's contempt.

For obvious reasons in a scholar as conscious as Astell of her age's conventional indifference to women, she celebrated friendships and other potentially nonexploitive relationships. Her praise of the affections that close and noncompetitive colleagueship could bring is as touching as Austen's equally tender fictional celebrations of those rare moments of family love that her life's experience had taught her to cherish. In fact, without acknowledging the infusion of Astellian ideas in Austen's fiction, however she arrived at them, readers are in danger of misreading Austen's novels at every turn.

For Astell, friendship is not only a solace for the types of social betrayals that women's novels so persistently portrayed, but it is a moral necessity: it is a "virtue which compounds all the rest." For women especially, it is "a kind of revenging ourselves on the narrowness of our Faculties, by exemplifying that extraordinary Charity on one or two, which we are willing but not able to exercise towards all" (*Serious Proposal*, 32).

II

Just as Astell and other Enlightenment rationalists had urged their readers to seek all possible causes of all effects, and especially to search for observable origins of diseases, in individual bodies and in the body politic, so did Astell's feminine successors, theoretical and fictional, seek for the causes of effects and struggle to separate ends and means. In the open rhetorical discourse expected of the analytical essay, or in the more elusive methods of plots, themes, and symbolic speech and action expected in fiction, they all sought historical or contemporary causes of the hostility between the sexes and its effects upon women's moral, intellectual, and physical health, upon the suspect institution of marriage, and upon the children born to embattled couples.

How Astell passed on her bleak vision to post-Enlightenment feminists, we may never know. But the list of arguments, metaphysical turns and returns, rebuttal and qualifications that the feminists of the 1790s and later had in common with Astell would fill a fat volume. They all exploited the same metaphors of morally maimed, blinded, or fettered women; of creatures fluttering in vain, like caged birds; and they all placed their hopes in "an Ingenious education," meaning classical, rather than domestically utilitarian, which would comfort women in loneliness and allow them to "*see through* and scorn those silly Artifacts which are us'd to ensnare" them (*Serious Proposal*, 58, 9; emphasis mine). A hundred years later, Wollstonecraft insisted that as long as women are required to take "reason . . . second hand," by the reflected "light" of male prejudices, they will always be treated as creatures "only created to *see through* a gross medium and to take things on trust." In the voice of Elizabeth Bennet insisting to her fatuous suitor that she is a "rational creature," Wollstonecraft echoed Astell's voice: "My own sex, I hope, will excuse me if I treat them like rational creatures," rather than mere "*modest* slaves of opinion" (Wollstonecraft, *Vindication*, 48, 53, 9, 51; emphasis mine).

The same metaphors occur repeatedly, if obliquely, in the fiction of woman-centered novelists such as Burney, Edgeworth, and Austen. They represent the moral stigmata afflicting almost all the minor women characters, which the heroines transcend only through lonely and heroic struggles hardly acknowledged by anybody else.

The opportunistic blinding of women's moral and intellectual vision also appealed to Catherine Macaulay as an apt metaphor for their failure of "original thinking." The "texture of the mind" requires that the thinker be supplied with a rational and dignified "object *in view*," otherwise she is easily captured by the sight of "any little triffle" dangled before her. Unfortunately, both sexes tend to form "their opinions on trust" and upon "mere authority," and this common habit "must stop the progress" of all genuine thinking and all "improvement" in national ethics (*Letters on Education*, 127; emphasis mine).

Mary Hays described intelligent women trying frantically "to force their way through *the artificial cloud* that envelopes them." They are blinded by men who are themselves "*blinded* . . . by strong passions and still stronger prejudices." In revenge, women deliberately create the "*false appearance*" of the various "virtues they assume," and "with a certain degree of management and cunning," the deceived women become the deceivers, and the deceivers become the deceived twice over, first by their own blinding prejudices and then by those whom they intended to blind (*Appeal to the Men of Great Britain*, 44, 140, 225; emphasis mine).

Hays offered a brilliant example of a rational woman's refusal to accept received opinions on trust. Christians should not celebrate the assumptions of "the Apostles and the immediate successors of Christ" that men should dominate women as "the constant and unalterable appointment of heaven." For what were these disciples "but men, subject to the passions and prejudices of men?" One must always "ascend to the fountain head for instruction," and Christ himself was very "far from considering women as in any degree inferior in point of understanding" to men. "On the contrary," she said, unlike modern men, Christ addressed women "on the subjects of the highest importance" and performed miracles before them, and even "at their particular request." A "literal interpretation" of any event by which men endeavor to enslave the other sex is as dangerous for women as the acceptance of any other "after-thought of designing men" (*Appeal to the Men of Great Britain*, 5, 14–17, 3, 9).

Hays joined Macaulay, Wollstonecraft, and their model, Astell, in urging women to draw their opinions "from common sense, from experience, and observations,—all very keen searchers of human character and conduct" (*Appeal to the Men of Great Britain*, 2–3), and all intellectual virtues very well fitted to the purposes of women novelists deprived of university education and largely denied any public experience.

That an Enlightenment and post-Enlightenment public tolerated fierce and unrelenting misogyny under the guise of satire may come as small surprise in the late 1980s to scholars already alert to such historical fads and currents. But that women from Mary Astell to Jane Austen revenged themselves, sometimes with equal fierceness and persistence and with the very weapons of satire that had been inflicted upon them, may surprise even some scholars who are now unearthing the social history of women. Astell created a devastating vision of pan-historical masculine pugnacity. In the ironic mode that was so useful to her successors, both theoretical and fictional, she asks why any woman should complain about her sex's "intire Subjection" to every man born. After all, men have performed "all the great Actions," conquering and destroying entire empires abroad and at home, making laws that they immediately "repeal and amend," forming and disbanding "Cabals," and with their pens and the masculine privilege of satire, destroying reputations, public "Worlds," and whole "Systems of universal Nature."

Astell's most serious charge had been that pugnacious men accepted "no bounds or Measures" against their imperial "Desires," for they ignored "the petty Restraints which honour and conscience" lay upon women. And since they found it impossible to treat one another with little more "due Applause" than they offer women, it should be woman's function and her joy "to hear, admire and praise them" (*Some Reflections upon Marriage*, 59–60).

Mary Astell's descriptions of men in power creating and destroying empires and entire theoretical systems as gleefully as a sadistic small boy destroys insects is a distinct model for the same charges of her successors. The historian Catherine Macaulay describes war and pillage as an archetypal method of male governance throughout history. Among other examples, she chose Rome, which first destroyed Carthage, then Greece, and then reached for further landed booty. She implicitly compared the captive "provinces, reduced to beggary by the rapacity of their governors," to women, who like other conquered peoples, "groaned under the yoke of a power which they had once looked up to for protection." Throughout this study, princes, generals, theologians, and other "political fathers" function as macrocosms for the traditional English husband, the unrestrained domestic law-giver. The "total and absolute exclusion of every political right to the [female] sex" represents a mass example of the wrongs that those with unchecked power always visit upon those in their control (*Letters on Education*, 253–255, 224, 210, 16).

To explain and "excuse the tyranny of man" over woman, as Astell and Macaulay had attempted before her, Wollstonecraft also resorted to history, a subject not always considered appropriate for women. The human male, she said, had become "accustomed to bow down to power in his savage state" and had learned to worship the model of force and to assign its privileges to himself as a private citizen. It was therefore very difficult for him to "divest himself of this barbarous prejudice," even to the extent that he himself had benefited in the modern world from far greater political and theological liberty than past centuries had granted him. Men seem to consider themselves entitled to women's obedience and service according to some ancient pagan model of vanquished women as booty for male conquerors. The military "camp," the perpetual masculine metaphor and presumed reason for men's contemporary dominance over women, "has by some moralists been termed the school of the most heroic virtues," even though "civilization determines how much superior mental is to bodily strength" (*Vindication*, 19, 46, 146).

In describing male control over the female, Mary Hays, Wollstonecraft's radical successor, also appealed to the metaphor of imperial lusts backed by absolute power: "you maintain it by the same law by which the strong oppress the weak and the rich the poor; and by which the great and powerful crush the friendless and him who has none to help him." By "law," Hays meant a jungle law: "you maintain your empire by force alone" (*Appeal to the Men of Great Britain*, 28).

Hays exploited a brilliant and brutal analogy for the sadism that all the radical feminists of the 1790s perceived to be at the heart of misogyny. Surgeons who discovered a patient with cataracts in both eyes would often pick one eye at random, which they left alone and which they called "the *male* eye." They gave no name to the other eye upon which they performed surgery, while leaving the male eye intact. "Needless to say," the eye that the surgeons had attacked, and that Hays exemplified as the female eye, "suffered . . . the most extreme anguish," whereas the cataract in "the male eye" then "dispersed, nobody knows how except by the power of sympathy, but certainly without any operations being performed upon it." Hays's final comment is worthy of Austen's most savage modest proposals in her letters, turning as they often did upon the barbarous state of obstetrics and other frightening experiences then common only to her sex. "I almost forgot to mention that the poor eye on which the experiment was made, soon 'closed in endless night.' " Hays then drew a deliberate analogy between these brutal medical experiments and any other social arrangement, such as male dominance over women, "where one part only suffers, and the other receives all the benefit" (*Appeal to the Men of Great Britain*; 50–51).

In their studies of the human malaise of which they were the primary sufferers, Macaulay, Wollstonecraft, and Hays all informed their readers, in these terms, that they are going to examine "first principles," the "necessity" that governs responsible thinking and behavior, "causes and effects," "ends and means," "the relations of things" to other things in their proper proportion, the difference between "expediency" enforced in the name of principle, and logical, scientific, and therefore trustworthy "first principles" themselves. The radical feminists' obsession with masculine violence was not merely prompted by the shock value of these rhetorical techniques but by their attempts to examine the social causes and effects of tyrannical husbands, who represented the most extreme private example of unchecked male power.

From Astell to *Pride and Prejudice*, Austen's most widely read novel, the nouns *pride* and *prejudice*, often in pairs, are code words to describe men's pride in their dominion and their prejudice against the sex they dominated through their presumed superiority. Mary Hays admitted that "the seeds of pride and vanity, are originally planted in the breast of every human being," but men are given license for these destructive attitudes, and therefore women "dare not be what they . . . ought to be, because it clashes with the . . . prejudices of the stronger party" (*Appeal to the Men of Great Britain*, 76, 75).

Mary Astell, the mother of this discourse, analyzed the persistent "Pride in the Minds of Man," meaning the male sex, which "flatters him that he can see farther and Judge better than this neighbour." Astell was one of the first, if not the first woman writer, to insist that original sin sprang not so much from female vanity and insubordination as from most men's "groundless prejudice" against allowing women to exercise their minds and souls. Men guilty of these prejudices cannot be rational, for "Rational Creatures" do not allow "pride and Conceitures" or "Prejudice and Errors" to impede other people's search for salvation (*Serious Proposal*, 160, 20, 58, 68). But "Man" is so "Proud and vain" of "the Dignity and Prerogatives of his Sex" that he obstructs women's opportunities for salvation (*Some Reflections upon Marriage*, 30). For men have "long unjustly monopolized" all access to the "tree of Knowledge" and kept women ignorant of its pitfalls and its salvific properties alike, so that they could neither guard against its dangers nor benefit from its inducements to salvation. Even women, or perhaps especially women, so beleaguered and unprotected as they are from masculine spoilage, must be guided by "Reason," which demands of all of us "that we shou'd think again, and not form our Conclusions . . . till we can honestly say, that we have without Prejudice . . . view'd the matter in Debate on all sides, seen in every light" and "have no bias to encline us either way" (*Serious Proposal*, 20, 68).

A hundred years later, Macaulay was condemning the "pride and prejudices of man," which appeared under many guises. Men's "sensuality," which reluctantly drew them to women, was "soothed" by their assumption of "superiority," which in turn increased their sexual lusts. But "I owe to you," she remarked candidly, "that my pride and prejudices lead me to regard my sex in a higher light than the mere objects of sense" (*Letters on Education*, 9, 212–213). She attributed the outmoded "notion of a sexual difference in the human character" not only to the "ignorance and vanity of women" but overwhelmingly to the "pride" of men. Macaulay observed this principle of tyranny and oppression throughout "the animal creation," including the human animal. Just as humans maltreat animals, who have equal claim with themselves to justice and compassion, so do men mistreat women, for the idea of equality and dignity between different types of God's creatures is "so mortifying to the fond prejudices and pride of our species," that we do not stop to think how "alarming" every new idea "is to the ignorant and the prejudiced" (*Letters on Education*, 1–2, iii, 203–204).

Following Macaulay, Wollstonecraft condemned the "pride and sensuality of man," the masculine "pride of power," the "arrogant pride of man," the "prejudices" of men induced by their "sensual reveries" of conquering debilitated women, and their persistent exploitation of false "reason to justify prejudices, which they have imbibed, they can scarcely trace how." The male "throne of prerogative only rests on a chaotic mass of prejudices," and the most destructive of these is the "prejudice" that beauty, "mere beauty of features and complexion," represents the only "perfection of woman" (*Vindication*, 44–45, 29, 11–12, 101). The "poor victims" of this masculine "pride" are forced "to remain immured in their families groping in the dark," because the combined pride and prejudices of men have distorted masculine reason: the male "sensualist," lost in "his voluptuous reveries" of fragile and perfumed women, insists that she and all her sex be forever denied "civil and political rights" so as to preserve her in an undefiled living death (*Vindication*, 154, 5, 24–25). In this circular example of masculine "reason on false ground," women's artificially preserved beauty becomes the badge of "prejudices broached by power" and unchecked lusts (*Vindication*, 69, 113).

On one page alone of *A Vindication of the Rights of Woman*, Wollstonecraft intoned a dirge of the noun "prejudice" nine times (*Vindication*, 113). And the whole of *Vindication* is a lament against the "fumes which pride and sensuality have spread over the subject" and "the number of human sacrifices" that are made to "that moloch prejudice" (*Vindication*, 26, 176). It was the belief of the feminist theorists, both radical and moderate, as it was the belief of woman-centered novelists including Austen, that this mass pride and prejudice sacrificed not only women and their children, but the intelligent happiness of men as well.

Hays acknowledged her debt to Wollstonecraft (*Appeal to the Men of Great Britain*, "Introduction," 7–10) as Wollstonecraft had acknowledged hers to Macaulay (*Vindication*, 198, note), and Hays resorted as fully as her utopian predecessors to the language of "pride" and "prejudice." "ALL PREJUDICES are inimical" to society's "happiness and interests," yet one must try "to manage with some degree of tenderness" the common run of "prejudices" and "to respect even *these* till the multitude can be persuaded" of their errors (*Appeal to the Men of Great Britain*, "Advertisement," 5th p.; n.p.).

Hays would no more defend the "obstinacy or pride of man" than she would excuse the "frivolous or inconsistent" habits into which the enforced sloth of many wealthy women had driven them. Either failing creates grave social misunderstandings and unhappiness. But those men who "pride themselves upon this rugged quality of mind," are "equally tenacious of right" or of "wrong," and their "pride and obstinacy" cause all the more domestic unhappiness (*Appeal to the Men of Great Britain*, 43, 42, 53).

Hays described marriage as a relationship ideally designed for the "perfecting" of the "human species." She asked the same questions that the satire and the sadness in the novels of Burney, Edgeworth, and Austen implicitly ask: How can the two sexes "discourage . . . vice in each other," or "reward" each other's "virtue" as long as men's "pride of heart," and their "old prejudices" and "overstrained notions of their own consequence and dignity" poison domestic relationships? Although especially "in this enlightened age . . . every prejudice ought to be laid aside," yet "every little opposition on the part of women" rouses "the men's pride and resentment" to an irrational pitch. As Astell, Macaulay, and Wollstonecraft had also insisted, some self-serving readings of national imperatives and scriptural literature and the dictates of "custom and prejudice," "imposed by the hand of authority," now prevented any serious attempts at the perfectibility of "reason," "passion" or common "sense" (*Appeal to the Men of Great Britain*, 138–139, 112–113, 128–129).

III

The essays of the moderate feminists, Priscilla Wakefield, Elizabeth Hamilton, Jane West, Clara Reeve and Maria Edgeworth, regressed in ways that were critical for Austen's fiction; she praised some of them and paraphrased them all. Astell and the 1790s radicals had hoped to be agents for systematic changes in law, theology, education, and social and economic practices affecting women. The moderates believed that women were mired in patriarchal systems incapable of change, and that therefore only heroic and piecemeal efforts on their own behalf could help them.

The moderates tended to shift their targeted readers from both sexes to women alone. Both sets of feminists tried "to account for and excuse the tyranny of man," but the moderates did so with less confidence than the radicals. Between their essays and those of the radicals many male conduct-book writers had emerged, whose main function was to act as policemen to aspiring feminists. The prefaces to the moderates' essays were full of appeasing comments: they did not intend to step out of their province; they did not dispute men's superior strength nor the biblical strictures against women in authority; they did not intend to cause domestic and national upheavals; and so forth. But they vehemently disagreed with men who claimed that they would be departing from "the necessary duties" and the "proper manners, graces, and accomplishments of [their] sex," whenever they attempted to "arrange, abstract, pursue," or "diversify in a long train of ideas," since God had not granted them the brains for these achievements (Bennett, *Female Education*, 88, 7). And yet, to publish at all, they now felt they needed to adopt that rhetoric of "Meekness," conventionally considered sexually "alluring" and in any case, a "duty . . . incumbent upon all women" (Duff, *Character of Women*, 256).

Just as alert readers have been aware of the muffled despair in

Austen, the loyal Anglican churchwoman, which sometimes erupts in satire, so did religious loyalties frequently muffle the voices of the moderates, which sometimes erupt into acerbic irony. Jane West imitated the male habit of associating women with animals by comparing men to predatory wolves, vultures, peacocks, jackasses, and braying donkeys, simultaneously playing the role of domestic emperor and spoiled baby. Austen's ridiculously self-important and self-indulgent suitors and husbands, her spoiled heirs, indifferent to their sisters' welfare, and her callous fathers of Mr. Bennet's stamp, who mocked his daughters while he enjoyed their miseries, emerge out of this school of feminine satire, no matter what else her own satire addresses.

The moderates thought no more highly of marriage than their radical predecessors. Jane West offered the bleak advice that "in the married state, women should never *expect* too much, nor feel to *keenly*," and this fact "can never be too deeply impressed on the ardent mind of youth," particularly of that sex whose hearts were said to be most properly at the permanent service of the other sex. " 'Hope deferred maketh the heart sick,' " and marriage is one long deferred hope: it is "John Bull's . . . prison house!" Throughout life, women "scarcely know the exercise of free will"; they cannot dispose "of their time or their fortunes," nor can they chose their "pleasures," their "friends," or even "the spot on earth where they would reside" (*Letters to a Young Lady*, III, 97, 130; II, 366, 372).

Elizabeth Hamilton, a favorite with Austen, described the painful discipline required of wives: "All the decorums of life, all the graces which constitute the charm of polished manners, are the offspring of restraint imposed on inclination; not till they have acquired the force of habit, are they adopted by nature as her own. Before this can happen, how many painful sacrifices must be paid!"[6]

Austen's letters to her sister Cassandra are full of this same sad resignation, chastened by the corrective of her irony. But then, not only did every male conduct-book writer urge women never to give way to self-pity, but also he often coupled this advice with the information that women suffered nothing to induce self-pity, while a few pages later, he might insist that the suffering that God had inflicted on women unfitted them for equality with men. In any case, irony can perform the function of allowing its practitioner to accept God's will with as much equanimity as possible, even though Austen's fiction and her correspondence indicate that she thought God was suspiciously partial to his own sex.

One evidence of the lost nerve from which the moderates understandably suffered after the worse excesses of the French Revolution and the discrediting of the radicals, was their difficulty in imagining that women would be permitted to form close and nourishing friendships. Astell and the radicals of the 1790s had offered imaginary glimpses of libraries, classrooms, and feminist colleagues talking back and forth to each other, thus exemplifying that "play of the mind" usually denied them. They all thought that women could remake themselves, enforce some respect from men, and thus ease their own sufferings. As Macaulay had remarked: the human creature "is as artificial a being" as a portrait "on the canvas of the painter," for it is the "distinguishing characteristic of our species . . . that we can make ourselves over again" (*Letters on Education*, 10).

One of the greatest aids in remaking oneself was the friendship of other struggling women, according to feminist wisdom. But if we think back to Astell's radiant apotheosis to friendships between women, it is sad to encounter some characteristic obstacles to women's friendships described by several moderates. Clara Reeve's allegorical Lady A______. cannot resume a friendship with Reeve's equally allegorical governess, Frances Darnford, without the "permission" of Lady A______.'s husband. Although Lord A______. "allows" them considerable frankness, their friendship is bound to be tainted by his previous attempts at seduction inflicted upon the vulnerable Mrs. Darnford.[7]

Priscilla Wakefield was particularly distressed over a social phenomenon familiar to students of group rebellions, which enforced additional isolation upon intelligent women. Those who struggle against oppression threaten members of their group who do not: "Of the few who have raised themselves to re-eminence by daring to stray beyond the accustomed path, the envy of their own sex, and the jealousy or contempt of the other, have too often been the attendants" (*Present Condition of the Female Sex*, 7). Even worse, among the disciplines that Elizabeth Hamilton catalogued as marital drawbacks was the necessity for women to temporize with women friends, even if the friendship had preceded the marriage. Jane West's anguished remarks about the discomfort that women's friendships often aroused in husbands, sadly repeat what the male conduct-book writers had merely announced as a fact: many men think of their wives' friendship with other women as a form of betrayal. "Friendship is not monarchical in its constitution, like love," but West said that "marriage is *constantly* the grave of female friendship." A woman's exertions to serve an old friend must be limited by the permission of her husband, and by what she owed to his interests and to those of her children. But despite the fact that a rich and trustworthy friendship with another woman is "an inestimable treasure, and we ought to feel its value," if husbands become jealous, "Should caprice . . . so cloud their judgments, I conceive that every humble entreaty, every temperate remonstrance which female eloquence can suggest should deprecate the privation; which, if hard necessity comples, female sensibility must with *slow* reluctance *painfully endure*" (*Letters to a Young Lady*, III, 83, 67, 72–73).

Although the moderates lacked the vivid vision of a reconstructed world that illuminated even the accusatory rhetoric of the radicals, Wakefield and Reeve both drew up very precise plans for women's education and for methods to facilitate their entry into the world of work and their survival there. Yet as they both admitted, the double standard about women and work was as cruel as the double standard about women's sexuality. Men of the middle and upper classes, they said, all too often posed as women's protectors by imprisoning them at home, then leaving them penniless and uneducated, and then refusing them any entry into work upon which they could survive without penury or indignity. When a woman was faced with the choice of working or starving, through no fault of her own, why should "degradation . . . attend" her merely because "her good sense and resolution enable her to support herself," and why should she be "banished from . . . the company of which she had perhaps previously formed a distinguished ornament?" (Wakefield, *Present Condition of the Female Sex*, 72).

Austen's semiauthorial voice, describing the anguished thoughts of Jane Fairfax, creates this same mournful scenario, including some of the same terminology. Jane's foster-sister had a dowry sufficient to purchase a husband, "while Jane had yet her bread to earn." Jane struggles with a profound depression brought on by her impending banishment from her lover and from "all the rational pleasures of an elegant society" and the "judicious mixture of home and amusement" in London. Jane and her foster-parents demonstrate "fortitude" and "good sense," but Jane's interior monologue describes her approaching "penance and mortification" as a "sacrifice" that entailed permanent exile "from all the pleasures of life of rational intercourse, equal society, peace and hope" (*E*, 164–165).

Maria Edgeworth's analysis of marriage and of woman's condition was the most damning of all five moderate feminists. Her collection of satirical feminist essays, *Letters for Literary Ladies*, includes a scathing attack on current gender relations called "An Essay on the Noble Science of Self-Justification." In this mock correspondence, Edgeworth's fictional female advisor describes marriage for women as a military "engagement" against that "enemy," the "husband." Throughout this wickedly satirical essay, "the enemy" is usually in immediate syntactical opposition with "your husband." The wife must train herself like an army officer, whose "choice of [her] weapon" should depend upon "those which [her] adversary cannot use." She must never "provoke the combined forces of the enemy to a regular engagement, but harass him with perpetual petty skirmishes." In this war, the conquered can never win, yet by creating an "incessant" military "tatoo," she may be able to manage a "defensive" survival ("Essay on Self-Justification," 7–8, 20–25). Austen particularly admired Edgeworth, and it is pleasurable to speculate whether she found this satire useful in her own satirical models of marital warfare between Mr. and Mrs. Bennet or Mr. and Mrs. Palmer.

Even the full title of Edgeworth's satire, "An Essay on the Noble Science of Self-Justification," is a clear echo of Wollstonecraft's comment about contemporary relationships between the sexes: "defensive war" is "the only justifiable war . . . where virtue can shew its face." Such a "just and glorious war" against a godless enemy "might again animate female bosoms." But even the impenitent Wollstonecraft felt she must assure her "gentle" readers of both sexes that although she had compared "a modern soldier with . . . a civilized woman," she was "not going to advise them to turn their distaff into a musket," but she did "sincerely wish to see the [male] bayonet concerted into a pruninghook" (*Vindication*, 145–146). These remarks do indeed deliver a warning that in the war of words, women now had the arsenal of secret self-education and even access to commercial presses.

From Mary Astell onward, metaphors describing the nature and the history of the bellicose male express a pervasive feminine terror about marriage, about men's primitive rights over the minds and bodies of women, and their association of these rights with themselves as God's designated scourge and warrior. Even Austen's favorite, the moderate Elizabeth Hamilton, described how in the past, "Alters raised to the God of heaven were polluted by human blood," while "parents resigned their children to the murderous knife," assuming that they were thus winning the "favour of the deity." But such "cruelties could not fail to make the people cruel," since they "believed that God delighted in injustice." It is true that "wars and revolutions" appear throughout human history, where "one event seems to grow out of another as natural and unavoidable occurrences," and that they represent "Divine Providence." Yet their immediate earthly cause is the "ferocity in the human mind," by which Hamilton here meant the male military mind (*Letters to the Daughter of a Nobleman*, II, 5–7, 40).

Radical and moderate feminists thought it small wonder that the average husband, taught neither to respect his wife nor to offer her those Christian attributes of courtesy or justice, should resemble a pillaging god of war, some Mars descending upon a weakened Troy, which his troops have infiltrated and then sacked. The moderate Wakefield's advice to women arises out of this pervasive feminine fear. Unlike men, she said, a woman must live, "not for herself only, but to contribute to the happiness of others." The purposes of this feminine appeasement quickly emerge: only by "bearing patiently" with her husband's irascible "tempter" and in learning "to soften his asperities," as though she were pleading for mercy from the emissaries of an advancing enemy, might she achieve the ambiguous blessing of peace in her time (*Present Condition of the Female Sex*, 36).

Clara Reeve was as diffident and as full of the terminology that characterizes appeasement as Wakefield or Hamilton. Yet in her *Plans of Education*, which defined a rigorous education for women of the gentry classes, she places her imaginary governess, Mrs. Darnford, in an ugly adversarial position with Lord A——. His attempt to seduce a penniless upper servant was merely another aspect of the war upon women that was engaging the moral condemnations of all feminists. Lord A——'s. son was at Eton, and readers would assume that his own education had been comparable. But one of the feminists' most frequent accusations, which have their oblique counterpart in the fiction of Burney, Edgeworth, and Austen, was that boys' education at the universities and at the great public schools lacked as much in ethical and moral training as women's lacked in intellectual. Since Lord A______. felt free to attack a defenseless woman, his own education had clearly been deficient not only in Christian concern for those stripped of power but it had also lacked that sportsmanship upon which Englishmen pride themselves.

In their war against oppressive conditions, the moderate feminists were as fully skilled as the radicals in adopting the weapons of classical logic, such as arguments about cause and effect, first principles and premises, and ends and means. But of these five moderates, only Edgeworth's series of essays in *Letters for Literary Ladies* fully spells out the rhetorical process necessary for women's defense. In her "Letters of Julia and Caroline," the war of "the woman question" has been declared between two women, each thinking about what women owe men, or what, if anything, they owe themselves. And just as Austen's Elinor Dashwood argues vehemently with her sister to try to protect Marianne against Willoughby's insidious attacks, and just as Elizabeth Bennet tries to arm her naive sister Jane against the male tendency to enter a town, capture female hearts, and escape for further conquests elsewhere, so does Edgeworth's Caroline argue with Julia in her attempts to save this pathetically craven young woman from the wretched marriage she is planning with an arrogant young nobleman. Caroline begs Julia to see how inconsistent she is when she assumes that the "*art*" of pleasing men is not only "instinct," or "nature," born of women's finer sensibilities, but that "the sole object of a woman's life" should be "*to please.*" Julia's lapses in logic are far more dangerous than her acceptance of "received opinion" and her confusion between the artifice of custom on the one hand, and on the other, those traits that she conventionally assigns to women as innate. And yet she condemns just the sort of metaphysical inquiry that Astell recommended and that Austenian readers have identified in Austen when they call her "Johnsonian."

As Caroline tries repeatedly to explain, those mental and ethical processes that Julia condemns as "vain systems! and theories and reasonings" inappropriate to women, would not only assist her in attaining her desired ends—her happiness—but they would also help her to realize that her means—marriage to a man who despised her—would fail to obtain her ends:

> Your object, dear Julia, is "to please." If general observation and experience have taught you that slight accomplishments, [and] a trivial character, succeed more certainly in obtaining this end, than higher worth, and sense, you act from principle in rejecting the one and aiming at the other. You have discovered the secret causes which produce an effect, and you employ them. Do not call this instinct or nature; this also, though you scorn it, is philosophy.
>
> Let us, however, distinguish between disapprobation of the object and the means. ("Julia and Caroline," 11, 12–17)

Edgeworth seems to have had Wollstonecraft's advice in mind, which is based on the familiar feminist strictures against easy acceptance of commonplace "prejudices," such as Julia's prejudice against analysis. "A measure rotten at the core," in which "expediency is continually contrasted with simple principles," may well fail not only in its ends but even in the "expediency" that was its goal. As Wollstonecraft had remarked with ironic humility: "I may be allowed to infer that reason is absolutely necessary to enable a woman to perform any duty properly, and I must again repeat, that sensibility is not reason" (*Vindication*, 12, 64).

Caroline argues in vain that Lord V______'s "family pride," his "personal vanity" embracing his sex and his "exalted station," and his inability to offer "equal friendship and confidence, or any of the delicacies of affection," would cancel the benefits of his "large fortune" and his "extensive connections" ("Julia and Caroline," 33, 35). Lord V______ is clearly a model for Austen's Fitzwilliam Darcy, but Julia is hardly a model for Elizabeth Bennet. For Julia's means are ignoble, since she intends to use a man as a mere object, just as men were said to use women. Even her ends were meretricious: she seeks happiness in things that she will be given rather than in intellectual or moral achievements that she would have to earn.

Edgeworth was not the only moderate feminist bringing subtle and sustained analysis to the management of women's predicament. They were all affected by the decombinative and recombinative itch of the responsible intellectual subversive, despite their anxieties—so easy to respect when one considers the hysterical climate gripping England after the French Reign of Terror. They all distinguished between the masculine myth of the innately serviceable feminine heart and their own understanding of how that heart is shaped from birth. In company with Astell and the 1790s feminists, and with the women novelists who learned from them, they wished to see the womanly heart transcending its previous instrumentality of other people's distorted myths and desires. And they wished also to see the feminine faculty of the heart combined with the intellectual faculties of seeking, comparing, and selecting ideas. Only when women's minds and hearts were taught to function comfortably together could they demand justice and compassion for themselves. And only then, the feminists all observed or implied, could women discern which members of their society and which policies deserved their allegiance, and which did not.

These same processes of investigation, comparison, and selection of both ideas and potential lovers and companions appear as pervasive motifs in the three novels that Austen praised in *Northanger Abbey*. Her comments about these novels and her own analytical habits in her fiction indicate as clearly as she thought politic that she considered herself the latest novelist in a tradition of "Enlightenment feminist" fiction.

IV

Over one hundred women writers published more than six hundred novels and other fictional forms between Aphra Behn's *Adventures of the Black Lady* (1684) and Austen's *Sense and Sensibility* (1811).[8] Yet the history of women's achievements is still so fragmented that we cannot be sure how many of these works were familiar to Frances Burney, before her epistolary frolic, *Evelina*, emerged in 1778 to delight and astonish the English reading public. But as Judy Simons has observed, beneath the surface glitter and sweetness that still deceive her readers, Burney "shows her concern for the plight of women. The subtitle of her last novel is *Female Difficulties*, and it could be applied to all her novels."[9] But *Evelina*, which enters the mind of a female nobody whose predicament was a rebuke to an imaginary society cheerfully ignoring it, nevertheless "was received with . . . undiluted acclamation" in the actual society that praised the novel so highly for its verisimilitude.[10] Perhaps its readers could deny its subversive quality all the more easily because it is so charming, and because they had not yet been alerted to danger by the 1790s feminists, whose works did not begin to emerge until over a decade later.

Austen was familiar with all of Burney's novels, not only because she admired them, but because she hungrily read all the novels by women that her library stocked, since she could seldom afford to buy books. Her own novels have clearly inherited the same "insidious feminist sympathies," which Burney's novels display, as well as permission to write fiction that is concerned "centrally with female survival" and with "the attempts of a young woman to maintain an independent identity in a world inimical to female interests" (*Cecilia*, x–xi).

All three novels that Austen praised so lavishly in *Northanger Abbey*, are "insidiously" feminist, and they could all be as appropriately subtitled *Female Difficulties* as Austen's novels. Burney's *Cecilia* and *Camilla* and Edgeworth's *Belinda* are worth studying in themselves, but they also illuminate Austen's work. They are also of crucial importance for scholars who are fascinated with the function of novels as social barometers, because Burney's *Evelina* anticipated so accurately the 1790s furor about the "woman question," and because Edgeworth's novels, and principally *Belinda*, reflect it with equal prescience.

The novels of Burney, Edgeworth, and Austen are often so insidiously feminist in their plots, their metaphoric symbols, their dialogues and monologues, and their authorial voices, that their covert imitation of the "*HE* . . . she" substructure that shaped the feminist discourse has been entirely overlooked. From Astell and the 1790s radical feminists to the most moderate of the moderates, the subject of investigation was what "*HE*" could do, and why throughout history "*HE*" had been permitted to do it, and what "she" could not do, and all the myths and all the masculine assumptions about feminine utility that had perpetuated women's predicament. These two implicit columns, "*HIS*" rights and "her" duties, which function as an official architectural principle throughout the feminists' discourse, now function with equal structural governance for Austen and her two fictional predecessors, however deceptively they draped this architectural principle with the surface good humor of their satire.

Burney, Edgeworth, and Austen all create debates of varying flippancy or seriousness about the feminine predicament. Anne Elliot's great dialogue with Captain Harville resonates with all the debates on this subject that had preceded *Persuasion*, from both feminist theorists and novelists. Burney, Edgeworth, and Austen all consider how much money their heroines and their minor feminine characters are allowed to accrue, how these women are permitted to spend it, and what restraint predators and busybodies placed upon their funds.[11] All three novelists treat ironically those of their male characters who have been granted a classical education and who despise it or abuse it. They all stress that among their heroines, who have been denied a thorough formal education, only the autodidacts have genuinely survived.

All three novelists, in fact, have somehow absorbed a complete and systematic feminist vision, which describes, however covertly, the circular connections between a callous patriarchy, feminine poverty, poor education, low self-esteem, and meretricious conduct where it occurs. They all display the same determination that Mary Evans identified in Austen's heroins alone: despite the landmines on all sides, all the heroines attempt, with various success, to be "active makers of their fate" (*Jane Austen and the State*, x). Austen's Fanny Price had painfully learned "all the heroism of principle" and she was "determined to do her duty" (*MP*, 265). Edgeworth's Belinda Portman was advised to practice the "civil courage" that "enabled the Princess Parizade, in the Arabian Tales to go straight up the hill to her object, through the magical multitude of advising and abusive voices continually calling her to turn back."[12] This excellent advice is also ominous; it suggests that in the war between the sexes, a woman would be surrounded by no well-wishers, but only a crowd of advisors urging that she rely upon received opinions alone. She must brave this opposition with all the courage of a single soldier storming a hill under a barrage of artillery.

All the heroines, from Burney's naive waif Evelina to Austen's mature and often quietly ironic Anne Elliot, lack conditions that allow them to act with self-respecting autonomy. They all struggle with varying success to substitute "civil courage," or the "heroism of principle" that earns readers' respect. It may well be, also, that the heroines' predictable triumph at the altar, with the men whom they chose, wisely or otherwise, allowed these novels to escape the public notoriety that their subversive material ought to have earned them. But since woman-centered novelists could then only imagine the moral triumph of exceptionally courageous or dutiful women, their readers need never consider whether the universal treatment of women was pernicious. These heroines were token survivors presumably exemplifying the possibilities for all women who behaved themselves and bore themselves with "mental resolution," "fortitude," and "patterns of firmness, composure, and resignation under tedious and painful trials." Gisborne claimed "that Providence" had "conferred" these morally utilitarian traits on "women in general," while paradoxically conferring moral inequality upon them (*Duties of the Female Sex*, 25–30).

Austen's heroines are indeed token survivors in her fictional world. Each of them, like their sister heroines in Burney and Edgeworth, is surrounded by exploitive men and shallow, opportunistic women, and readers sensitive to their difficulties will interpret their internal monologues as silent cries for help that arrives, when it does, in the conventional form of a husband who could never solve their difficulties even if he were aware of them.

Austen's heroines are systematically made to feel almost as guilty as Cecilia, Camilla, and Belinda. They apologize as often, whether they are guilty or not, and their apologies are as often taken at face value, both by the inhabitants of their fictional world and by modern readers. They also feel the same excessive "gratitude" to anyone who treats them kindly, and their profound gratitude to the man who has finally chosen them after placing them on trial after trial, is as heartfelt as all the male conduct-book writers said that it ought to be. They are all provided with false tutors and tutors who may be benevolent enough but who are bound to obey patriarchal discipline.

Here, too, Austen had her models: Burney's Mrs. Delvile, disgusted by the ugly role she is forced to play against Cecilia, the daughter-in-law she really yearns for, "gravely yet with energy exclaimed" to Cecilia:

> How few there are, how very few, who marry at once upon principles rational, and feelings pleasant! Interest and inclination are eternally at strife, and where either is wholly sacrificed, the other is inadequate to happiness . . . the young are rash, and the aged are mercenary: their deliberations are never in concert, their views are scarcely even blended; one vanquishes, and the other submits; neither party temporizes, and commonly each is unhappy. (*Cecilia*, 488)

The semiauthorial voice in *Sense and Sensibility* echoes the same mournful dirge. Elinor Dashwood is separated from the man she loves by the pride and prejudices of his widowed mother, who has tried to rule him as fathers rule daughters. She has threatened to disinherit him unless he marries Lord Morton's daughter, an heiress to £30,000, and she has created a son who lacks moral autonomy and who is full of feminine "self-mortification":

> Elinor placed all that was astonishing in [Edward's] way of acting to his mother account. . . . His want of spirits, of openness, and of consistency, were mostly attributed to his want of independence, and his better knowledge of Mrs. Ferrars's disposition and designs [for him]. The shortness of his visit, the steadiness of his purpose in leaving them, originated in the same fettered inclination, the same inevitable necessity of temporizing with his mother. The old, well-established grievance of duty against will, parent against child, was the cause of it all. (*SS*, 102)

The metaphor of the double feminine punishment—both incarceration and exile—is an obsessive motif in all three of these novelists. Cecilia Beverley's enforced removal to London from the friends and the county she loves is as melancholy as the journey into another exile that the Dashwood women endure. Although Cecilia is an heiress, she is permitted no more autonomy than Austen's wealthy Emma Woodhouse or than historical heiresses of that time were usually able to command. "Reluctantly, she complied," which became Cecilia's motto for survival, was also the implicit guide for all these heroines, whether their conscience or their temperament allowed them to obey or not.

All these heroines were just as apt to be kept at home, so as to ensure feminine passivity or for reasons of parental convenience or indifference, as they were to be abruptly banished from home. Burney's Camilla Tyrold stays at home, while her mercurial lover comes and goes for years at a time. Once Cecilia Beverley is in London, she has endless constraints upon her movements, in shocking contrast to the speed with which her status as an orphan precipitated her exile. Edgeworth's Belinda Portman is forced to shift uneasily from her family home to the home of a titled woman who abuses her, and from London to a suburban house of an affectionate couple, from which she is periodically summoned back to London. The Dashwoods' banishment from Norland and their exile to Devon is matched by Fanny Price's first banishment from Portsmouth to Mansfield Park, then back to Portsmouth as a punitive measure, and a final return to Mansfield when the reason for her second banishment has simply been forgotten. But after her banishment from her first home, she is kept prisoner in the house and on the grounds of Mansfield Park for a decade, since nobody cares enough about her to see that she enjoys a rational social life.

Catherine Morland's journey to Bath to find a husband is a most unusual event for an Austenian heroine, as her creator admits. Mrs. Bennet's obsessive fear of expulsion from Longbourn, accompanied by five marginally dowered daughters, carries the same echoes of similar reasons for feminine distress that readers encounter from Astell's *Serious Proposal* through *Persuasion*.

Austen's Anne Elliot is another victim of the double fate so often suffered by these heroines. Her marriage portion has been appropriated by her greedy father, who will not allow her to travel with him while he luxuriates in county houses and in London with his eldest daughter. But his greed forces him to rent Anne's beloved Kellynch Hall which she has preserved and cherished during his long months of absence. Her reward is an enforced exile in Bath, which she loathes with all the passions of a squire attached to the land and its responsibilities.

Burney, Edgeworth, and Austen all supply their novels with at least one truth-telling female monster, who makes comments about the female predicament that are meant to shock readers happy with received opinions. One of them, Emma Woodhouse, is a heroine. Lady Catherine de Bourgh's tart comment that male entail, the descent of land and money through the male line, works great hardships on women is a painful truth for the Bennet sisters. Equally true and painful is Lady Catherine's casual comment that fathers have little use for daughters. Mrs. Arlbery, a shallow, fashionable widow, has a tender concern for Camilla, the naive victim of a misogynist lover, whom Mrs. Arlbery accuses of false "pride" and an unwarranted sense of sexual superiority.[13]

In *Belinda*, Mrs. "Freke," a despicable figure meant to disarm readers as a caricature of the radical feminists, in fact, quite often does the opposite. She initiates one of the most intelligent debates in all the feminist literature, condemning the euphemistic language of the male conduct-book writers and the falsehoods by which women are governed and silenced. Mrs. Freke's impassioned outburst—"you may say what you will, but the present system of society is radically wrong;—whatever is, is wrong . . . I'd have both sexes call things by the right name"—resonates throughout and beyond this novel. The prophetic cry of the biddable but highly analytical and speculative Belinda, "give her air—

give her air, air, air!" takes on an equally ominous resonance, within and beyond the novel (*Belinda*, 209, 421).

Austen's most obvious borrowing occurs in the title of *Pride and Prejudice*. The pair of nouns, *pride* and *prejudice*, appears so often in *Cecilia* as to function with almost allegorical significance. The Delvile male "pride" in rank and wealth, as well as their "prejudice" against Cecilia, are emblems of London's proud and privileged citizens and their "prejudices" against disenfranchised or displaced people of all sorts—women, the poor, respectable artisans, condemned criminals, the old, and the sick and dying. Lady Honoria Pemberton mocks the "pride" and the "prejudices" of the Delviles in these terms. Dr. Lyster, a genial truthteller and a confidant of rare good sense and integrity toward women, informs Cecilia and her lover that their whole sad estrangement had "been the result of *PRIDE* and *PREJUDICE*" exhibited by two excessively patriarchal males. But if the battered couple were entitled to charge their prolonged miseries where the accusation belonged, upon a Dean of the established church and a titled landowner, they also owed their journey's loving end to "*PRIDE and PREJUDICE*" as well. Just as Elizabeth Bennet's condemnation of Darcy's hollow pride in his title of gentleman stimulates his desire to behave like one, so Dr. Lyster's tongue-lashings of Lord Delvile for the same sins of pride and prejudice perform the same function (*Cecilia*, 908).

Yasmine Gooneratne's *Jane Austen* describes the isolation in which Austen's heroines live, so mournfully reminiscent of the experiences of Cecilia and Belinda, and even of Camilla, whose worthy parents are for understandable reasons largely oblivious to the forces arrayed against her, including their own benevolent selves. Gooneratne was quite explicit about the social "defects and injustices," aimed exclusively at women, from which Austen's heroines "suffer":

> Her heroines marry men who appreciate their virtues and their moral (and sometimes their intellectual) superiority to their immediate world, but never does it even wish them well. . . . To Marianne Dashwood in London, to Fanny Price in her parents' home at Portsmouth, and to Anne Elliot, entering her father's new lodging in Bath, life becomes a burden, creating a sickness of heart that agonizes and seems almost like death.

Gooneratne sees in Austen's novels the sustained satire that tries to mask grief and anger with as decent a covering as possible. Yet "a careful reader cannot miss the irony implicit in the maxim that only the fair deserve the rich, with its criticism of a society that provided no satisfactory alternative to marriage for women, pretty or plain."[14]

But by 1811, when Austen was revising *Sense and Sensibility*, a decade had elapsed since Napoleon's most frightening successes had terrified England. The national anxiety was now considerably eased, and Austen's letters reveal a diminished fear for her two naval brothers, and a renewed interest in her writing.

This first published novel combines several Austenian voices in addition to the voice of the post-Augustan moralist and satirist already universally acknowledged. *Sense and Sensibility* is often drenched in a deep sadness, and this grief, which clearly afflicts both the heroines and their creator, discomforts most lovers of her work so much that they ignore its presence or dismiss it as mere melodrama. For the same reason, perhaps, traditional criticism has ignored an innate quality in abundance, which I think is Austen's alone. Yet it is a quality that subliminally appeals to feminists, patriarchs, and readers committed to no position at all about "the woman question," and which differs profoundly from satire; for satire signifies social distress of some sort.

These novels also express Austen's marvelously irrepressible delight, not only in ridiculous moments, which is the gift of satirist, but in lovely and touching ones as well. It is a celebratory quality that I can only describe as Austenian joy, although there is a clear precedent in Shakespearean comedy, which she or her characters often quote or paraphrase. It is comedic gift that exhibits her intellectual and psychological vigor, as well as an ebullient moral resilience that signifies grace under prolonged adversity. It is a capacity similar to the instinctive courage of a soldier who rejoices when a single bird sings during a lull in the bombing.

By no means, as Austen's detractors have insisted, does she ignore the poignant spectacle of young people at their discreet sexual play. In her novels, there are dances, picnics, fireside confidences, gentle flirtatious teasing, tense lovers' quarrels, and above all, the healing penultimate scenes in all the novels, where heroines and heroes become reconciled to each other in the blessed privacy of benign English gardens and invigorating open spaces. Belinda Portman's poignant cry, "Give her air—give her air, air, air!" which she directs toward the rescue of her lover's stifled ward, may well have resonated in Austen's imagination. For air is what she does provide for her heroines under siege, and there is enough air in all six mature novels to obscure feminine suffering from readers unaccustomed to thinking about it, and to relieve the anxieties of those who recognize it.

3

The Author's Province

Just as Elizabeth Bennet once remarked with teasing affection to her sister Jane that a young courting man ought to be "handsome . . . if he possibly can" (*PP*, 14), so Elizabeth's creator might have said that a satirical woman novelist should be born to intelligent parents as irreverent about most pseudo-pieties as her own father and mother, "if she possibly can." The Austen children were all encouraged to develop talents to amuse the family circle, and among Austen's scribbling, sketching, and painting siblings, her own wildly hyperbolic juvenilia may not have seemed as savage as it actually was. Far from complaining about her modest proposals, which attacked not only every sort of patriarchal abuse but the very principles of patriarchy itself, her family was delighted when she began to amuse the world of Steventon and St. John's College with her bleak imitations of Augustan satire.

When Austen was born, her father accepted the birth of a second daughter with none of the apparent contempt that Edgeworth's fictional misogynist displayed to the fictional father. Austen's own experienced father thanked "God" that his wife had once again been spared the horrors and the dangers of childbirth, and was now "pure well of it," and he prophetically consigned the baby "Jenny" to her sister as "a plaything," and to her older brother Henry as the male tutor frequently assigned to baby girls at birth to teach them their subordinate place in the universe (*LL*, 22).

In a large family, then and now, a potential woman writer should arrange to be born near the end of the sibling row, if she can, so that she will not be prematurely forced into the role of "free nurse or a kind of mobile upper servant," as one parent or well-to-do Austen brother or another expected of the unmarried sisters throughout their lives.[1] Readers owe Austen's correspondence with Cassandra to this customary exploitation of spinsters, since one sister or the other, usually Cassandra, was so often functioning as free housekeeper in some brother's house.

Mr. Austen's most important gift to the one genius among his children was his choice of his genial, intelligent, and affectionate son Henry as her male mentor. James, the eldest son, despised his second wife and his two daughters. Edward, the next brother, was no scholar and no reader, and he was already adopted by rich relatives in need of a male heir, before Austen was out of the schoolroom. Witty, charming, and self-indulgent Henry was the perfect choice as a male definer of women's limitations; he was as indulgent with her as with himself. If it had not been for Henry, there might well have been no *Sense and Sensibility*, "By a Lady," nor the other five published novels that followed it. After Mr. Austen's death, Henry successfully took over his heretical father's attempts to publish his daughter's fiction, since women rarely conducted their own business.[2] It is no wonder that Austen loved Henry dearly, despite his usual indifference to his sisters' needs in most other respects.

Austen's correspondence and the family biographies all stress how serviceably the Austens' talents for family living spread from themselves to relatives in shock or trouble. A cousin lost a husband to the guillotine; she found refuge at Steventon. A relative's daughter lost her father just before her marriage. She was brought to the rectory to be soothed and to be married from there shortly afterward. A sickly young ward of Mr. Austen's was nursed by Mrs. Austen, who grieved when he died. James's wife died leaving a two-year-old daughter, who lived and played with her two older girl cousins for several years until her father remarried and reluctantly summoned her home, perhaps initiating her scribbling aunt's life-long preoccupation with the double theme of women's vulnerability to summary exile or prolonged incarceration. A brother's ailing wife died and he came to his sisters for consolation. Edward's prolific wife died after her eleventh child was born. Both unmarried sisters then took their turn soothing the shocks and meeting the needs of a dozen or more family members.

For weeks after the death of her sister-in-law in child-birth, Austen begged to have two of the boys sent to her for consolation. When they finally arrived, Austen's reception of her two small motherless nephews is one of the most touching revelations of her deeply affectionate heart and her confident intelligence. She knew her Ecclesiastes and she knew that with children, and especially with grieving children, as with everybody else, uncritical love has its seasons; she also knew that judgment and gentle discipline have their seasons too. She comforted these motherless nephews with her effective combination of maternal tenderness and bracing care—a healthy crispness toward children then considered impossible or unfashionable in women. Of one of the newly motherless Austen-Knight girls, Austen wrote: "Your account of Lizzy is very interesting. Poor child! One must hope the impression *will* be strong, and yet one's heart aches for a dejected mind of eight years old" (*Letters*, 221).

There speaks the writer for whom even the most wracking grief is "very interesting"; and there also speaks the loving aunt, and the Christian, conscious of suffering as a vale of soul-making. Austen's description of her grieving nephews' visit indicates how thoroughly acquainted she herself was with grief, and how tactfully she could minister to it. First she looked and listened: "George sobbed aloud, Edward's tears do not flow as easily." Then she consulted another spinster whose sex assigned her to the care of small children: "Miss Lloyd, who is a more impartial judge than I can be, is exceedingly pleased with them." Above all, she consulted her own extensive experience with her brothers' small children: "*They behave extremely well* . . . showing as much feeling as one wishes to see"—but not too much—and "speaking of their father with the liveliest affection." And then, after looking, listening, consulting, and calling upon experience, she devised a splendid program designed to begin her nephews' healing process without denying them the need for mourning. She was interested that George was equally unabashed on board a river ferry, "skipping" and "flying about from one side to the other," as he was in his grief, while Edward, the heir to his father's estate, could neither weep nor play with as much spontaneous abandonment (*Letters*, 225–227).

Soon Austen got the boys outdoors to play "bilboacatch, at which George is indefatigable, spillikins, paper ships," and then she urged them indoors again for a change of pace, so that they could play "riddles, conundrums, and cards," while from a window they could be archetypally soothed, "watching the flow and ebb of the river," and stretch their muscles and ease their grief "with now and then a stroll out," so that altogether Austen reported that all these activities "keep us well employed."

But if there is a time for grief, there is a time for light-hearted play: "In the evening we had the Psalms and Lessons, and a sermon at home, to which they were very attentive; but you will not expect to hear that they did not return to conundrums the moment it *was over*. . . . While I write now, George is most industriously making and naming paper ships, at which he afterwards shoots with horse-chestnuts, brought from Steventon on purpose; and Edward equally intent over the 'Lake of Killarney,' twisting himself about in one of the great chairs" (*Letters*, 227–229). A few days before the boys left for home, their aunt achieved a trip for them upstream on the river: "it proved so pleasant and so much to the satisfaction of all that . . . we agreed to be rowed up the river; both the boys rowed a great part of the way, and their questions and remarks, as well as their enjoyment, were very amusing. George's enquiries were endless, and his eagerness in everything reminds me of his Uncle Henry" (*Letters*, 228).

Austen's own artless "eagerness in everything" to do with warm-hearted, attractively brought up children appears at its finest in *Pride and Prejudice*: "As they drove to Mr. Gardiner's door, Jane was at a drawing room window waiting their arrival. . . . On the stairs were a troop of little boys and girls, whose eagerness for their cousin's appearance would not allow them to wait in the drawing-room, and whose shyness, as they had not seen her for a twelvemonth, prevented their coming lower. All was joy and kindness." Once again the Gardiner children became symbols of domestic equality between the parents, and therefore of family felicity and of sensible parental discipline: "The little Gardiners, attracted by the sight of a chaise, were standing on the steps of the house, as they entered the paddock; and when the carriage drove up to the door, the joyful surprise that lighted up their faces, and displayed itself over their whole bodies, in variety of capes and frisks, was the first pleasing earnest of their welcome" (*PP*, 152, 286).

Elizabeth Bennet witnessed both these delightful family scenes, which Austen has placed with infinite craft between scenes where two young men have betrayed two of the Bennet daughters, one with and one without the daughter's active collusion. In the first scene, where "all was joy and kindness," the principled but duped Jane Bennet was visiting the Gardiners and trying to recover from the shock of Charles Bingley's casual courting and equally casual disappearance. In the second scene describing the Gardiner children's appealing capers and frolics, Elizabeth and the Gardiner parents have just discovered George Wickham's perfidy in his elopement with the unprincipled Lydia Bennet. The shocking disjunction between loving couples with happy children and irresponsible courtships is no accident.

Post-Enlightenment parents were particularly confused between Pauline injunctions; the feminists stressed that "we, being many, are one body in Christ, and every one members one of the other," and that in Christ, "there is neither bond nor free, there is neither male nor female." The male conduct-book writers, on the other hand, emphasized St. Paul's patriarchal corollary: that "as we have many members in one body . . . all members have not the same office." Wollstonecraft described the customary acceptance of Paul's modification as purely opportunistic, based on a male principle of female "utility" shaped always by male "convenience" (*Vindication*, 51).

For all Mr. Austen's reputation for kindness, he was spending his funds and training his boys for "the widely differing professions and employments into which private advantage and public good require that men be distributed" (Gisborne, *Duties of the Female Sex*, 2), whereas from their earliest childhood, the two Austen sisters were taught that they "had not the same office" as their brothers, nor the same needs, and that they therefore did not require the same resources. Elizabeth Bennet once remarked that well-to-do men enjoyed "great pleasure in the power of choice" (*PP*, 183), a luxury that almost no women could command. And Eleanor Tilney's sad comment to Catherine Morland—"you must have been long enough in this house to see that I am but a nominal mistress of it, that my real power is nothing—" is true of all

Austen's heroines and all her chaste yet witty minor women characters (*NA*, 225).

Throughout her life, in all matters to do with education, funds, travels, books, pen and paper, clothing, or any other personal property, Austen and her sister were severely deprived compared with their brothers. But despite the clear bitterness that these deprivations bred in both Austen's fiction and her correspondence, all her writing displays the spontaneous wit and affection that she poured into her own family. She performed the same chaste yet witting and even passionate service for her fictive heroines and heroes, struggling to mature under very harsh and artificial assumptions about marriage and gender distinctions. One of her most admirable traits, both as a novelist and as a member of a close-knit family, was her refusal to demand too much of fallible and suffering humanity, and an equally discerning refusal to demand too little. She wrote of a despondent Henry: "I hope he comes to you in good health, and in spirits as good as a first return to Godmersham can allow. With his nephews he will force himself to be cheerful, till he really is so" (*Letters*, 244). From Enlightenment sources she had clearly learned that responsible habits and desires can produce responsible conduct fully as much as innate talents and temperament—a desperately necessary acknowledgment for a member of a sex often considered intellectually and morally defective from birth.

A brilliant girl-child in training to become a satirist ought to be born to a witty mother, "if she possibly can," a rare feat among the daughters and granddaughters of Anglican clergymen, which Austen managed to accomplish. Her great uncle on her mother's side was Theophilus Leigh, Master of Balliol, whose reputation for slightly irreverent wit "and agreeable conversation extended beyond the bounds of the university" (*Memoir*, 6). This great-uncle was certainly one founder of the Austenian school of wits, who served as inadvertent tutor to his niece, Cassandra Leigh; and her fiction-writing daughter matriculated in the same school. Whatever outrageously self-important received opinions amused Austen were also likely to amuse her mother, in her daughter's fiction and elsewhere. The "strong common sense," the "lively imagination," and the "epigrammatic force and point," in Mrs. Austen's "writing and conversation" were legendary, even before her daughter became famous. When she was dying and in pain, she remarked to a great nephew, "Ah, my dear, you find me just where you left me—on the sofa. I sometimes think that God Almighty must have forgotten me, but I dare say He will come for me in his own good time" (*Memoir*, 11–12).

Nonetheless, all family accounts suggest that Mrs. Austen was jealous of her precocious daughter. Austen's increasingly irritated comments about her mother imply that she suffered keenly from the covert maternal jealousy that mothers are often taught to inflict upon their most intelligent daughters. This daughter was usurping the male privilege of writing—with the father's tacit encouragement, too—which he would hardly have sanctioned in his wife. There was apparently no gross abuse, but all the evidence suggests that as Austen matured and began to publish, she did not receive the critical yet unresentful support in her feminine ghetto that writers need. There is a sting in Austen's life-long comments that she has commanded her mother to get well or stay well, and that she fully expects her mother to follow her commands, so that she can finish a chapter, make a dearly desired visit, or allow herself some badly needed respite. And her teasing contrast between Cassandra's "starched notions" about what women writers ought and ought not to write, and Wollstonecraft's contempt for just such "starched rules of [feminine] decorum" suggests distinctly divergent opinions on a subject crucial between writers and their readers (*Letters*, 300; *Vindication*, 98).

Mrs. Austen was descended from county families with one or two distinguished members, whereas her husband had sprung from respectable rather than socially acceptable stock. He supported his family almost entirely through his priestly living, and Mrs. Austen was almost as poorly dowered as her daughters. She was said to be "somewhat proud of her ancestors" (*LL*, 1–9, 16), and she may very well have "found herself obliged to be attached to the Rev. Mr." Austen, a man "with scarcely any private fortune" (*MP*, 3), as the authorial voice described the predicament of the grotesquely cruel Mrs. Norris. Mrs. Austen's life seems to have been one more "proof of how unequally the gifts of fortune are bestowed," a daily example of "the melancholy disproportion" between the empowered and the unempowered that forms so large a part of Austen's fictional preoccupations (*Letters*, 348, 508–509). To make ends meet, Mr. Austen could accept some private pupils; Mrs. Austen's contribution could only take the form of relinquishment. Riding, which she had once loved, was too expensive for her after her marriage, but not for one of her boys, for whom she cut up the riding habit that she had brought with her when she married (*LL*, 18).

Whatever feminine renunciations had been forced upon Mrs. Austen, of the sort so often described in her daughter's fiction, the sanguine-tempered and highly talented man she married was to create for her and their children anything but a pinched or dour parsonage. All the family biographers zestfully describe the entertainments that the rectory family loved to provide for neighbors, visiting relatives, and vacationing sons returning from Oxford or from a gentleman's continental tour. Mr. Austen's own Oxonian education had turned him into an unpretentious gentleman scholar, and his healthy delight in humanistic pleasures allowed the family to "mix in the best society of the neighbourhood, and to exercise a liberal hospitality," so that he was able to make the rectory "a sort of center of refinement and politeness" (*Memoir*, 23–24; *LL*, 52). The Austen family loved to read aloud to each other, and their unashamed sampling of every kind of novel, French and English, silly and serious, Gothic and satirical, and above all novels by both sexes, allowed Austen to absorb fictional techniques almost before she could write.

In other light-hearted ways that nobody considered an insult to honest piety, the Steventon rectory resembled a small post-Renaissance provincial court. Austen read French well and a little Italian, and she became familiar with the great poets and essayists (*Memoir*, 88). Her brothers all rode and hunted whenever they could afford or borrow horses, for "part of the good training at Steventon consisted in making the boys . . . manly, active, and self-reliant" (*LL*, 23–24).

Although "it must be borne in mind how many sources of interest . . . were then closed . . . to ladies" (*Memoir*, 37), dancing was no less an appropriate occupation for ladies and gentlemen at the Austen rectory than it had been at Castiglione's court. The "stately minuet still reigned supreme, and every ball commenced with it." Later in the evening, romping dances were popular. "Hornpipes, cotillions, and reels were occasionally danced, but the chief occupation of the evening was the interminable country dance, in which all could join." Austen's Victorian nephew could not resist reporting something that his aunt would have enjoyed as a record saved from the past. For the "ladies and gentlemen were ranged apart from each other in opposite rows, so that the facilities for flirtation, or for interesting intercourse, were not so great as might have been desired by both parties" (*Memoir*, 34–36).

Eliza Hancock, Comptesse de Feuillide, Austen's first cousin, offered some delightful descriptions of this latter-day minor squire's court that Mr. Austen had erected in Steventon parish. Eliza herself was later to benefit not only from Steventon's gracious pleasures but from its compassion. After her husband, Comte de Feuillide, was guillotined by the French revolutionaries, she "escaped through dangers and difficulties to England [and] was received for some time in her uncle's family" (*Memoir*, 26).

Eliza Hancock de Feuillide "was a very pretty, lively girl, found of amusements, and perhaps estimating her own importance a little too highly" (*LL*, 37). Even in the unusually equitable Austen family where the battle of the sexes was concerned, a woman possessing too much overt self-confidence no doubt faced mild but persistent censure. Eliza appears to have been one of those charming and frivolous women who enraged the feminists of both persuasions, for she had been trained to be deliciously appealing to men. As a "clever woman, and highly accomplished after the French rather than the English mode" (*Memoir*, 26), she had been taught as thoroughly as any young Englishwoman "the whole science of pleasing, which is cultivated with unceasing assiduity, as an object of the most essential importance," as Priscilla Wakefield remarked in distress (*Present Condition of the Female Sex*, 30).

Eliza recognized something that her disapproving male descendants did not: a woman's survival usually depended upon her genuine pleasure with the particular society in which she found herself. The Reverend John Bennett had himself commanded every woman "to see the heart in all its folding and recesses. She should know how to *multiply* and *variegate* herself as exigencies require" (*Female Education*, 112). Eliza was able to multiply and variegate herself according to each of the feminine exiles she suffered, from India to England, from England to Paris, and back and forth across the dangerous channel several times, until in her lonely widowhood she finally married Austen's older brother Henry. She was merely demonstrating as best she could in Paris, and later at Steventon, her capacity to achieve the feat that Gisborne had insisted was divinely "implanted" in all women—"a remarkable tendency to conform to the wishes . . . of those for whom they feel a warmth of regard" (*Duties of the Female Sex*, 116).

Eliza's descriptions of prerevolutionary teas and royal balls in Paris (*LL*, 38–39) indicate how thoroughly she had taken to heart the orthodox demand that women enjoy the life their husbands provide for them as though it represented a free choice, and how artlessly she entered into her aristocratic husband's elegant and decadent society. But she obviously aroused the "pride and resentment" of her English male relatives, who wanted her to be womanly in the English way rather than the French (Mary Hays, *Appeal to the Men of Great Britain*, 101, 128).

There is something very charming in Eliza's frank enjoyment of her pleasures and her own pretty face and captivating manners. There is something equally charming about her handsome clergyman uncle, Austen's father, who inspired her to write him about a miniature she was sending him: "It is reckoned like what I am at present. The dress is quite the present fashion of what I usually wear" (*LL*, 37). The miniature is delightful: it shows a lovely small and piquant young face. The hair is slightly powdered and artfully draped off the face by a rich-textured ribbon of silk or satin fastened at the back of the head. The combination of the slight drift of gray in the full-bodied head of hair, and the young elfin face is particularly poignant. The bodice is gracefully but not unduly provocatively sculptured so as to exhibit the throat and the barely risen little breasts. Eliza seemed indeed to have been anatomically constructed to practice the whole science of pleasing men.[3]

The artlessness of this young woman ostensibly begging her ecclesiastical uncle to notice the latest Parisian fashions, but covertly suggesting that Uncle George should notice how pretty she had become, also says something reassuring about this rector. Eliza seems completely to have avoided the male conduct-book advice that women were to strive in every way to arouse men's sensual appetites by their flattery and their looks and ornaments, and yet to be completely unaware that they were trying to do so. And no young woman, no matter how artless she was, would have written to a clergyman in the Church of England in such a confident manner, if he had been among the breed of men who insisted that "Confidence" in women " 'is a horrid bore' " (Bennett, *Female Education*, 107).

Another serious conduct-book lapse on the Austens' part was their love of private theatricals. Eliza de Feuillide appears to have enjoyed "the prologues and epilogues" written by James Austen, the oldest son who eventually became a pompous and self-opinionated model for Mr. Collins. James wrote these amateur pieces to support the family repertory company, for the Austen parents "several times indulged" in plays for themselves and their close neighbors, "having their summer theatre in the barn, and their winter one" indoors (*Memoir*, 26–27).

Eliza's own letters indicate that she had as much pleasure at the rectory as she had described in prerevolutionary Paris: "I assure you we shall have a most brilliant party [at Steventon] and a great deal of amusement, the house full of company, frequent balls. You cannot possibly resist so many temptations, especially when I tell you your old friend James is returned from France and is to be of the acting party." Eliza was offering these bribes to her rather sour cousin Philadelphia Walter, and she was earnestly seconded by the rector's wife, that robust conversationalist, who wanted as many gay and intelligent young people around her as she could stuff into the expandable rectory during the holidays, providing there was no pious assumption that acting was a crime: "for my Aunt Austen declares 'she has not room for any *idle young people*' " of the sort that the self-righteous Philadelphia appears to have been (*LL*, 65).

Eliza wrote admiringly of both her girl cousins. She thought them "equally sensible . . . to a degree seldom met with"; but "still," she said, "my heart gives the preference to Jane, whose kind partiality to me indeed requires a return of the same nature" (*LL*, 61).

Young Jane Austen adored her worldly cousin who appreciated affection as readily as she gave it. She also exemplified for Austen, the neophyte novelist, the bleakly realistic vision of women's limited marital choices, which even the most urbane parents in a provincial rectory were hardly likely to stress to dowerless daughters. Eliza had married a man for whom she felt merely the "preference" of "gratitude" so often described by male conduct-book literature. She was a living example of a woman gallantly accepting a solution to her penniless spinsterhood that found its way into many Austenian motifs and dialogues. Furthermore, Eliza's predicament, which was the exact replica of her mother's, offered Austen the spectacle of feminine truths universally unacknowledged that forms so violent a part of Austen's juvenilia and so distinctive a component in her mature satire.

Although one must regard some of the family biographies of this famous member with measured skepticism, since the male biographers tend to stress how much they or their fathers taught this genius, and the female biographers stress how much she taught them, yet one can agree, on the whole, with Austen's nephew, the memoirist. Austen's "early years were bright and happy, living as she did with indulgent parents, in a cheerful home, not without agreeable variety of society" (*Memoir*, 44). Eliza de Feuillide is the most reliable biographical source, in one way, because she did not know that her cousin was to become famous, when she wrote those cheerful letters validating the Austen members' habit of taking pleasure in each other and creating amusements for each other. Eliza's records are also validated by the sunny ebullience that illuminates much of Austen's fiction, despite many of its dark and painful origins. Like Austen's own Catherine Morland, there were often times when she was so "soothed," so "surrounded, so caressed, she was even happy! In the joyfulness of family love everything for a short time was subdued" (*NA*, 233).

The trouble arose as one older brother after the other left for university or naval schooling. Mr. Austen merely did what he thought was customary for a man of his social rank and limited income. When sons were plentiful and funds were scarce, daughters were neglected. But by supplying his daughters with a hospitable home, he may have hoped to attract enough young men to his cheerful rectory to provide eventual husbands for them, with hardly any extra expense or effort on his part. He had simply ignored what all the feminists could have told him, that rich men's sons do not marry poor men's daughters, and poor men's sons cannot afford to do so.

According to R. W. Chapman's last calculations, Austen began her first juvenile efforts in 1787 (*MW*, 1); and according to Jane Aiken Hodge's precise documentations of dates and family bills, Austen came home from boarding school in 1787. She apparently began her scribbling just after she had finished her few years of formal schooling and had been brought back to the rectory, and just as it was being rapidly emptied of its boys. In fact, she and Cassandra had been sent away in the first place, because their bedroom was needed by a series of boy boarders whom Mr. Austen prepared for the universities (*Only a Novel*, 20–21).

The persistence and the severity with which Austen exploited the Augustan parallel yet adversarial rhetorical structures and motifs, even as a twelve-year-old girl, indicate how clear it already was to her that when *HE* goes out into the world, she must come home to save money for *HIS* schooling, but that she cannot come home until *HE* leaves home. This child's breezy mockery of various assaults upon young women is a classical demonstration of the way dreams, childlike fantasies, and fiction often present metaphoric and symbolic conditions quite literally. In Austen's mature fiction, three married women, Mrs. Tilney, Mrs. Woodhouse, and Lady Elliot, were yoked to a tyrant, a hypochondriac predator, and a solipsistic snob, and Austen implies that these women's early deaths symbolized almost a blessed relief, as though the confinement and the finality of the grave were scarcely worse than the confinement and the finality of marriage to such men.

If confinement by tyrannical or selfish keepers was grim, desertion by men or by patriarchal systems was even worse: What was a young woman to do after "she was turned out of doors by her inhuman Benefactors"? The ambivalence in the oxymoron is revealing. The answer is to steal, and if necessary, to kill. But this young female criminal's earliest introduction to abandonment took place on the day of her birth: her mother had left her in a field to die, "dreading" the father's "just resentment at her not proving the Boy [he] wished" (*MW*, 34, 39).

During the crucial year of 1787, James, Frank, and Edward left home for good, and Austen's beloved Henry was about to leave for Oxford (*LL*, 46–49; *Letters*, Index I, Item IV). The shock of returning home because four boys were going out into the world seemed to have established Austen's life-long fictional occupation with feminine poverty, feminine incarceration, and feminine exile and abandonment. It also initiated her into the grim knowledge that even in the kindest families, women's lives were never schools for intellectual and professional opportunities, but on the contrary, they were schools for patience and resignation, just as the male conduct books had described as proper and agreeable for women.

Austen took some deliciously zany revenge on absent brothers. No matter how shrunken was Mr. Austen's court of its male courtiers, there was this ridiculous child, not weeping for lost brothers, as she might well have longed to do, but mocking customs inimical to girl-children, as though she had been licensed as a young female court-fool. It is a striking fact that all Austen's satirical juvenilia and almost all the fragments she left unfinished at her death bear the unmistakable marks of some psychic blows, some as yet unresolved traumatic experience or series of experiences, which her satire resolutely kept at bay. Familial and sexual violence of all sorts is coolly accomplished and gloatingly contemplated. Theft, adultery, and excessive drinking are equally coolly appraised as characteristic modes of family life. And even as Austen matured, family hostilities are far more common in these fragments than warmth or generosity; cruelty to the disempowered, which therefore renders them even more vulnerable, occurs as an accepted social fact.

One is also struck by the hopelessness in many of Austen's mature fragments. In *The Watsons*, one impoverished daughter says to the other: "You know we must marry . . . my father cannot provide for us, & it is very bad to grow old & be poor & laughed at." Their brother Robert, "carelessly kind, as became a prosperous Man & a brother," does all the talking, since he does not care to "let his attention be yielded to the less national, & [less] important demands of the Women" (*MW*, 317, 349, 356). Lady Susan's daughter is a mere cypher, crushed by a monstrous mother and a system that has evolved no machinery for rescuing her. But one might wonder which is the greater victim, an impoverished and predatory widow who has no home, or her daughter who has no willpower.

D. W. Harding's description of Austen's comic monsters and the nightmares that her heroines endure is even more prominent in her fragments and her juvenilia than in her six mature novels.[4] By the time she was sixteen, she had already learned how to treat women's limited choices without comic hyperbole. Such phrases as "hopelessness of sorrow," "tho' all were her relations, she had no friends," "her separation from her sister," and "she usually wrote in depressed spirits" all suggest far more than a taste for fictional sorrow. This grief is pervasive, and it is personal (*MW*, 195).

These grieving women are early Austenian examples of female exile; but there are just as many early and unfinished examples of female incarceration in the women's quarters of an estate. Annis Pratt calls the feminine ghetto a "tarnished enclosure," within which women lacked "the basic element of authencity," the liberty "to come and go" as men did, and "the right to make decisions about one's own time, work, and other activities."[5] Priscilla Wakefield described the same predicament from personal experience: "Feminine action is contracted by numberless difficulties, that are no impediments of masculine exertion" (*Present Condition of the Female Sex*, 9). Knightley's comment that "there is nobody hereabouts to attach [Emma]; and she goes so seldom from home" (*E*, 41), anticipates Lady Russell's internal monologue about Anne Elliot's isolation: "Anne had been too little from home, too little seen. Her spirits were not high. A larger society would improve them" (*P*, 15). Mary Hays harshly summed up this feminine deprivation as systematic and ubiquitous:

> In matters of great and important concern, women are generally soon taught to understand, that they ought to have, and can claim to have, no weight whatever. They then naturally think that the lesser ones, mere family matters, of ornament or fashion, may be left to them; but even here they are mistaken and misinformed; for their share in the management of home, and domestic concerns, lies entirely at the mercy of husbands, who except they are more than human, will rather be guided their own caprice, than by the exact rules of equity.

Since "the wife is acknowledged to be, even in domestic concerns, the upper servant of her husband only . . . the iron hand of authority lies desperately heavy, in even the trifles of life" (*Appeal to the Men of Great Britain*, 87–88).

Austen had apparently never experienced "the iron hand of authority" which Hays describes as a common feminine fate. But as a young woman who had barely reached her majority, Austen did indeed suffer from the exasperating knowledge that she "ought to have, and can claim to have, no weight whatsoever." Enforced incarceration or enforced exile was always a personal problem for her. She was neither summarily expelled from one estate nor kept a virtual prisoner in one, according to the fate of Fanny Price, Catherine Morland, the Dashwood sisters, Emma Woodhouse, and Anne Elliot. But all her adult life she suffered shifts of residence—from Steventon to Bath to Southampton to Chawton, or to the bedside of a sick relative. These shifts were always initiated for someone else's benefit, and they gave "no weight whatever" to Austen's own health, her publishing deadlines, or a rare visit already planned to some friends who loved her for her own sake.

Austen's rueful jokes at her helplessness began early and continued throughout her life. She enjoyed writing to her sister, her nieces, or her friends that she had intended to mount the box herself and direct the horses to carry her to them, since they, too, were as helpless about coming to see her as she was to go to them, but, as she frequently bemoaned, some malign fate intervened or was sure to intervene. Once she wrote Cassandra four letters over a period of a month, complaining that one after the other of her five brothers refused to fetch her home after there was no more need of her services where she was, and where she had clearly worn out her welcome. She jokingly compared herself to Frances Burney's Camilla Tyrold, whose irresponsible brother and heir to the family goods had locked his sisters in a summer house for hours by running off with the ladder, which was the only method of entrance or exit. Austen was particularly exasperated with her brother Frank, who would neither sanction her return by stagecoach nor come for her himself. After applying once or twice again to all her brothers, including her host, the rich Edward, Austen wrote in satirical exasperation: "My father will be so good as to fetch home his prodigal daughter . . . unless he wishes me to walk the Hospitals, Enter at the Temple, or mount Guard at St. James." Her final comment about her eventual return was ironically despairing: "the time of its taking place is so very uncertain that I should be waiting for *Dead-men's Shoes*" (*Letters*, 9–18).

In Austen's threat to become a physician, a barrister, or a member of the household cavalry, there are some quietly bitter allusions to what *HE* can do and she cannot. And her ominous reference to "*Dead-men's Shoes*" suggests how enormous the strain must have been to subdue constant anger and frustration over constant indifference to her needs.

Austen's yearly allowance of £20 partially explains why she joked so often about forbidden male professions that would have eased her constant niggling anxieties about money. Her correspondence is filled with ironic remarks about what profession she or some other woman had adopted or should adopt: the "science" of music, "the study of Medecine" (*sic*), of the navy, the law, or English history, "The Civil & Military—Religion—Constitution—Learning & Learned Men—Arts and Science—Commerce, Coins & Shipping—& Manners." She ironically included those whom she considered history's martyrs, such as Mary, Queen of Scots, or a witch who was burned at the stake. Nor did she ignore women's primary disenfranchisement upon which all the others rested: she even cracked a joke about voting for a candidate who was seeking a constituency so that he could stand for Parliament (*Letters*, 50, 40, 89, 233).

Austen's father died in 1805, and soon Austen began to dwell on legacies and particularly on those who received them and those who did not—namely, herself, her sister, and her widowed mother. Various relatives and prominent people already reasonably wealthy were inheriting even more funds than they needed to function most comfortably, whereas the Austen widow and the spinsters were counting not pounds, as they estimated the cost of food, clothing, pens, writing paper, tips, and presents to tenants and the extended family, but pence; and saving not yards, but inches of fabrics for refurbishing shoddy dresses, underslips, caps, and bonnets. Austen wrote with her particular brand of tart yet wistful irony: "Indeed, I do not know where we are to get our Legacy—but we will keep a sharp look-out" (*Letters*, 207; Hodge, *Only a Novel*, 99). "The rich," she once said mockingly to Cassandra, "are always respectable," as the poor are not (*Letters*, 195).

Austen's open contempt for her brother James and his wife, Mary, at least in her letters, does not make pleasant reading, but the sources of her grief and anger against them are even more unpleasant. Their worst offense to this affectionate aunt was that they treated their daughters with all the varieties of hostility and contempt that Fanny Price's two families inflicted on her. And their indifference to the plight of James's mother and sisters is contemptible. They flaunted their new carriage and pair, their trips, and their plentiful servants, while the little band of women who were now classified with "the genteel poor," scrimped and hoped for tips and presents from wealthy relatives. Mary complained of everybody's housekeeping except her own, and James infuriated his fiction-writing sister by visiting the three women whenever he became bored with his wife, and by behaving in a boorish fashion, slamming doors, and demanding instant service as a male right.

James must have been a rather unpleasant man even as a young curate. When Mr. Austen relinquished his ecclesiastical living in favor of James and then retired to Bath, James coolly bargained for all the household goods at Steventon, for the books, pictures, and silverware, in exactly the same cheap and contemptuous way as did the John Dashwoods in *Sense and Sensibility*. The cruelest "melancholy disproportion" of all was that Austen's precious piano and her equally precious books, which she had been able to purchase out of her annual allowance of £20, all had to be sold, not only to finance her father's retirement in the city of Bath, which she hated, but even more bitter, to help

James's acquisition of the Steventon living from which she was now being expelled. Austen wrote Cassandra with understandable rancor that even Mr. Austen's tractable and sweet-going little mare had now deserted him, to trot over and pay permanent court to the crown prince of the Steventon rectory, before Mr. Austen and his family of women had even removed to Bath. Yet James had but recently "bought a new horse; & Mary [had] got a new maid." The pictures, the flatware, and other household goods went to James, while Mr. Austen was frantically "doing all in his power to increase his Income by raising his Tythes" (*Letters*, 75, 101–103, 126). When Austen remarked, "The whole World is in a conspiracy to enrich one part of our family at the expense of another" (*Letters*, 133), she was expressing the very economic underpinnings of *Sense and Sensibility*, especially the monstrous chapter where John and Fanny Dashwood defraud his mother and three penniless sisters of the funds and goods which his father—and theirs—had designated for them.

As the years without a settled home wore on, and as Austen continued to find that her published novels failed to relieve her financial worries, she began to demonstrate a symptom of distress in her correspondence from which she did not recover until just before her death. She started to make inventories of one "poor woman" after the other, married or single, and women of every class and economic condition, but always bullied or neglected at home, or else impoverished and abandoned. There was "the sad story" of three women "almost frozen to death in the late weather." One of them was "likely to lose the use of her limbs." There was the "melancholy history . . . of a poor Mad Woman, escaped from Confinement"; there was a governess, first to Edward's children and then living most precariously thereafter, who was "born, poor thing! to struggle with Evil—" and whom Austen described as "hard at it, governing away—poor creature! I pity her though they are my Nieces" (*Letters*, 248, 261, 278).

Austen wrote with particular compassion of a rector's sister who was to suffer the exile and dependency common to the widows and daughters of modestly endowed rectors:

> We are very anxious to know who will have the Living of Adlestrop, & where his excellent sister will find a home for the remainder of her days. As yet she bears his Loss with fortitude, but she always seemed so wrapt up in him, that I fear she must feel it dreadfully

when the fever of business is over—There is another female sufferer on the occasion to be pitied. Poor Mrs. L.P.—who would now have been mistress of Stoneleigh had there been none of that vile compromise. (*Letters*, 316)

Austen's distress about "that vile compromise" alludes to another occasion when a tortuous will ensured that "as so often, there was money about" and money changing hands, "but none of it coming their way" (Hodge, *Only a Novel*, 99). She was particularly distressed that "Edward has driven off poor Mrs. Salkeld.—It was thought a good opportunity of doing something toward clearing the house." One cleared out the house by clearing out the housekeeper (*Letters*, 351). Mrs. Stent, "an earlier friend of rather inferior position in life, and reduced from family misfortunes, to very narrow means," was a model for Miss Bates: "poor Mrs. Stent! it has been her lot to be always in the way; but we must be merciful, for perhaps in time we may come to be Mrs. Stents ourselves, unequal to anything & unwelcome to anybody." But Austen's sense of her own precarious condition did not prevent her from satirizing Mrs. Stent, who "will now and then ejaculate some wonder about the Cocks & hens, what can we want" more amusing for an evening's entertainment? (*Letters*, 154, 89, and note to 89).

Austen's grief over the hazards that women suffered in childbirth was centered most painfully upon her novel-writing niece, Anna, one of the despised daughters of James and his wife. Austen was obviously distressed not only that Anna had endured three painful pregnancies within three years of marriage—"Poor Animal, she will be worn out before she is thirty—" as indeed she was, but that this niece had been her writing colleague, whose husband actually offered "encouragement & approbation" for her work, which for women used to disparagement, "must be quite 'beyond everything.' " This was the niece who was "but *now* coming to the heart & beauty" of her writing, when she married and began the frightening process of bearing seven children almost yearly (*Letters*, 488, 401, 404). Twenty years earlier, Austen had worried about a recent pair of maternal deaths: "Mrs. Coulthard and Anne . . . are both dead and both in childbirth. We have not regaled [the pregnant] Mary with this news" (*Letters*, 29).

Austen's pity was bound to be stirred by the example of Princess Caroline, whose husband had installed one of his mistresses as his foreign bride's lady-in-waiting, just after the royal pair were married. Her failure to give birth to a boy probably angered him more than all the injudicious comments she said about *HIS* scandalous conduct and the unfortunate friendships she made during the long, lonely years of her ordeal. "I suppose all the World is sitting in Judgment upon the Princess of Wales' Letter," Austen wrote to a relative: "Poor woman, I shall support her as long as I can, because she *is* a Woman, & because I hate her husband—but I can hardly forgive her for calling herself "attached" & affectionate to a Man whom she must detest . . . but if I must give up the Princess, I am resolved always to think that she would have been respectable, if the Prince had behaved only tolerable by her at first."

In the next paragraph, Austen mourned over a poor tenant, another dead rector's sister, who was to be thrown out of a leaking house, so that the landlord's son could have it. Austen reported that all the townspeople were "anxious . . . to get her decently settled somewhere. . . . & if anything else can be met with, she will be glad enough to be driven from her present wretched abode" (*Letters*, 504–505). The conditional grammar with which Austen discussed the forlorn predicament of these two "female sufferers," the rejected princess and the superfluous female tenant, indicates how thoroughly saturated Austen was by 1813 with the grammar of women's contingent position: "*if*" Princess Caroline's gross husband "had behaved *only tolerably* by her," and merely "*at first*," she could have behaved respectably; "if anything else *can be met with*," Miss Behn will be glad to move from her "*present wretched abode*." Austen was now mourning over intolerable facts that she had only dimly imagined in the childhood prescience of her juvenilia. Now, even when a family member "feels less interest" in James's "branch of the family than any other," Austen takes it for a mere ironic fact that somebody will benefit and that it will not be James's two despised girls: "I dare say she will do her *duty* however, by the Boy" (*Letters*, 198).

Austen's sense of deprivation occasionally became so deep that she exhibited symptoms of withdrawal, which is a common protective mechanism in prisoners, hospitalized patients with long illnesses and no relatives, or women who are incarcerated by prolonged and exaggerated domestic isolation: "I do not want people to be very agreeable, as it saves me the trouble of liking them a great deal." A close family friend was to visit, but Austen assumed that something would happen to put off the visit, as she reported a dozen or more times that her visits to friends or theirs to her were put off. She then made the ominous comment: "and if it does, I shall not much mind it on my account, for I am now got into such a way of being alone that I do not wish even for her" (*Letters*, 43, 213).

Austen was quite aware that she risked debilitating depressions, especially when her eyes became inflamed, and she was forced to give up first her writing, and finally, as she often complained, "*even*" the free needlework she did for her brothers and their wives and children. These commonplace renunciations found their way into Austen's fiction: there is an ironic yet sad little vignette in *Northanger Abbey*, when Catherine Morland is at last home and grieving over General Tilney's betrayal and her loss of Henry. Her mother scolds her for her manifestations of shock and mourning, "still perfectly unsuspicious" of its cause, "which, for the parents of a young lady" who has been visiting a young man for several weeks, "was odd enough!" Mrs. Morland insists not only that Catherine read a male conduct book called "The Mirror," but that she accept her responsibilities for sewing her brother's neckties: "I do not know how poor Richard's cravats would be done, if he had no friend but you" (*NA*, 235, 240–241).

Austen had early perfected several techniques to keep despair at bay. For instance, even as a young marriageable woman, she had adopted the whimsical habit of pretending that she and Cassandra could plan their lives as their brothers did, and even control the elements. She would thank Cassandra most profoundly for ordering such good weather, scolded her for not choosing more handsome and charming partners to dance with than those with whom her sister had reported herself to have been afflicted, begged Cassandra to enjoy the next dance and to arrange a dance for her—from a distance of several counties—and other imaginary assumptions of an autonomous will. She also informed Cassandra that some trifle, such as an unexpected letter or a good pudding at dinner or the successful hemming of an old shabby gown had sent her into "the utmost pinnacle of human felicity," or into "utter unimaginable human joy," which Cassandra was to take with all the salt she chose.

One of Austen's most charming techniques for disrupting depression was her habit of personification. She loved to tell Cassandra that various household goods, such as furniture, scarves, gowns, or silverware missed her, loved her, and sent her their most respectful duty. She enjoyed informing her nieces and nephews that the farm animals often spoke of them and longed to see them. The saddest example of personification occurred when she wrote to her niece Caroline, who loved her dearly and whose memoir described a woman with great affection and respect for children. Caroline was a daughter of the selfish pair, James and Mary. Austen was then clearly very ill, but she wrote with the playfulness that was designed both to express her sadness and her longing to see Caroline, and to hide these feelings if Caroline could neither accept them nor arrange to visit her aunt—which she was unable to do until just before Austen left for medical care in Winchester: "The Piano Forte often talks of you—in various keys, tunes, & expressions . . . but be it Lessons or Country Dances, Sonata or Waltz, *you* are really it's constant Theme. I wish you c^{d} come and see us, as easily as Edward can." A yearly earlier, she had also written to Caroline with the sad humility that age and her genteel poverty had taught her: "I will say no more, because I know the [ere may be?] many circumstances to make it inconvenient at home . . . but if she does feel disposed to pay us a little visit & you could *all* come, so much the better" (*Letters*, 473, 445–456). "She" was Mary Austen, who was apparently not so disposed.

The cause of Austen's early death is still a mystery. It may have been Addison's disease or Hodgkin's disease,[6] but in any case, both these diseases have opportunistic habits. They are not caused by stress, but the time of their onset, their severity, and the speed of the patient's death are now recognized by many physicians to be influenced by conditions that are often beyond the patient's control. Austen's early and life-long renunciations, and perhaps even worse, the legitimate complaints that she was customarily supposed neither to acknowledge even to herself nor to express in public, obviously created breeding-grounds for diseases that turn inward and attack entire somatic systems.

Most fatal of all were the two severe shocks to which Austen had been subjected before the onset of her own final illness. She went to London to nurse her beloved brother Henry; he had recently suffered bankruptcy, and in the process, he had lost all his sister's savings. He was able to recoup his own funds by becoming ordained and finding a curacy: but for Austen herself, no such deliverance was possible.

And then to find that her selfish brother James had inherited money from Mrs. Austen's brother, and that not one penny had gone to Mrs. Austen or her daughters, was piling distress upon distress.

In the last months of Austen's illness, her correspondence began to express those exaggerated attitudes of feminine gratitude, which the male conduct-book literature considered only seemly in women, and which to me, at least, are infinitely painful to read. If she were to live longer, she says, she could never be as well-cared for as she is now; she is grateful for kindnesses immeasurably beyond her deserts; her family is so kind to take her illness as seriously as they do; she is so ashamed to be such a nuisance, and so on. Yet even now, her ironic novelist's courage did not desert her. Any novelist who could earlier laugh in a private correspondence at a dancing woman who looked like "a queer animal with a white neck" or another who "appeared exactly as she did in September, with the same broad face, diamond bandeau, white shoes, pink husband, & fat neck," or who could find vast amusement at the naked cupids on one of the ceilings in a girls' boarding school, could never altogether lose the healing gift of laughter. With typical Austenian whimsy, which functioned both to appease others and to comfort herself, she described her rides on a tractable donkey, when she could no longer walk, and the violent discoloration of her skin, as though she had temporarily donned a pantomime costume to amuse the children (*Letters*, 120, 91).

Such a spirit, which quietly arranged its own entrances not only into the woman's province of the heart, but into the community of the "Mind," with all its "lovely display of what Imagination does," is indomitable. Austen's sweet sentence praising her niece Anna, her young novelist colleague—"You are but *now* coming to the heart & beauty of your book"—is one of those artlessly generous Austenian moments that resonate so courageously throughout her correspondence, and with even greater sonority throughout her mature fiction (*Letters*, 478–479, 401).

Austen had more than a little in common with her probing and questioning heroine, Elizabeth Bennet. The conduct-book males might inform her, as the narrator's voice, half authorial and half internal monologue, advises Elizabeth, that "it was her business to be satisfied," but there was no question either that it was "certainly her temper to be happy," and that "to fret over unavoidable evils, or augment them by anxiety, was no part of her disposition" (*PP*, 239, 232). Austen did her best to follow her own advice as often as she humanly could. She obviously fooled her male relatives and her neighbors; the miracle she performed was that she has fooled almost two hundred years of the reading public as well.

Austen's prayers that she wrote for herself are full of good counsel about the sin of rancor and of despair (*MW*, 453–457). Her fictional voice and her vision are both truly mediative and often truly androgynous, according to Caroline Heilbrun's own provocative vision: in describing "the absolute androgyny of Jane Austen's genius," Heilbrun identifies Austen as one of the first reliable and authentic fictional recorders of women's redemptive values: "More than any other novelist she wrote about women who were potentially complete human beings, not handicapped in the race of life by either innate or socially conditioned imperfections. Nor did she see the sexes as born to warfare, one with the other."[7] As a Christian, Austen could not believe that the sexes were *born* to perpetual warfare, but she knew that they were *trained* to little else. Heilbrun's qualifier—"potentially complete human beings"—describes the heroines more than the heroes: except for Edward Ferrars and Colonel Brandon, all Austen's heroes are born to confident autonomy, reasonable liberty, and the governance of women. That the author allows her heroines and heroes to transcend this asymmetry, to the extent that they do, is both a psychological and a professional triumph.

Part II

The Heroines' Province

4

The Eve Principle and the Schooling for the Penitent Heart

The great feminist debates of the 1790s, as well as their harbingers and their unfinished aftermath, were bound to address the whole vexing quarrel over women's education. There was as yet no national policy dictating or facilitating rigorous and extensive education for gentlewomen, and questions as to what, how much, for how long, where, and by whom young girls of all classes should be taught varied from father to father, parish to parish, class to class, and decade to decade.[1] As orthodox theorists began to be slightly reshaped by the Enlightenment, they became less threatened by any connection between women and the civilized arts. For example, Gisborne and Burton were less rigid in their plans for women's curriculum than Halifax, Gregory, Bennett, or Fordyce, or even the early nineteenth-century Duff, and these men were all slightly less primitive than Rousseau, who was less overtly hostile, if nothing else, than the Renaissance misogynists in *Book II* and *Book III* of Castiglione's *Book of the Courtier*, those delightful examples of the great French and Italian "Querelle des Femmes." Since Castiglione's aristocratic women defend themselves against their attackers and defamers at Urbino's court, and since they are even defended by the genial Platonist, Cardinal Bembo, the tone of this work is infinitely more civilized than those of the misogynist church fathers during the Middle Ages.

Nonetheless, post-Enlightenment conduct-book males still tended to discuss the matter of women's learning from the masculine perspective alone, as though such luminaries as Christine de Pisa, Marguerite of Navarre, Lady Jane Grey, Queen Elizabeth, or Mary Astell and the 1790s feminists had never lived nor left any record at all. Duff, for example, constantly drummed into his feminine readers' heads that they must consider everything "from the relation they bear to the other sex" (*Character of Women*, 19), and he wished women's education to consist largely in learning humility before divinely ordained male authority and brilliance. Women's education should therefore never rigorously emphasize intellectual subjects and techniques for their own sake; the "singular activity" of the male "mind and body" equips men to address themselves to all the "splendid and envied" intellectual "spheres" from which "providence" itself has "debarred" all women. Duff sensed something inappropriate about his rigid separation of the male intellectual "province" from the female, since he felt called upon to make a qualified apology for it: "To exclude you from the paths of literature and science might appear illiberal and invidious. . . . But the extensive and hidden fields and intricate paths of learning . . . are not in general your native province" (*Character of Women*, 98–99).

The orthodox presumption about women's ineducability as an "original defect" in mind and body always stressed profound gender differences in that complex, ambiguous Enlightenment term, "Understanding." Post-Edenic women were said to suffer from so grave "a deficiency of understanding" that "the peculiar characteristics of the female mind" fitted women only for an intellectually passive and supportive role rather than any active or initiatory functions (Bennett, *Female Education*, 88; Duff, *Character of Women*, 107; Gisborne, *Duties of the Female Sex*, 76).

There was an intellectual confusion in this assumption that male conduct-book literature never attempted to explain. If the human understanding "of both sexes issued immediately from the fountain of light," and yet if "knowledge . . . was not communicated equally to both sexes" from the outset (Bennett, *Female Education*, 18), then Eve, "Poor

Wretch," was already placed "*en Penitence*" even before the fall, in fact, from the moment of her birth. What, then, was her sin before her original sin? (*Letters*, 149). It was illogical to claim that understanding was denied Eve and her descendants from the moment of her creation *and* as a punishment for her "pride of knowing" during the fall.

In any case, the ideal conduct-book gentlewoman was to be carefully trained into a condition that enlightened modern physicians now often recognize as containing seeds of physical or mental pathology. In *Pride and Prejudice*, Austen created two models of this pathology in girl cousins reared under the same conditions. Readers never hear a single word spoken by Anne de Bourgh, daughter of the autocratic widow Lady Catherine de Bourgh. Georgiana Darcy, trained into silent docility by Lady Catherine's equally autocratic nephew, Fitzwilliam Darcy, is equally silent throughout the entire novel. Lady Catherine remarks with an odd pride in her daughter's social pathology, that she is too shy to play the piano in public or to make her debut in London. Georgiana is so excruciatingly shy that in the presence of visitors she can hardly speak to her governess above a murmur.

Austen was well aware of the psychological damage that the most orthodox vision of a young woman's appropriate education could do to female mental health. In 1807, she described a visit from an appealing child named Kitty Foote:

> she is now talking away at my side & examining the Treasures of my Writing-desk;—very happy I beleive [*sic*];—not at all shy, of course. . . . What has become of all the Shyness in the World? Moral as well as Natural Diseases disappear in the progress of time, & new ones takes their place.—Shyness & the Sweating Sickness have given way to Confidence and Paralytic complaints.

"The progress of time" indicates that Austen was quite aware of the debate on "nature or nurture," and how much environment contributed to heredity.

Austen was "highly pleased" with this "nice, open-hearted girl, with all the ready civility which one sees in the best children in the present day," and "so unlike anything that" she was permitted to be at her little visitor's age. In fact, despite her utter delight in this child and others equally natural and open-hearted, Austen was "often all astonishment and shame" (*Letters*, 178–179). Family biographers frequently stress how shy she had been, despite the geniality of her immediate family.

The radical and moderate feminists identified agoraphobia as one of the pathologies that tended to accompany the orthodox female education. Mansfield Park produced two such women: Lady Bertram had been so flattened into submission by her looming husband that she seldom left her sofa and she had to ask him to identify her own desires for her. Her niece, Fanny Price, is a study of many neuroses associated with feminine deprivations: except for her mind, which is hungry for books, she is another derivative person, shaped entirely by the contempt that her dependent status elicits. Her struggles to overcome the complete moral calcification of Mansfield Park summon up her gallant but tragic "heroism of principle" (*MP*, 265). She, too, fears exposure to strange places and people; but she also yearns for them.[2]

Austen's comments about charming Kitty Foote, and her treatment of her women characters, indicate how thoroughly aware she was of the delicate subliminal decisions that the minds of young girls had to undergo—and particularly the minds of intelligent young girls. To accept passive renunciation may ultimately be less complicated, despite the agony of mind and spirit it may produce, than the difficult and subtle task that the mind must undergo as it tries to decide how much active will and energy to put forth, when energetic and clear-thinking women were the objects of so much national cant.

If "our first mother was betrayed by the pride and knowing," and if therefore, a woman's "unstudied innocence" was all that stood between her and damnation after death and the stigma and isolation of spinsterhood during adult life, at what moment in the infant struggles of her fresh young mind would a nursery scholar decide, not only "that the more profound researches of philosophy and learning are not the pursuits most improving to the female mind" but that any learning at all might be dangerous? If astronomy and abstract philosophy had in the past "unmade the women" and had improved their "understanding on the ruin of their graces,"[3] the morally sensitive young Christian girl was bound to ask herself where she would be safest from mortal sin. Should she avoid all secular "understanding," to say nothing of Christian understanding? How far did the massive prohibition against abstract thinking go? Was all rational thinking forbidden, or only some, and about what, and where? In the schoolroom but not in the ballroom or in mixed company? Before puberty but not afterward?

Another conflict faced young women anxious to think but not too much. Their mentors were supposed to be men, functioning in divine imitation of "our first father," Adam, who taught Eve those mental rudiments necessary for her to serve him, even, it would seem, before the fall (Bennett, *Female Education*, 18). But the male conduct-book literature said that it was beneath the dignity of men to teach young women. Yet a woman teaching herself was suspiciously like a woman making love to herself, and a woman teaching other women suggested to orthodox thinkers the horrid spectacle of women making love to each other, although the sexual terms for these assumptions never appear in this literature. Who, then, could a young girl trust? If men ought not to teach her, and other women were not fit to do so, where could she learn? In all feminist and para-feminist literature of this time, it was the more ambiguous question of feminine intelligence, even more than the matter of Christian conduct *per se*, which most painfully exercised the consciences of England's most intelligent women. For what Ruth Kelso remarked of earlier centuries was true of Austen's: "The ideal set up for the lady is essentially Christian . . . and the ideal for the gentleman essentially pagan."[4]

The debates of the 1790s and afterward overtly allude, again and again, to Locke's *Essay Concerning Human Understanding*, and covertly, to Astell. The male literature for women never quotes Locke's descriptions of "the *Understanding*" as "the most elevated faculty of the soul." Yet Locke's description of this quintessentially human faculty foreshadows Astell's *Serious Proposal*: "Its searches after truth are a sort of hawking and hunting, wherein the very pursuit makes a great part of the pleasure. Every step the mind takes in its progress toward Knowledge makes some discovery, which is not only new, but the best too, for the time, at least" (*Concerning Understanding*, I, 7–8). One could even say that the Christian humanist Locke sounds in places like the Christian humanist Austen; for they both tend to "search out the bounds between opinion and knowledge; and examine by what measure, in things whereof we have no certain knowledge, we ought to regulate our assent and moderate our persuasion" (*Concerning Understanding*, I, 26–27).

If one compares Locke's advice to his own sex with Gisborne's advice to "intelligent women" not to become "absorbed in the depths of erudition" lest they lose "all esteem," one might well wonder how Austen escaped Gisborne's prescription for a feminine "cultivated understanding," which is "a memory stored with useful and elegant information" and a "polished taste," rather than the mind of the thoughtful and discriminating moralist she became (Gisborne, *Duties of the Female Sex*, 270, 271).

Other "strictures" on female education combined pseudo-pastoral and pseudo-anatomical rhetoric to describe the passive, retentive "nature" of women's "faculties and the texture of their understanding," as though every man was sufficiently adept with that centuries-old instrument, the microscope, to anatomize every living woman's brains (Bennett, *Female Education*, 87).

Fanny Price's cousins, Maria and Julia Bertram, who could "repeat the chronological order of the kings of England, with the dates of their accession, and most of the principal events of their reigns!" are satirical stereotypes of such women who have been carefully taught to respect rote learning and to despise the capacity for "human understanding," in Locke's and Astell's terms. They jumble "all the Metals, Semi-Metals, Planets and distinguished philosophers," as well as "the Roman emperors as low as Severus, besides a great deal of heathen Mythology" all together in their minds, and they are unable to compare one fact with another so as to distinguish the most important. As to intellectual and moral ideas, they cannot compare and thus judge any, since they are taught none. It is even more satirical that "their favorite holiday sport of the moment" was "making artificial flowers or wasting gold paper," both feminine occupations approved by *The Spectator* and some of the male conduct-book literature (*MP*, 18–19, 14).

Feebly taught gentlewomen were particularly vulnerable to "The School of Sensibility," which ran parallel to "the school of the heart," as distinguished from the school of satire and the austere classicism upon which the age still prided itself. Fordyce's *Sermons to Young Women*, first published in 1766, took full advantage of the cult of sensibility as a mode of address most appropriate for subjecting women to orthodox "persuasion," since it was the only mode of address considered appropriate for women themselves to speak or write in. The cult of the feminine heart was an offshoot of the cult of sensibility; it guaranteed that woman's mental faculties would remain attenuated.

In case a woman rebelled against so flaccid an intellectual diet, she could be taught to take comfort in the fact that under her "snowy bosom" lay this great feminine heart, as large as a man's mind, innately ready, after the proper penitential schooling, to dedicate itself "to the man, to whom she has plighted, at the altar of God, her vows and affections" (Bennett, *Female Education*, 75, 76). Phrases like "the affections of the heart," "the school of the heart," "the schooling of the heart"—for "well-regulated sympathy and benevolent affections" toward men and children, "the sweet power of the gentle, pleading, innocent, untutored female *Heart*," "the delicate, responsive quality of the female *Heart*," "the training for the innocent *Heart*," "the education of the *Heart*," "the absolute loyalty of the female *Heart*," and so on, drip through the male conduct-book literature, with or without italics.

These unctuous phrases occasionally invade the language of the moderate feminists, even the most angry members of this persuasion. After the scandal of Wollstonecraft's radical *Vindication*, hardly any but the most intrepid feminist would have dared to write an overtly feminist book, nor would she have been likely to have had it published. Therefore, most moderate feminists offered appeasing statements that women's great hearts still palpitated toward the male sex, but that it would be an even greater compliment toward men if women were schooled to emulate men's most civilized achievements, modestly, of course, rather than merely to adore these achievements from a distance.[5]

These appeasing feminine flatteries were largely ignored by masculine advisors to women. Dr. Gregory had warned his daughters that men "generally look with a jealous and malignant eye on a woman of great parts, and cultivated understanding" (*Legacy to his Daughters*, 31–32). Warnings of this type were commonplace, and Gregory's prohibition against "great parts, and cultivated understanding" clearly identifies his purposes. Everything except women's swollen hearts and nurturing bosoms should be small and stripped of function. Locke's version of "human understanding" was not for them.

Locke's and Astell's context for their visions of human understanding thus differed in crucial ways from the commonplace concept of women's understanding. For just as code-nouns such as "law," "justice," "love," "equality," "benevolence," "health," "intelligence," "care of offspring," "marriage," "divorce," "occupation," "cultivation of the arts," "heroism," and even "piety toward one's maker" meant profoundly different things for each sex, so the code-noun "understanding" was also part of that "melancholy disproportion" that Austen mourned in one of her last letters.

In his ground-breaking study, *Jane Austen and the Drama of Woman*,

Leroy Smith remarked, "Austen defines a woman as de Beauvoir does," as a creature who cannot "be free" unless she is permitted "to possess self-knowledge and self-respect, judge for her self and be true to her self in making judgments, and insist on being judged as an individual and not by a stereotype." This passage is embedded in a section describing Austen's preoccupation with women's pitiful education. Both Austen and de Beauvoir, says Smith, "believe that woman has the reasoning power and potential for learning needed to break free from unreasonable external restraints and to move from ignorance and faulty perception to knowledge."[6]

Unfortunately, however, vague phrases such as "the dispositions" of the woman's "heart" were invariably coupled with the male concept of women's "understanding," as though Astell, Macaulay, Wollstonecraft, and Hays had not already explained why mere static virtue in Christian women can no more displace understanding than understanding can ever be offered as a satisfactory displacement for virtue (Gisborne, *Duties of the Female Sex*, 5).

Priscilla Wakefield's sad comments on the intellectual predicament hampering women of all classes puncture these assumptions. Women's minds have been so cramped "by narrow and ill-directed modes of education" that "the energies of which they are capable" have "thus . . . been concealed, not only from others, but from themselves." And by observing that stupid women envy intelligent women, who had to face as well "the jealousy or contempt" of men, Wakefield offered at least two causes of customary deficiencies in both "the heads" and "the hearts of the [female] sex" (*Present Condition of the Female Sex*, 5, 7).

Elizabeth Hamilton, one of Austen's favorites, was as good as other serious students of women's condition at analyzing causes and effects and ends and means. The signature of all these thinking women is also an Austenian signature: they all insisted that the mind thinks through the heart as often as the heart thinks through the mind. Therefore women should never be denied an education "which is thought to qualify" them for thinking, since the rigorous cultivation of the female "understanding" is by no means "foreign to the cultivation of the heart" (*Letters to the Daughter of a Nobleman*, I, 170, note).

Whether Austen in her fiction and these moderate feminists in their theoretical essays were aware of all their sources, or not, they were all quietly connecting "the natural qualities of the female mind" with its capacity to seek a truly enlightened understanding, which is to say, a truly Christian understanding, quite contrary to the unverifiable "doctrine of innate ideas, and innate affections" in the two sexes (Macaulay, *Letters on Education*, 203).

Wollstonecraft went so far as to charge "the very constitution of civil government" with placing "almost insuperable obstacles in the way to prevent the cultivation of female understanding." It appeared essential to her, as it did to all the feminists, "to go back to first principles," and to separate "the axioms upon which reasoning is built" from the mere "words" or "the conduct of men" (*Vindication*, 54, 11). Yet Wollstonecraft's *Thoughts on the Education of Daughters*, written five years before her explosive vindication of her sex, stated clearly and sadly that repressive customs now largely prevented women from undertaking scrutinies by means of either their minds or their hearts. At that time, she could not thoroughly articulate all "the needful correctives" that *Vindication* was to supply. Now she felt she must warn women that "the school of adversity" is a feminine academy and that each woman's most reliable instructor in a more benevolent curriculum will of necessity be the woman herself.[7] In fact, the feminists of either persuasion all describe women's customary education in terms of "a chaos," "a bundle of contradictions," "intellectual starvation," "intellectual deprivation," all built upon the ridiculous assumption that active Christian virtue can be produced by absolute unthinking obedience.

Alert readers of *Cecilia*, *Camilla*, and *Belinda* soon discover that these heroines must all confront the sexual dichotomies that governed the post-Enlightenment concept of "human understanding." Each heroine must struggle with a hero and others who exaggerate their own capacity for understanding and disparage hers, usually to her face. She must spend months or years begging the hero to believe that she is a rational creature worthy of respect. All three heroines enjoy reading and they speak with the polished diction of well-taught young women. Each heroine is comforted during her prolonged ordeal by the intellectual furniture in her mind as well as the model sensibilities of her heart. Each young woman finds a supporter who reassures her that her human understanding is intact and that she can trust it against all nay-sayers.

In all three novels, there are debates as to what the female intellect innately is, what it has been constructed to be, and what it ought to be to satisfy men. All three novels have truth-telling female monsters who disturb the patriarchal universe by refusing to speak in cant about the presumed intellectual or moral weaknesses of women and the superior mental and moral stature of the heroes. Since these female monsters are often seemingly condemned by the authorial voice and by other characters, they can only covertly condemn the heroine's unnecessary sufferings, and by implication, the whole system of "melancholy disproportions" that make such suffering inevitable.

Austen was fully as distressed by the false concept of women's understanding as her two fictional predecessors. All her heroines eventually clear their minds of cant, to some extent, if they have not already done so when the novel opens. They all know or struggle to accept that human understanding is the capacity, among other things, to blend sensible caution, based on experience, with rational optimism, based on Christian hope, a hard lesson indeed, when their experience provided far more need for caution than reasons for optimism. Above all, they must learn that it is their right to refuse to expect good wishes from grossly mean-spirited people, or benevolent outcomes to issue inevitably from bizarre social customs. Fanny Price and Catherine Morland have been so undernourished for love or respect that readers do not expect them to accomplish this feat of maturity to any great degree.

All seven Austenian heroines were forced to create the materials for their own human understanding through a rather tortuous attention to mundane details and distressing experience, and they had to make as rich and as accurate use of their limited intellectual resources and privileges as possible. They were all autodidacts, or what one of Burney's male characters rather disparagingly called "closet reasoners" (*Cecilia*, 10), whether they are described as readers and thinkers, or not. What mentors they do encounter as they mature, all appear accidentally, and the materials they are given with which to exercise judgment are largely associated with human relations, especially sexual relations. But it is clear, either from the initial or eventual syntax of their speech patterns, and the complexity of their mental processes, that they, too, are readers and that they have read to some purpose. Elizabeth Bennet politely amuses herself with the contents of the Netherfield library while members of the Darcy-Bingley party are playing games for money, which she cannot afford to do. Catherine Morland learns to appreciate people who combine a respect for history and a pleasure in it equal to the pleasure they take in Gothic novels; in the process, her syntax matures. Fanny Price only needs her Edmund Bertram, a benevolent tutor who is also a serious reader, to absorb as much as he can bring her from Eton and Oxford. Emma Woodhouse gently mocks Knightley because he reads nothing but the estate reports and agricultural manuals, whereas she reads—but what she reads even Austen dares not say. Anne Elliot reads both solid prose and poetry, and she seems to know what to read for pleasure, what to read for moral medicine, and when each is appropriate. Marianne Dashwood reads the wrong books and absorbs unbalanced ideas from them.

Catherine Morland's schooling had hardly created a young woman with a sturdy understanding. As the novel opens, Catherine appears as another Kitty Foote: "her heart was affectionate, her disposition cheerful," and she possesses no "conceit nor affectation." Unfortunately, "her mind" is "as ignorant and uninformed as the female mind at seventeen usually is." She and the next sister, as the two oldest daughters, "were inevitably left to shift for themselves."

The results are predictable. James, the heir to the father's modest estate, is selfish and indifferent to his sister's welfare, and she prefers boys' sports to "anything like useful knowledge," since she already knows which of the two sexes is the valued one. But Catherine was privately grooming herself as a heroine of sensibility as she grew prettier and more conscious of the role expected of her. With Gray, she mourned that like herself, "Many a flower is born to blush unseen, / And waste its fragrance on the desert air," and she feels a sympathetic pang for the plight of Isabella's doomed brother in *Measure for Measure*:

> The poor beetle, which we tread upon,
> In corporal sufference feels a pang as great
> As when a giant dies.

If Shakespeare had already taught her woman's role—to sit, "like Patience on a monument, / Smiling at grief"—James Thompson offered her a glimpse of a vision customarily forbidden to her sex: "It is a delightful task, / To teach the young idea how to shoot" (*NA*, 13–18). Austen's satire at the expense of the male conduct-book literature was never more overt than in this ironic quotation. Catherine's very paucity of experience and the fragility of her understanding is just what Henry Tilney is looking for, a woman with limited verbal and mental skills and a heart made easily grateful.

Austen's praise of Burney's *Camilla* in *Northanger Abbey* is an apt part of the satire. The authorial recommendation of Catherine's "natural folly," that innate intellectual weakness so consistently celebrated as one of woman's greatest deficits and perhaps her greatest charm, is immediately followed by an ironic comment intended to do "justice to men." Although "to the larger and more trifling part of the [male] sex, imbecility in females is a great enhancement of the personal charms, there is a portion of them too reasonable and too well informed themselves to desire any thing more in women than ignorance." And, as Burney's *Camilla* had also mockingly observed throughout that novel, "a good-looking girl, with an affectionate heart and a very ignorant mind, cannot fail of attracting a clever young man" (*NA*, 111).

Henry Tilney is the archetypal male pedagogue, pleasantly and condescendingly instructing a young woman who adores his Oxonian polish as much as he relishes her ignorance. "Nay," he says, when they are engaged in one of their flirtations disguised as a tutorial, "if it is to be guess-work, let us all guess for ourselves. To be guided by second-hand conjecture is pitiful. The premises are before you" (*NA*, 151–152). Henry speaks to his pupil as Locke or Astell would have spoken to theirs. But the irony here is that Henry himself is "guided by second-hand conjectures." He is drawn to Catherine for her conditioned deficiences, and he relishes the control over the relationship that they offer him. His ironic comments about Catherine's distaste for Europe's imperial history and his mocking assumption that, even in letter-writing, women lack the most rudimentary skills are obvious indications that he does indeed think it a "misfortune" if women know "any thing," and that a woman with such a blemish should "conceal it as well as she can" (*NA*, 110–111).

One of the gentlest moments of quiet wit at the expense of the male conduct books occurs during this same scene when the three young people on holiday in Bath take a walk to Beechen Cliff. Henry lectures Catherine and his sister on drawing and the picturesque. His "instructions were so clear that she soon began to see beauty in every thing admired by him, and her attention was so earnest, that he became perfectly satisfied of her having a great deal of natural taste." Feminine "taste" is a code word meaning admirations for male accomplishments. Henry is "delighted with her progress," but his mind is so imbued with popular maxims about women's feeble brain matter and short attention span that he is "fearful of wearying her with too much wisdom at once." He "suffered the subject to decline," for as the male conduct books said, the man had the right to direct all conversations according to the dictates of his interests and his judgment. Henry then moves easily from specific scenes of beauty and utility to national problems of agriculture, land enclosures, "waste lands, crown lands, and government." When he finds himself discoursing on politics, "it was an easy step to silence," since "the state of the nation" was a taboo subject for men to discuss in front of women (*NA*, 111).

When Henry discovers that Catherine has been harboring suspicions of his father as the murderer of his mother, he is shocked. His distress is understandable, yet it is one of the emblems of his blindness, for he loves Catherine because she is so ignorant and so inexperienced.

> Dear Miss Morland, consider the dreadful nature of the suspicions you have entertained. What have you been judging from? Remember the country and the age in which we live. Remember that we are English, that we are Christians. Consult your own understanding, your own sense of the probable, your own observation of what is passing around—Does our education prepare us for such atrocities? Do our laws connive at them? Could they be perpetrated . . . in a country like this, where social and literary intercourse is on such a footing; where every man is surrounded by a neighbourhood of voluntary spies, and where roads and newspapers lay every thing open? Dearest Miss Morland, what ideas have you been admitting? (*NA*, 197–198)

This monologue is full of sad ironies. Henry now condemns those traits in Catherine that he had earlier found adorably reassuring to his brittle self-confidence and that he had therefore deliberately promoted with his constant teasing and his sly tales of ghosts at the Abbey. He now follows his condemnations with vague comments about "our education," although he knows that Catherine has had none, and he enjoys rectifying her intellectual deficiences despite her "natural folly." His equally vague recommendation that she respect English laws completely ignores the fact that most women would have no opportunity to learn firsthand what the laws were and, furthermore, that women lived almost entirely without any legal protection. Henry's final blunder takes place when he boasts that English "roads and newspapers lay everything open." The roads of England were open only to those gentlewomen fortunate enough to be permitted to travel and to be able to procure or afford a chaperon, as Catherine's creator all too frequently could not. And Henry ought to have known that the "inclusion of newspapers in the male catalogue is significant," and that male conduct-book literature urged women not to read them. Merely for example, women "were not allowed to express an opinion on politics" (*E*, "Manners of the Age," 510).

Sense and Sensibility does not provide either heroine with a male tutor during the course of the novel, and its quiet defiance of courting customs may partly explain its relative lack of public approval. Marianne Dashwood, the younger of the two heroines, was a specialist in the art of feminine sensibility. Her elder sister Elinor knew "that what Marianne and her mother conjectured one moment, they believed the next—that with them, to wish was to hope, and to hope was to expect" (*SS*, 21). Elinor possesses "a strength of understanding" that forced her to become the moral tutor of her mother and her sister. But she has more than the sane wisdom to analyze causes and effects, ends and means. "She had an excellent heart;—her disposition was affectionate, and her feelings were strong" (*SS*, 6).

Edward Ferrars, Elinor's diffident lover, represents a deliberate reversal of those roles that each sex is expected to play. He is "too diffident to do justice to himself," and he lacks the ambition that his "good understanding," his solid Oxonian education, and his travels should have provided for him. He shares many of the traits that feminine deprivation creates: neither his plight nor his good "understanding" is entirely an innate condition; each depends to a considerable extent on social engineering (*SS*, 15).

Austen exploits Lucy Steele to represent the mental poverty that women's education frequently created in them: "her powers had received no aid from education, she was ignorant and illiterate," and Elinor pities her, even while she despises her, for "the neglect of abilities which education" might have fostered (*SS*, 127). She is deplorably deficient in the schooling of both the mind and the heart.

Marianne's case is far more subtle than Lucy Steele's. She constantly confuses the female heart with human understanding, or the untutored promptings of the emotions with integrity, a disastrous mistake that Willoughby exploits. The conduct books of all persuasions informed women that the cult of sensibility was often a mask for selfishness—

even while the male literature vigorously promoted it—and young Marianne was indeed selfish. She caused herself and her family months of anguish, while she recovered from Willoughby's perfidy, which she had refused to anticipate. Her delightful feminine artlessness has fooled some readers as easily as it fooled Colonel Brandon, as though as readers we were sometimes suspended in a gender-bound uncertainty as to whether we are judging heroines too harshly or not harshly enough.

Austen often resorts to the code-noun "understanding" in a quietly ironic way that would have been familiar to her contemporaries, however subliminally. When the family of Dashwood women is about to be introduced to the Miss Steeles, Sir John Middleton, their host, assures them that these young women are "the sweetest girls in the world." Such "commendation as this, however," does not fool Elinor, who knew all too well that marriageable women were customarily required to be "sweet," and that the sweeter they were, the less genuine "understanding" they were likely to have acquired (*SS*, 119).

Marianne has to go through the agony of searing experience before she can profit from lessons in the art of human understanding. There is a drenching sadness in the London scenes where Marianne is forced to confront Willoughby's betrayal, and these pages seem to sum up all the grief of the moderate feminists. Marianne can only weep, shriek, and rock herself back and forth in her agony, and Elinor can only sit and drip tears, even while she speaks soothingly to Marianne as though to a suffering child.

In the months to come, Elinor's compassionate wisdom, so disagreeable to most readers, is selflessly placed at Marianne's service. Elinor's task is delicate. She must simultaneously convince Marianne that a rake might feel an intense momentary tenderness toward the object of his hunting proclivities—and Willoughby hunted both women and animals—but that mere tenderness is not commitment, and that Marianne's "happiness was never his object." Elinor comforts her sister with bracing commendation for the long and painful road that Marianne has traveled: "You consider the matter . . . exactly as a good mind and a sound understanding must consider it" (*SS*, 351, 350).

The commonplace critical opinion of *Pride and Prejudice* is that Elizabeth has to reconsider her willfully obtuse "prejudice" against Darcy's legitimate "pride," in himself and in his legitimate public humiliation of her. Only readers of eighteenth-century periodicals and of Austen's novels would know that Darcy's inexcusable rudeness to her is similar to the rudeness of *The Spectator* wits to Mary Astell and of Emma Woodhouse to Miss Bates. Darcy appears to assume that a woman freely thinking in public does not deserve a gentle and loving proposal. Elizabeth does take pride in her judgments of people, and in Darcy's case she was initially profoundly just.

It has always seemed to me that Austenian studies persistently offer some very peculiar special pleading on this man's behalf. Darcy's training has been as deficient in the school of the heart as Catherine Morland's has been in the school of the mind. For all his great privileges, including an extensive library from which he has failed to learn good manners, he refuses to adapt himself rationally and pleasantly to the various social circles to which his rank and his sex introduce him. He lacks social kindness. His type stalk their way not only through the feminist literature of the time, but through the novels of Burney and Edgeworth as well.

Elizabeth Bennet's conduct and her speech patterns are supposed to indicate to alert readers that she has resorted to reading, observation, and experience, as well as the Enlightenment feminist imperative to think for herself. She has even had to teach herself "to think on serious subjects," which is a code word for "religious subjects," although as a woman, her creator could not say so (*PP*, 283). The disgraceful marriage of her parents and her repugnance for contemporary dictates about male dominance as she saw it practiced all around her were in conflict with her own ideas of theological and social justice. Darcy's rudeness to her neighbors and to herself offended her understanding of a Christian gentlemen's manners.

Elizabeth's conduct-book reading would have warned her not to aspire to Darcy. The men warned women against the sin of social ambition, and the feminists warned them that the Darcys have "tutors and masters in abundance. But all for the head, and none for the heart. . . . By being taught" to consider themselves only "as heirs to a great fortune," they "lost" that "delicacy of the moral feeling" without which the earth's privileged creatures predictably refuse to recognize the social claims of lesser mortals. The "consciousness of . . . elevated rank, and splendid fortune" ought not to "give birth to pride" in one's birth-privileges and to prejudice against those born without them, but all too often it does (Hamilton, *Letters to the Daughter of a Nobleman*, I, 164, 165,169, 109–110).

Elizabeth has had to teach herself the curriculum of both the head and the heart, since her parents refuse to do so. Her observations on the state of affairs between the sexes have been very depressing. Her father had married a stupid woman because he thought too little of women to hope that he might find an intelligent one. He mocks his daughters as "silly girls" throughout the novel, and locks himself in his library, but his books have taught him neither patience with his lot nor kindness to his daughters, whom he has left without any dowries.

Elizabeth's neighbor, Sir William Lucas, is genial compared with her misogynist father, but he prefers to go to the expense of playing the village squire rather than providing for his daughters. His delight in his oldest daughter's outrageous marriage is sad commentary on his care as a father.

Elizabeth's first and second marriage proposals from two different men both strip her of self-respect. She has watched her sister Jane suffer from a flirtatious suitor, who casually takes advantage of the fact that Jane is all heart and no head. The marriage of Charlotte Lucas to Collins is another shock to Elizabeth's sense of the "melancholy disproportion" between the sexes, which is as sharp as her creator's.

Elizabeth's first refusal of Darcy is the product of experience and, as he later handsomely admits, of his public rejection of her and his officious meddling in her sister's love affair. But Elizabeth does demonstrate one failure of understanding. Because Darcy and Collins have both treated her as though she deserved no respect, she assumes that charming young George Wickham is trustworthy about facts because he exerts himself to be very attentive to her for self-serving reasons. Wickham tells her one truth that the whole village already knows: Darcy may be an aristocrat but he does not behave like a Christian gentleman when he is bored, and Elizabeth therefore assumes that Wickham, a truth-teller about one subject, is reliable on all subjects. Because Wickham is tender toward Elizabeth, she assumes that he has integrity—which he does not. Because Darcy is crassly arrogant, she wrongly assumes that he lacks integrity in family matters. Once he has taken the trouble to show her that he can be as gracious to her and her relatives as a squire should be, she can accept that a man may be a social disaster in public and a caring benefactor to all his dependents in private.

Elizabeth's healing of her pathologically shy sister-in-law is one of those marvelous moments when Austen combines irony with tender and reconciliatory feelings: Georgiana Darcy has been her brother's ward for a decade, and his patriarchal style has badly damaged her. His new understanding that kind manners make the gentleman and brother, as mere rank, money, and fraternal authority never can, now extends to his sister, whom he graciously consigns to Elizabeth's bracing love, until the "attachment" of the two women becomes "exactly what Darcy," in his new generosity, "had hoped to see." For her part, Georgiana now learns a new understanding about men and women: "Her mind received knowledge which had never before fallen in her way. By Elizabeth's instructions she began to comprehend that a woman may take liberties with her husband, which a brother will not always allow in a sister more than ten years younger than himself" (*PP*, 387–388).

Fanny Price, the adopted waif of *Mansfield Park*, is an example of the benefits that autodidacticism under affectionate management can create for the most bereft young woman. Edmund Bertram coaches Fanny just as Astell and Locke advised benevolent tutors to do. Edmund's coaching was "of the highest importance in assisting the improvement of her mind, and extending its pleasures." He had early discovered what nobody else wished to know, that she was "clever," and that she had "a quick apprehension as well as good sense, and a fondness for reading, which properly directed, must be an education in itself." He was that rare post-Enlightenment tutor to a woman who addressed both her serviceable feelings and her objective mind: "he recommended the books which charmed her leisure hours, he encouraged her taste, and corrected her judgment." If this ideal pedagogue does not sound like the Edmund who later tries to force Fanny into an outrageous marriage for self-serving reasons, readers need only accept this description as Austen's oblique statement that the intelligent nature of women flourishes under kind tutelage, and that any education commonly considered good for a gentleman is equally good for a gentlewoman. Edmund "made reading useful by talking to her of what she read, and heightened its attractions by judicious praise" (*MP*, 22). He is a good tutor: he expects her to put forth her best efforts. Yet neither he nor she has any fears that she will ever outdo him.

The abandoned schoolroom at Mansfield Park, with its cast-off furniture and nicknacks, and its fireplace with an empty grate—courtesy of the monstrous Mrs. Norris—all symbolize Fanny's capacity to manufacture her own school with her own books, when Edmund goes off to Eton and Oxford.

Fanny's difficulty is that the artificial split between the giving heart and the judging, deciding mind is never healed. She comes to Mansfield Park already a complete masochist, the eldest daughter of a lower–middle-class military father who despises women, and a mother whose "daughters had never been much to her," although "she was fond of her sons" (*MP*, 389). Fanny has already been turned into a free nursery-governess at home, teaching her younger brothers and sisters and rescuing them from parental neglect. She arrives at Mansfield Park as a thin, undernourished lower–middle-class girl-child adopted as a fetcher-and-carrier for her aunts and cousin members of the landed gentry. Her clothes are shabby, her memory is wretched, and her spirits are crushed—her training in the penitent heart is already complete.

One of the most charming scenes that addresses the question of women's education takes place in Portsmouth, when Fanny makes a disastrous visit to her birth-family, after a ten-year absence. "There were no books in her father's house; but wealth is luxurious and daring—and some of hers found its way to a circulating library." She now takes her abused sister Susan under her protection, delighted "to be having any one's improvement in view in her choice" of books. Her pleasure in her new role as instructor and mentor to another damaged woman suggests how derivative a creature Mansfield Park has made of her, and her dawning recognition of something amiss in her own education.

Fanny's pedagogical technique with Susan represents one of several Austenian examples where women are able to become healers to other people. Fanny is as gentle with Susan as Edmund had been with her, as Elinor Dashwood was with Marianne, and as Anne Elliot was with Lieutenant Benwick, and with the Captain Harville during the fine debate that ends *Persuasion*, and that effectively ended Austen's writing life. Fanny quickly comes to "admire the natural light of [Susan's] mind which could so easily distinguish justly." She assumes correctly that pedagogical gentleness would be as efficacious with an independent young woman made irascible by neglect, as it was with Fanny herself, who had simply been made unnaturally diffident, and she refuses to "censure the faults of conduct" and of thinking, which Susan's treatment at her parents' hands had bred in her. Fanny "gave advice; advice too sound to be resisted by a good understanding, and given so mildly and considerately as not to irritate an imperfect temper." Susan, whose parents had treated her with no "tenderness" at all, not even enough "to buy her off," and who therefore need feel "no gratitude for affection past or present" (*MP*, 396–398), flourishes under this benign care.

In the feminine school of adversity, Susan had learned to defend herself with radically different techniques from the defensive and masochistic responses into which Fanny had been driven. Where Fanny shrinks before her abusers and attempts to appease them, Susan attacks. Fanny's reward is to see Susan gradually mature and become gentler but no less self-respecting. She accompanies Fanny back to Mansfield Park, to comfort her uncle and aunt after Maria's disgrace and Fanny's marriage to Edmund.

But Fanny had not bred another conduct-book woman such as herself. Her creator would not allow it, and her own soft heart would not wish any woman to suffer as she had suffered. In fact, one of the last paragraphs in the novel should disabuse readers of any assumption that Austen ratified these two pernicious ways of educating daughters, the way of Portsmouth or the way of Mansfield Park: "Susan's more fearless disposition and happier nerves made everything easy to her" at the park. "With quickness in understanding the tempers of those she had to deal with, and no natural timidity to restrain" any healthy spontaneity, she became, "perhaps, the most beloved of the two" nieces (*MP*, 472–473).

Austen is clearly paying off some old and bitter scores in *Mansfield Park*: "When Jane Austen's elder brother James suffered a small diminution in his income, he very naturally cut down on his daughter's education. It is eternally to the credit of [James's son], the author of the *Memoir*, that he instantly offered to give up his hunters rather than let her suffer" (Hodge, *Only a Novel*, 33).

Those few contemporaries of Austen who were familiar with all three types of conduct-book literature would recognize the satire of *Emma* as a battle of the conduct books. In a rarely perceptive essay called "Reading Characters: Self, Society and Text in *Emma*," Joseph Litvak describes this novel "as a contest between Emma and Knightley" or "between two equally compelling interpretations of the self—especially the female self—and society." While candidly admitting that "Emma is frequently 'wrong,' " as indeed she is wrong, fully as wrong as Darcy, Litvak claims that "she is 'right' to question the absoluteness with which Knightley" pronounces "the distinction between them. . . . Patriarchal criticism of *Emma*, of course, takes Knightley's side," in which his "right" seeks to correct her "wrong." Litvak is one of the few students of Austen's fiction who insists that readers must "give Emma some respect and construe the conflict" partly as a difference in two distinct perspectives, the male and the female.[8]

Many of the dialogues and some crucial authorial comments in *Emma* address the problem of Emma's education, and implicitly, the education of gentlewomen. Emma's governess was beautifully trained to teach her pupil the feminine understanding of the heart, but she fails dismally because she is sadly deficient in human, or mental understanding, and so she can do nothing to ease the "intellectual solitude" from which Emma suffers (*E*, 7).

Emma is often quite prescient about what is wrong with her education: when she is to be left as nursery governess to her nieces and nephews, her sister charges her to love them and her brother-in-law insists that she discipline them. She replies that she can satisfy both charges, since "happiness must preclude false indulgence and physic" (*E*, 311). As a governess, she will not separate the heart (maternal indulgence), from the head, or "physic," that is to say, from cool medicinal treatment when necessary. Readers who enjoy demolishing Emma should look again at a charming scene where she is cuddling an eight-month-old niece, who is "happy to be danced about in her aunt's arms," and all the while, Knightley is giving her one of his scolding sessions, which always contain great justice to his own position, and almost none to hers (*E*, 98).

Austen's analysis of Emma's "intellectual solitude" may well have emerged partly from her favorite, Thomas Gisborne. While bemoaning the "general contempt" under which women labored, Gisborne nonetheless laid the blame for many women's "mental indolence" upon the women themselves: "disappointed at not perceiving a way open by which they, like their brothers, may distinguish themselves and arise to eminence; they are occasionally heard to declare . . . that the sphere in which women are destined to move is so humble and so limited as neither to require nor to reward assiduity" (Gisborne, *Duties of the Female Sex*, 10–11).

Emma's incapacity for "steady reading . . . industry and patience," and a preference for "fancy" rather than "understanding," for which Knightley condemns her (*E*, 37), are all symptoms of her restless mind, which has never been rewarded for the "assiduity" it does possess. She is about to make a sketch of Harriet Smith and she "produced the portfolio containing her various attempts at portraits, *for not one of them had ever been finished*, that they might decide together on the best size for Harriet." The rest of this authorial description contains a quiet, sad rebuke for a system that had produced this creative apathy in a woman of Emma's quirky brilliance: "her many beginnings were displayed. Miniature, half lengths, whole lengths, pencil, crayon, and watercolours *had all been tried in turn*" (*E*, 44; emphasis mine). Any instructor of troubled youth, particularly troubled women, will recognize this symptom.

The contrast between Emma, who is without rigorous and kind instruction, and Jane Fairfax, who "had received every advantage of discipline and culture," is deliberate. Jane lived "with right-minded and well-informed people"; "her heart" and her "understanding," and even "every lighter talent had been done full justice to." No wonder these two women are suspicious of each other. Emma had been trained to be a surrogate wife and free nurse-companion to her father. Jane had deliberately been offered the best education possible for a woman, precisely because her feminine poverty forced her to undergo the classical fate of the governess. Now, with "the fortitude of a noviciate," Jane steels herself "to complete the sacrifice and retire from all the pleasure of life, of rational intercourse, equal society, peace and hope," and to abandon herself "to penance and mortification for ever" (*E*, 165).

There are four spinsters in this novel, whose education—or lack of it—defines them. Intellectually polished Jane is frantic about her future; the impoverished and untutored Miss Bates, a poor clergyman's fatherless daughter, has none, and Harriet's education has left her as ignorant and as vulnerable as her illegitimacy. Emma has had no companion who could "meet her in conversation, rational or playful" (*E*, 7). But there is something very grim about the fact that the three women whose minds had been neglected were trapped at home, whereas the one woman who had been well trained, is now facing exile. There is something even grimmer that Emma and Jane, the two most intelligent women characters, should both be placed "*en Penitence*." Emma's struggles with the deliberately created split between her head and her heart often leave her morally exhausted with humility and a profound desire to "repress imagination all the rest of her life" (*E*, 142).

Emma's crimes of the heart, her jealousy of Jane's fully developed talents, her self-serving association with Harriet Smith, and her cruelty to Miss Bates have been so thoroughly canvassed that they have obliterated the intellectual poverty and the other social deformities that have engendered such outrageous behavior. Readers need to consider carefully the plight of a woman such as Emma, who watches over an agoraphobic father so carefully that she can barely leave the house, who grieves for the loss of her governess, even while she rejoices that Miss Taylor has found security in marriage, and whose strong maternal streak has been as thoroughly exploited as her mind has been neglected.

Anne Elliot, the heroine of *Persuasion*, is twenty-seven when the novel opens. She is an interesting model of the sadder and less indignant of the moderate feminists such as Wakefield, Reeve, or Austen's favorite, Hamilton, rather than a fictional version of the warrior woman represented by Wollstonecraft and Hays. Her age makes her predicament more poignant and more potentially fatal than the predicament of other Austenian heroines: "She had been forced into prudence in her youth"; now she shares with other intelligent reading heroines of Austen, Burney, and Edgeworth the capacity to muse over her experiences and to make some independent judgments. She "had learned romance as she grew older—the natural sequence of an unnatural beginning" (*P*, 30). That suggestive verb, "forced," and the quietly ominous phrase, "unnatural beginning," describe the difficulties of all Austen's heroines as they begin their perilous journey toward their socially prescribed destiny.

As the novel opens, Anne is musing over the eight years of "suffering" that had followed her anguished refusal of the intelligent and witty naval lieutenant, Frederick Wentworth, at her godmother's behest. Anne thinks not only of "the misery of parting" and of the lonely years with a hostile sister and father, during which she had "hardly anybody to love," a fate she shares with all the heroines, but she is also considering the causes and effects of a renewed crisis of the heart (*P*, 28, 26). Even as she prepares herself to face an angry Frederick's return, she is able to separate her mature response—that she need not have refused Frederick as matters turned out—from the received wisdom of her original acquiescence, firmly dictated by all the male conduct-book literature—that subservience to older and presumably wiser heads was appropriate at the time.

Anne Elliot has the elegant speech patterns of Elinor Dashwood,

Elizabeth Bennet, Emma Woodhouse, and Eleanor Tilney, the charming young woman who will eventually become Catherine Morland's sister-in-law and her female instructor in human understanding. With the exception of Emma, they all try to use their intelligence to instruct defenseless people of either sex in the art of self-protection, as though the role of instructor eased their own "intellectual solitude."

Anne becomes the bereaved Captain Benwick's tutor in his recovery from grief, in which she has had almost a decade of practice. Like the ideal governesses and tutors, from Astell and Locke to the moderate feminists, Anne's principal tools are "the persuasion" of interest and sympathy under the control of judgment, and exact advice about specific bad habits. In this case, Benwick has collapsed into the dangerous practice of nourishing grief rather than working through it. Anne "had the hope of being of real use to him in some suggestions as to the duty and benefit of struggling against affliction . . . and to say, that she thought it was the misfortune of poetry, to be seldom safely enjoyed by those who enjoyed it completely." She recommended "a larger allowance of prose in his daily study," such as "memoirs of characters of worth and suffering, as calculated to rouse and fortify the mind by the highest precepts and the strongest examples of moral and religious endurance." Anne sounds like Elizabeth Hamilton, whose most pervasive prescription for suffering women was prayer, endurance, and the consolation of bracing literature.

Anne may have been properly solemn with Captain Benwick; as a sensitive woman, she knows from experience that it would be the height of crudeness to laugh at suffering or to brush it off. She comforts him and advises him because she is "emboldened" to teach the arts of self-healing, "feeling in herself the right of seniority of mind" and of suffering, since he has been in mourning for his dead fiancée for less than a year. But as she says to herself, "he has not, perhaps, a more sorrowing heart than I have. I cannot believe his prospects so blighted forever. He is younger than I am; younger in feeling, if not in fact; younger as a man. He will rally again, and be happy with another" (*P*, 100–101, 97).

Anne knows herself very well, although she cannot conquer the unhealthy habit of public diffidence that the early death of her mother and her father's irritable hostility have taught her. Yet she can legitimately lay claim to the province both of the mind and of the heart.

Her own "submissive spirit" and her "patience" in the feminine school of adversity have not prevented her from acquiring a "strong understanding" of books and people, which she knows from sad experience can "supply resolution." But she admits that she lacks "that elasticity of mind" with which to repair the internal damage done to her by her father and sister.

In some ways, Anne does less than justice to herself and her own gentle humor, which in itself had almost been able "to counterbalance every other want" (*P*, 154). She is constantly amused to find other people "caught" in the "too common idea of spirit and gentleness being incompatible with each other," an archetype as dangerous as the assumption that separates women's minds and hearts. As to whether "a persuadable temper" in a woman improves a man's happiness more than "a very resolute character," she ironically asks herself whether "it might not now strike" Frederick "that, like all other qualities of the mind," female resolution, and even male, "should have its proportions and limits" (*P*, 172, 116).

Even after Frederick's profound apologies to Anne that he had not earlier "learnt to distinguish between" her "steadiness of principle," and Louisa Musgrove's "obstinacy of self-will" or between "the resolution of a collected mind" and the needless "darings" of an undisciplined heart, Anne will not exploit his newly learned generosity. If she should wish to redirect the reigns of her marriage to Frederick, she will simply copy Sophia Croft's tactfully persuasive habits with her own commanding naval husband. Frederick's new-born respect for Anne's "perfect excellence of mind" will allow her to do so, because she is artless in the delicacy of her human understanding. Her mind is even more acute than her modesty will admit to herself; in fact, it is almost as "excellent" as Frederick, in the second flush of love, thinks it is (*P*, 242).

5

Dancing and Marriage: The Province of the Ballroom

The treatment of ballroom dancing in Austen's mature novels is a classical example of Austenian joy. In the novels of Burney and Edgeworth, the ballroom scenes are full of satire: the antics of the undesirable suitors, and sometimes the theoretically desirable ones, suggest the muffled savagery of a rite of passage, and thus these scenes symbolize women's lives as Austen's ballroom scenes also do. But in Austen's fiction, the balance between dance as dance and as a sanctioned and delightful erotic pleasure, on the one hand, and on the other, as an introduction to a business deal in which all the advantages lie with the initiating partner, is often shifted in favor of the benevolent and mythic qualities in the human art of the dance. Austen's ballroom scenes and the authorial allusions to dancing are almost always joyful, for all their ominous implications, which Austen observed with her customary irony. Even when she was well beyond marriage age and playing dance music so that her nieces and nephews could enjoy this domestic pleasure, she still wrote with gusto about how much the young people enjoyed dancing as she once had. And her heroines share with their creator the capacity to celebrate what is intrinsically fine in social dancing, despite its secondary co-option into the mercantile and patriarchal scheme of things.

Austen obviously cherished the "animal spirit" of young people when they were released under circumstances where they could safely be given full reign. She condemned them in her didactic creations, Lydia Bennet and John Willoughby, because in Lydia they were vulgar and dangerous, and in Willoughby they approximated a chase after a beautiful animal. But when Austen's two most psychologically flattened heroines, Catherine Morland and Fanny Price, momentarily forget their diffidence and allow their youthful spirits to rise before or after a ball, their creator heartily approves of this wholesome event. When Edmund asks Fanny for two dances at the ball given in honor of her visiting brother,"She had hardly ever been in a state so nearly approaching high spirits in her life. Her cousins' former gaiety on the day of a ball was no longer surprising to her; she felt it to be indeed very charming, and was actually practising her steps about the drawing room" (*MP*, 272–273). Catherine Morland experiences the same exhilaration after she has been dancing with Henry Tilney, who enjoys dancing and who invites her to go walking the next day. While she is carried home from the ball in a sedan chair, "her spirits danced with her, as she danced in her chair all the way home" (*NA*, 81).

Austen clearly loved all the poignant and tender associations of the dance with that anticipatory period that she called "the season of happiness" (*SS*, 54). But she must also have loved the dance as an art that simultaneously demanded energy and strict attention to rhythm and harmony, as well as the social discipline of courteous and benevolent attention to one's partner. She was irritated with her brother James because he would not take the trouble to dance well. She believed that "an artist" in living "cannot do anything slovenly" (*Letters*, 30). But James was a man who paid no more serious attention to impoverished women than the puffed-up Mr. Collins paid to any woman except his august patroness, the autocratic widow Lady Catherine de Bourgh.

So clear-headed a country woman as Austen had obviously observed the sequential connections between all those family balls on her brothers' account, and their subsequent marriages and fatherhood. Henry Tilney enjoyed teasing Catherine with the slightly suggestive comment that "a country dance" is "an emblem of marriage." His assumption that it is the "duty" of each partner in each type of partnership "to give the other no cause for wishing that he or she had bestowed themselves elsewhere" (*NA*, 76–77), suggests that underneath his brittleness, he will be quite capable of giving flesh to his light-hearted symbol: in paraphrasing the Anglican prayer book on marriage as an "engagement between man and woman, formed for the advantage of each, and that when once entered into, they belong exclusively to each other," Henry momentarily reveals, however ironically, that he would enjoy an exclusive relationship with an artless woman who would never wish to stray.

Austen was obviously playing upon experienced readers' acknowledgment that the dance, "WHEREIN ALL THE FIGURES USED IN THAT POLITE AMUSEMENT," possesses erotic implications not so polite (*E*, facing p. 502), of which the innocent Catherine is not aware. Austen's fictional demonstration of this fact is as sly as her demonstration of many another universal truth that everybody knows and nobody is supposed to admit: "It may be possible to do without dancing, entirely," remarks the authorial voice in *Emma*: "Instances have been known of young people passing many, many months successively, without being at any ball of any description, and no material injury accrue either to body or mind;—but when a beginning is made—when the felicities of rapid motion have once been, though slightly felt—it must be a very heavy set that does not ask for more" (*E*, 247).

Robert Polhemus has provided a delightfully frank gloss upon this passage that does not ignore its symbolic implications:

> Dancing is as permanent and as old as warfare. And that precise, yet generalizing, elegant, typically Austenian phrase, "the felicities of rapid motion," extends the irony further. All dances are essentially mating dances, and the end, as well as the means, of dancing, is the felicity of rapid motion. Through such prose and such manifold strands of irony Austen brings home the importance of the "little things" she writes about and of the whole tenor of women's belittled lives.[1]

Dancing without any opportunity to flirt later with one's partner would have been to Austen what sexual fore-play is without consummation—had her century enabled her to articulate such a shocking idea. But Austen often offered shocking ideas by authorial innuendo or through her characters' mouths: "Mrs. Weston proposed having no regular supper; merely sandwiches, &c. set out in the little room; but that was scouted as a wretched suggestion. A private dance, without sitting down to supper, was pronounced an infamous fraud upon the rights of men and women; and Mrs. Weston must not speak of it again" (*E*, 254). How slyly and how whimsically the authorial voice stresses, almost a quarter of a century after Wollstonecraft published her *Vindication of the Rights of Woman*, that on the ballroom floor, at least, women are granted a few of the same rights as men.

As a young marriageable woman who was already seriously practicing the craft of fiction, Austen was aware of the roles that balls were designed to play, if young women were to perform their proper function of attracting a husband. Well into her middle thirties, her letters were still full of ironic comment as to male dancers both attractive and unattractive, with whom she danced or was not asked to dance at various county houses. Perhaps because all the Austen boys had left home by the time she had reached her dancing days, her letters contain no indications that balls were ever given for her at her father's rectory. Visits to richer cousins and family friends were therefore her only sources of potential marriageable material. But the pervasive social anxiety about "the felicities of rapid motion" and sexual intercourse, as well as the unfortunate connection of these two "motions" with the mercenary arrangements that marriage entailed, had always been a source of ironic amusement for Austen since her juvenilia.

An early letter to Cassandra, when Austen was just twenty-one, contains an elusive blend of irony and fleeting romantic dreams:

> I shall be extremely anxious to hear the Event of your Ball, & shall hope to receive so long & minute an account of every particular that I shall be tired of reading it. Let me know how many besides their fourteen Selves & Mr and Mrs Wright, Michael will contrive to place about their Coach, and how many of the Gentlemen, Musicians & Waiters, he will have persuaded to come in their Shooting Jackets.

Then there follows some good-natured banter about whether a certain gentleman, of whom Cassandra had previously given her sister "a good report," had indeed danced with her, whether "J. Harwood deports himself with the Miss Biggs" in ways the sisters would approve, and "which of the Miss Marys will carry the day with my brother James" (*Letters*, 11).

When Austen wrote this letter of September 1796, Cassandra was already engaged to Thomas Fowle, and the letter before this one teased Cassandra with the delightful news that people had begun to gossip about her pleasurable occupation as she sat making her trousseau. What follows in this letter is exactly what one might predict from an accomplished ironist with a well-developed heart and a dancing body, and an equally well-developed sense of duty. Even though Austen had been raised by parents with sound social taste and good sense about marrying for affection, Austen knew perfectly well that her mission in life was not to perfect and publish her fiction but to supply herself with a living through the agency of a husband.

Austen's early letters to Cassandra often demonstrate the combination of longing and ironic laughter that was passing through her head, even while her limbs and her smiles were officially and not so officially directed at all the most appealing young dancing men who might make her an offer of marriage. Balls and dancing clearly meant far more to young women than flattery and the politely erotic motion of the dance. They were as emotionally laden as is the interview for modern professionals seeking to survive or to climb a few perilous steps higher on a rickety corporate ladder.

After Austen had described what dancing news she wanted to hear from Cassandra, she proceeded to amuse and no doubt reassure her sister that she too had been paying attention to business by enjoying herself on the ballroom floor: "*We* were at a ball on Saturday, I assure you. We dined at Goodnerstone & in the Evening danced two Country dances and the Boulengeries.—I opened the Ball with Edwd Bridges. . . . We supped there, & walked home at night under the shade of two Umbrellas" (*Letters*, 11–12). The first sentence, with its italics and its factually unnecessary incremental clause—"I assure you"—sounds as though Austen were engaged in some genial sisterly competition with Cassandra as to which one of them could most successfully perform her duties to her family and to society by getting a husband. The last clause—"We . . . walked home at night under the shade of two Umbrellas"— suggests Austen's customary treatment of romantic topics at this time. It is both elusive and resonant with everything that a polite young woman does not say.

But there is some private wit involved here. Why do they need shade at night? Only Cassandra would know precisely what the joke was and what sensations were also in the head of her sister, that young dancer and writer, who was seeking both the human means of her only socially acceptable profession and material for her novels. But any novelist who could create such psychologically flattened heroines as Fanny Price and Catherine Morland, and still endow them with the capacity to become privately ecstatic about dancing and its erotic and social implications, must have had some complex ideas and fantasies floating through her head while she and her companions "walked home at night under the shade of two Umbrellas." And the romantic pleasures were not yet over; two weeks later, Austen wrote Cassandra: "We have been very gay since I wrote last: dining at Nackington, returning by Moonlight" (*Letters*, 13).

Austen's unabashed delight in the dance, both as a "*beau ideal*," as Cardinal Newman said in quite another context, and as a socially sanctioned form of sexual display, was one of her most endearing traits. In the first place, her own vigorous spirits required exercise, and gardening, walking, and chaperoned dancing were the only exercises customarily sanctioned for women members of the minor gentry. In the second place, dancing relieved, if only temporarily, the accumulated stresses inherent in women's predicament even while it created other stresses. It also placed the two sexes in positions of relative equality, since the steps of the dances were already patterned, and so the partners faced one another in positions of similar spatial dignity in the same public event. And under ideal conditions, the dance represented the community at its best, just as marriage undertaken for reasons of genuine sexual attraction, serious commitment, and mutual love and respect represented the community at its best.

Austen's sanguine pleasure in dancing was much closer to that of the feminists than the traditionalists. Although her fiction and her letters often mock the young woman who has been taught "only . . . 'to dance, to dress, to troll the tongue and roll the eye,' " and to engage in "frivolous pursuits" and "low artifices" in order to catch a husband, as Jane West complained (*Letters to a Young Lady*, I, 38–39), Austen's family life as a young girl, and her fictional descriptions of the dance might have come right out of Macaulay:

> When the little family are become adepts in the art [of dancing], I would advise the parents to treat them with a ball once a week;

> for whilst employed in dancing, they can enjoy the society of their young friends, without that intercourse which might infect them with the errors of their neighbour's education; and dancing is a wholesome exercise in a large well-aired room, when not continued till too late . . . in the evening. (*Letters on Education*, 59–60)

Clara Reeve's description of the ideal governess sounds engagingly like Emma Woodhouse's description of how she will function as governess to her nieces and nephews, and how, in fact she does function: the governess "is to be their friend, their companion, and sometimes their play-fellow; she should take a share in their pastimes, [and] should sing and dance with them," because children absorb good intellectual and moral habits most easily through the agencies of legitimate pleasures (Reeve, *Plans of Education*, 48–49).

For orthodox theorists, the archetypal connections between problematical woman and dancing created as many anxieties as their connections between problematic woman and thinking. Orthodox Anglicans did not want to forbid dancing altogether or to dampen women's pleasure in it so decisively as to make them unappealingly awkward on the ballroom floor, since its primary function was to introduce people of marriageable age, so that they could discover whether their dancing steps and other permissable modes of defining themselves were to fit each other in reasonable comfort. A dancing woman who liked dancing neither too much nor too little was presumed to be a woman who was ready enough to marry, but not unduly so. Such a woman was presumed to be able to conform to her subordinate role in marriage.

Nevertheless, the orthodox literature described vigorous feminine "motion," change, or progress of any kind, either geographical or metaphorical, in very modified and even guarded ways. Male conduct books often described married women as benevolent "fixtures" in their husband's country houses; travel or dancing, and above all, the London season, was thought to disrupt the mode of life most congenial to their happy seclusion and subordination. Burton, for example, asked his readers where the courting male might be expected to find the ideal woman, as fixed in her isolated province as she was fixed in her ideas of her proper role. The "blushing fair one," he warned, would not be found "in Crowds and Assemblies, but in the sequestered walks of domestic retirement." The "prudent and discreet" young "female" whom every man sought, a woman capable of "the tender affections of Wife and Mother," is one who would prefer "privacy and retirement" to "public resorts." But Burton was as ambiguous about women and dancing as any of his orthodox colleagues:

> Dancing, under proper regulations, may be innocent and useful. But let me remind you, my young Audience, of its principal design; which is, to improve the attitudes of the Body, and render the gait easy and graceful. . . . Dancing should likewise be considered as affording you that kind of exercise, which you seem to require more than the other sex, because your employments are more sedentary, and your amusements less athletic. (*Female Education*, I, 213, 132, 138)

Gregory had earlier placed the same strictures upon female dancing: "In dancing, the principal points you are to attend to are ease and grace. I would have you to dance with spirit; but never allow yourself to be so far transported with mirth, as to forget the delicacy of your sex.— Many a girl dancing in the gaity and innocence of her heart, is thought to discover a spirit she little dreams of" (*Legacy to his Daughters*, 57–58).

Wollstonecraft condemned the prurience in such advice: "Dr. Gregory . . . actually recommends dissimulation, and advises an innocent young girl to give the lie to her feelings, and not dance with spirit, when gaiety of heart would make her feel eloquent without making her gestures immodest" (*Vindication*, 28). "Besides," said Wollstonecraft, "what can be more indelicate than a girl's *coming out* in the fashionable world? Which, in other words, is to bring to market a marriageable miss, whose person is taken from one public place to another, richly caparisoned. Yet mixing in the giddy circle under restraint, these butterflies long to flutter at large" (*Vindication*, 170).

Gisborne admitted that dancing was "an amusement in itself both innocent and salubrious, and therefore by no means improper, under suitable regulations, of course." But he was troubled by its intrinsic invitation not only to female indelicacy, but also to female "vanity" in the favored women, and "envy" in those not chosen, since both these emotions were detrimental to the maintenance of male domination over women. He moves backward and forward on this issue so momentous to nervous patriarchs: one moment he claims that women's sexual attractions are part of the divine plan—"But to protect weakness from the oppression of domineering authority, those whom He had not qualified to contend, He has enabled to fascinate"—and the next moment he demonstrates a typical orthodox anxiety about the results of God's plan: "In the ballroom, however, a young woman has more temptations to encounter than she has experienced" before her debut (*Duties of the Female Sex*, 20, 180–181).

Hannah More was usually so orthodox that it comes as a surprise to find her describing the young gentlewoman's debut with such sympathetic irony:

> If, indeed, women were mere outside form and face only, and if mind made up no part of [woman's] composition, it would follow that a ball-room was quite as appropriate a place for choosing a wife, as an exhibition room for choosing a picture. . . . The two cases differ . . . in this, that if a man select a picture for himself from among all its exhibited competitors, and bring it to his own house, the picture being passive, he is able to *fix* it there: while the wife, picked up at a public place, and accustomed to incessant display, will not, it is probable, when brought home, stick so quietly to the spot where he fixes her; but will escape to the exhibition room again, and continue to be displayed at every subsequent exhibition, just as if she were not become private property, and had never been definitely disposed of. (*Female Education*, II, 162–168)

Despite Austen's contempt for More, this usually orthodox woman here demonstrates some feminist irony worthy of Austen's own. More's passive voice—"*picked up*," "*brought home*," "*displayed*," "*definitely disposed of*"—and the italicized emphasis upon the man's right to *fix* his woman in one spot for life, as though she were an inanimate object, are almost Austenian. So are More's ironic stress upon the unpleasantly mercantile aspect of women's debuts, and her stark acceptance of the woman's undignified role in such marriages.

Gisborne joined his conduct-book colleagues of all three persuasions in condemning the spectacle of a feminine nursery larva, "[m]ewed up from every prying gaze," who has nevertheless been "taught to believe that her first [public] appearance is the subject of universal expectation," and thereafter, "from that time forward thinks by day and dreams by night of amusements, and of dress, and of compliments, and of admirers." The naive Catherine Morland had her head stuffed full of thoughts by day and dreams by night that she was dressed as she ought to be, looked as she ought to look, and had captured at least one admirer, and Austen gleefully accepts the necessity for Catherine's metamorphosis. But Gisborne deplored the presumed necessity of dragging innocent young women "from London to Bath, from Tunbridge to Weymouth, that the young woman may be corrupted into dissipation, folly and misconduct, and exposed as in a public market, to the inspection of bachelors of fashion" (*Duties of the Female Sex*, 93, 391).

In *Northanger Abbey*, Austen provided a nice covert joke at the idea that any young woman would prefer to be "*fixed*" at home, rather than seeking young men at balls. Even the diffident Catherine Morland, who was completely dependent upon other people's opinions, once she passed puberty, was "all blissful happiness" on the way to Bath and balls. But then, neither her mentors who took her to Bath, nor her parents, who were "all compliance" over the idea of the trip, were themselves the least fearful of any harm that might come from this sensible scheme. On the contrary, they were quite aware "that if adventures"—in the shape of potential husbands—"will not befal [*sic*] a young lady in her own village, she must seek them abroad" (*NA*, 17), just as her creator had been forced to do.

There is no question, though, that Austen's pleasure in the dance, as a social institution allowing her access to a public event and as a legitimate symbol of mating, is darkened by her own sense of its undignified exploitation for the mercantile purpose of getting a daughter "disposed of" in marriage. The authorial voice observes tartly: "Happy for all her maternal feelings was the day on which Mrs. Bennet got rid of her two most deserving daughters" (*PP*, 385). But there was a worse fate then marriage and life-long subordination to a man who treated a woman with reasonable affection and respect, and that was finding no man at all and living at home with scornful parents.

In "The Glorious Anxiety of Motion," William Walling accounts for Austen's paradoxical pleasure and pain over the idea of travel as arising from her own ambivalent tensions between a static country world and a modern world full of new geographical and psychological "accelerations" and "nomadic" habits. Walling centers his descriptive symbolism in Austen's fictional journeys, when all the heroines, at one time or another, with the significant exception of Emma, experience this oxymoronic "glorious anxiety of motion" during coach journeys. Each journey symbolizes both opportunity and displacement for the heroine.[2] But then, changes of any kind were bound to create both hopes and anxieties, to a considerable extent because the journeys were so exceptional for these country gentlewomen and because they were always accomplished through the agencies of others.

The dance was full of just as much "glorious anxiety" as travel, for Austen's heroines. Although the dancing couple followed the same patterned steps, the protocol of the dance imitated the protocols of male choices and female acquiescence, as the ironic Henry Tilney takes pleasure in reminding Catherine Morland. In discussing the symbolic similarities between dancing and marriage, Henry archly remarks, "You will allow, I think, that in both, man has the advantage of choice, woman only the power of refusal . . . he is to purvey, and she is to smile" (*NA*, 77).

The dance provided other examples of what *HE* could do and *she* could not. According to F. B. Pinion, "It was not etiquette for unengaged couples to dance more than two consecutive dances; more would provoke comment."[3] Charles Bingley refused to honor this protocol, and he danced two sets with Jane Bennet and paid other marked attentions to her, thus exposing her to "misery of the acutest kind," to her mother's careless gossip, and to "the world's . . . derision for disappointed hopes" (*PP*, 12–13, 191). There were other restraints upon a woman who wanted to be free to further an acquaintanceship with one man, unencumbered by the unpleasant attentions of another; "if she refused an invitation" to dance with one man, "as Elizabeth refused Mr. Collins after the interval at Netherfield, it was out of her power to accept another partner during the remainder of the ball" (Pinion, 48).

Even though the man had exercised his choice to engage a woman for two dances in a row, he was free to desert her if he felt so inclined, and during that set, she could not accept an invitation to dance with anybody else. John Thorpe displayed his gross unfitness to be the hero to Catherine that he fancied he was, when he engaged her for the first two dances at the Bath Assemblies, and then forgot about her in the pleasures of the card-room, to which he repaired as soon as their party arrived at the Pump Room. Much later, Henry Tilney saw her sitting forlornly and engaged her to dance. No sooner had they started dancing than John arrived to claim his two dances, which had been over for some while. Mr. Collins engaged his cousin Elizabeth for the first two dances at the Netherfield ball, a mark of distinction that he expected her to receive with humble gratitude, but that angered her because it presumed upon a casual relationship. With him, Elizabeth endured "dances of mortification." Mr. Collins, "awkward and solemn, apologising instead of attending, and often moving wrong without being aware of it, gave her all the shame and misery which a disagreeable partner for a couple of dances can give" (*PP*, 90). This passage demonstrates Austen's habit of making a man's fitness as a dancing partner an emblem of his potential fitness as a husband or merely as a cooperative and friendly member of a tightly knit community.

One of the most gracious scenes in an Austenian ballroom occurs in Austen's fragment called *The Watsons*. "The first winter assembly in the Town of D." introduces the young, intelligent, impoverished spinster Emma Watson to ten-year-old Charles Blake, who had been publicly snubbed by the county Miss Osborne, almost as callously as Darcy snubbed Elizabeth Bennet at the Meryton assembly. Emma Watson, whose sex and poverty have already acquainted her with multiple humiliations, immediately steps forward to offer herself as the partner of this small boy, precisely because his face is crimson with mortification, and his eyes are about to drip unmanly tears: "Emma did not think or reflect,— she felt & acted—. 'I shall be very happy to dance with you, Sir, if you like it,' " says Emma, therefore addressing small, vulnerable, and insulted Charles as though he were a grown man, tactfully preserving his masculine privilege of choosing his partner. He need accept only if he should like the idea.

Charles does like the idea immensely: Emma has held "out her hand" to him "with the most unaffected good humor.—The Boy in one moment restored to all his first delight—looked joyfully at his Mother and stepping forward with an honest & simple Thank you Maam was instantly ready to attend his new acquaintance" (*MW*, 314, 330–332). In the Austenian world, "heroism of principle" takes place even on the dance floor.

The couple must have made an odd-looking pair, for Emma, no doubt, was a head taller than Charles. But their joy in one another is utterly infectious. The boy "is bent cheifly [*sic*] on dancing" because he does not want to shame himself or discomfort his partner. But Emma and Charles do talk; and Charles eagerly offers exuberant information about his mother, his sister, his brothers, and his uncle. He describes where he lives, what he is studying—Latin—and what he most likes to do—horseback riding. Anybody who has ever been entertained by an intelligent and gracious child, when the affectionate parents are elsewhere, knows how rare and unforgettable such moments are (*MW*, 331).

Austen's ironic interest in dancing as a symbol of male domination emerges as early as 1787. In her short story called "Jack and Alice," the twelve-year-old satirist staged a masked ball, and she took advantage of some traditional symbolic puns. Face masks in this satirical romp symbolize attempts of individuals to hide unsocial impulses: "Of the Males a Mask representing the Sun, was the most universally admired. The beams that darted from his Eyes were like those of that glorious Luminary tho' infinitely superior. So strong were they that no one dared venture within half a mile of them." This resplendent male is exceedingly clever, for "he had therefore, the best part of the Room to himself," so that everybody, even the lesser males, huddled "together in one corner of the room." When "he half shut his eyes . . . the Company discovered him to be Charles Adams in his plain green Coat, without any mask at all" (*MW*, 13).

Austen's first extant description of a ball mercilessly mocks traditional images of the man as the woman's celestial luminary, around which she circulates in a private orb much smaller than his, at a distance from his, but controlled by his "never failing genius" (*MW*, 14). But within two pages, readers discover that Charles's mask hides his cruelty, for he creates animal traps—or rather, woman-traps, in which unwary women who love him find themselves locked.

Almost a decade later, a more mature Austen was still fascinated with balls, assemblies, and dancing, but in a personal way. She had now left her juvenile modest proposals behind her and she had already begun her first full-length attempts at mature fiction (*Memoir*, 49; Chapman, *Facts and Problems*, 42). Austen's first few letters that Cassandra did not destroy also reveal that the young fiction writer was almost as fascinated with birthdays as she was with dancing. She was approaching her twenty-first birthday when she wrote her first surviving letters to Cassandra.

Austen's letters of this period indicate that she was laughingly intoxicated with her awareness of two maturing powers, the power to attract men and to be attracted by them, and the power of artistic self-confidence and ambition. Her ironic comments indicate that she wanted fame, money, and a kind and charming husband. These painful yet exhilarating muscle-flexings of a young feminine mind just beginning to realize its unusual powers were coupled with the normal stirrings of her feminine heart and body, and they reveal traces of mandatory feminine guilt, just when Austen was at the zenith of her dancing days.

In the very first sentences of her first surviving letter, Austen says archly that young Tom Lefroy has just had his birthday, his twentieth, in fact, a few weeks after her own. Austen was writing her older sister Cassandra to celebrate Cassandra's twenty-third birthday, and she mockingly said that Cassandra, at twenty-three, was "very near of an age" to Tom, who, in fact, was Austen's age (*Letters*, 1 and Indexes I and II). Austen was in love with Tom Lefroy, a fact that her family tried to obliterate for understandable reasons, since it was something of a social disgrace, as all the conduct-book males and some of the Augustan wits had observed, for a woman to fall in love with a man before he had announced that he had fallen in love with her: "It is a maxim laid down among you, and a very prudent one it is," intoned Dr. Gregory to his daughters, "That love is not to begin on your part, but is to be the consequence of our attachment to you" (*Legacy to His Daughters*, 80–81). Austen's gentle irony neatly spears such an utterly unnatural assumption: "if it be true . . . that no young lady can be justified in falling in love before the gentleman's love is declared, it must be very improper that a young lady should dream of a gentleman before the gentleman is known to have dreamt of her" (*NA*, 29–30). That Austen is describing a heroine dreaming with innocent eroticism of her first balls and her first potential lover is crucially symbolic.

Austen's first letter thanks Cassandra for scolding her and stimulating her guilt because she and Tom Lefroy had behaved with noticeable impropriety at one of the neighborhood balls: "I am almost afraid to tell you how my Irish friend [Tom Lefroy] and I behaved. Imagine to yourself everything most profligate in the way dancing and sitting down together." They are behaving as Charles Bingley and Jane Bennet behaved at several balls, with the same futile results.

Austen wrote that she was expecting a proposal from Tom, that she would have to refuse him, "unless he promises to give away his white coat," that she does not "care a sixpence" for him, but that after he has left for good, as he was about to do, she knew she would weep bitterly "at the melancholy idea" (*Letters*, 1–6). Tom Lefroy *had* been dreaming of pretty, lively, witty Jane Austen. His remembrance of her almost half a century later candidly revealed how much she had appealed to him (*LL*, 89; Chapman, *Facts and Problems*, 58).

Tom's disappearance into Ireland without proposing, perhaps because he had no money and she had no dowry, was exceedingly painful for Austen in ways that neither her family nor her readers have ever fully acknowledged. His disappearance, and his inability to express what he felt or to allow her to express what she felt, exemplified the masculine habit of abandoning the female, and this time it was associated with the delights of dancing, of flirting, and of the engagements that her older brothers and her sister had been contracting one after the other.

In these letters describing Tom's charms as a "gentlemanlike, good-looking pleasant young man," so painfully reminiscent of Jane Bennet's heart-stirred descriptions of Charles Bingley, Austen later reassured Cassandra that since Tom had left for good, she would postpone her entrance into the province of women and undertake instead her first tentative journey into equally dangerous feminine territory, the province of the mind. She seems already to have begun or to be thinking about *Elinor and Marianne*, the original epistolary version of *Sense and Sensibility*, and she wrote to thank Cassandra for her "commendation" (*Letters*, 2, 5). That all her dancing days were to come to nothing, and then an official estate in the province of the heart as a wife and mother was forever to be denied her, she could not yet know. That her successful entrance into the province of the mind would only be acknowledged anonymously a decade and a half later, she could not then know either.

By now one can recognize the painful signs of the code of feminine silent suffering. Almost three years later, Tom Lefroy's aunt, a close friend of the Austen family, visited the Steventon rectory:

> Mrs. Lefroy did come last Wednesday [and] . . . in spite of interruptions from both my father and James, I was enough alone to hear all that was interesting, which you will easily credit when I tell you that of her nephew [Tom Lefroy] she said nothing at all. . . . She did not once mention the name of [Tom] to *me*, and I was too proud to make any enquiries; but on my father's afterwards asking where he was, I learnt that he was gone back to London on his way to Ireland, where he is called to the bar and means to practice. (*Letters*, 27)

This letter displays something painful in Austen's muffled irony. Cassandra too was now on the spinster's shelf; Tom Fowle, her fiancé, had been dead for almost two years. Only to Cassandra could Austen indicate by her italicized admission that Mrs. Lefroy "did not once mention the name of [Tom Lefroy] to *me*, and I was too proud to make any enquiries" about a man now engaged to an heiress (*LL*, 88) and that she had loved her Tom and dreamed of him with something of the same dancing hopes that Cassandra had dreamed of *her* Tom.

The male conduct-book literature identified this peculiarly feminine form of shame and humiliation: when women's sexual interests have been aroused, usually described by another more decorous emotion, they will feel something akin to what their mother Eve felt when she first knew she was naked:

> Though a woman has no reason to be ashamed of an attachment to a man of merit, yet nature, whose authority is superior to philosophy, has annexed a sense of shame to it. It is even long before a woman of delicacy dares avow to her own heart that she loves; and when all the subterfuges of ingenuity to conceal it from herself fail, she feels a violence done both to her pride and to her modesty. This I should imagine, must always be the case where she is not sure of a return to her attachment. (Gregory, *Legacy to His Daughters*, 67)

It is "proper" for women "to be secret" and silent about their feelings for any man who has not yet proposed, not only "from motives of prudence" but to comply with the dictates of postlapsarian female diffidence (Gregory, *Legacy to His Daughters*, 66). But this mandate for secrecy itself increased feminine anxiety and guilt, and Austen laughingly assured her sister that she felt properly penitential over the pathetic Tom Lefroy affair, which began and ended so swiftly on ballroom floors.

Even when a man has indicated that he is likely to propose, said Gregory, "Nature has made [her] blush when she is guilty of no fault" (*Legacy to His Daughters*, 27). Bennett associated this easily aroused feminine sense of culpability with her longing for the male, which only his proposal and her deep gratitude will appease. He described a woman's awakening passions in such dazzlingly hyperbolic language that only Austen's irony could have punctured this discourse:

> In the intercourse of Love, which forms an essential part in the history of the [female] sex . . . how generous is her breast! How noble is her conduct. . . . She has but this *one* object in view, and it engrosses her soul. . . . She risks friends, character, fortune, ease for the sake of her *idol*. In *privacy*, she broods over the beloved image,

and if mentioned in *publick*, she tinges it with blushes. This man has become her *Universe*; for him *alone* she lives; with him she would *die*! (*Female Education*, 97–98)

To my knowledge, no Austenian student has ever commented upon Elizabeth Bennet's drastic shift of attitude toward Darcy, after he has made his second proposal. To be sure, this time he speaks to her with respect, even with ardor. But Elizabeth had already begun to express proper orthodox penitence that she had ever felt contempt for this authoritarian man. During her internal monologues, she repeatedly intoned the equally orthodox expressions of "gratitude," "gratitude," "gratitude," as soon as she had reason to believe that Darcy now loved her, and she continued to do so in the anxious weeks before his final proposal. She was now willing to forgive a man who had committed the same casual crimes of the heart against several vulnerable people that readers enjoy identifying in Emma Woodhouse. When he proposes for the first time, he lets her know that only sexual passion, which has left him feeling humiliated, has driven him to do so.

Elizabeth's self-flagellation is so unlike her as to seem a change of motivation for which there has been no artful planning. But her misplaced shame and her "gratitude" make sense if one has studied the male conduct-book literature. Bennett's unctuous phrases about women in love could have been written to describe Elizabeth during her weeks "*en Penitence*": "If a woman loves, it is the *man* himself. . . . Pride, ambition, vanity, dissolve into tenderness, and are humbled by the passion" (Bennett, *Female Education*, 97).

Gregory assumed that the intense excitement of "gratitude" that a woman feels for a man's "attachment" to her was her substitute for the unmistakable male sexual drive (*Legacy to His Daughters*, 82). These orthodox theorists and others of similar persuasions may partially explain why Elizabeth is acting out a feminine stereotype so foreign to her nature. But once Darcy has made his second proposal, Elizabeth recovers her nerve. She loves him no less, but she is privately less craven: she "longed" to tease Darcy about his autocratic ways with friends and enemies alike, but she "remembered that he had yet to learn to be laughed at, and it was rather to early to begin" to teach him (*PP*, 371).

It is important to remember that Darcy committed his primary crimes of the heart on dance floors. He originally damns himself in the eyes of any right-thinking dancer, including his creator, by his loud refusal to dance with anybody. When the chance is offered him, he surveys the dancers while remarking that it would be "insupportable to dance" at "such an assembly as this," and particularly since "there is not another woman in the room, whom it would not be a punishment to stand up with." When Bingley points out that Elizabeth is without a partner, Darcy remarks "coldly": "She is tolerable; but not handsome enough to tempt *me*; and I am in no humour . . . to give consequence to young ladies who are slighted by other men" (*PP*, 11–12).

Darcy commits another social atrocity with one particularly cruel and insensitive comment. At a small dance that Sir William Lucas has convened, Sir William remarks, fatuously to be sure, "What a charming amusement for young people this is, Mr. Darcy!—There is nothing like dancing after all.—I consider it as one of the refinements of polished societies." Darcy answers his host with an observation as contemptuous of the indigenous populations that England's colonial ventures were just beginning to exploit, as his first proposal is to Elizabeth: "Certainly, Sir—and it has the advantage also of being in vogue among the less polished societies of the world.—Every savage can dance" (*PP*, 25).

With the exception of Anne Elliot, all the heroines either meet their lovers at balls or their creator provides them with a crucial scene at a ball. Catherine Morland first learns to feel anxious and ashamed of herself in the presence of the mocking Henry Tilney when he begins his assaults upon her ignorance while they are dancing. Henry's conduct is very artful in stimulating her distress over her gauche comments. And moreover, she fits the stereotype of the conduct-book female who falls in love with a man long before he declares himself, and so she feels even more self-hatred when she faces Henry's condemnations at Northanger Abbey. Henry's teasing imitation of courtship, during their first dance and thereafter, is calculated in every way to inflame her vulnerable heart without necessitating any overt commitment on his part.

Marianne Dashwood also feels appropriate sexual guilt and shame, after Willoughby had flirted with her on and off the ballroom floor; but there again, her guilt is excessive. Her agonized admissions that Elinor was right about Willoughby, the seducer, would have been enough. To blame herself so thoroughly that she falls sick and almost loses her life, suggests how symbolically lethal much of the advice given to women could be, especially when women's dancing passions were aroused. Even Elinor feels an unusual twinge of feminine guilt and shame, after Willoughby had visited the Dashwood sisters at Cleveland, because she finds in him some of the seductive attraction that had almost caused Marianne's death.

Tom Bertram, the extravagant and irresponsible heir in *Mansfield Park*, satirically describes a bizarre metamorphosis between two equally extreme feminine stereotypes: girl larvae in the nursery, quiescent, humble, socially ignorant, and their appearance as butterflies the next season. This conversation takes place when Mary Crawford casually asks whether Fanny Price "is out or not out." In one case, Tom wittily described a nursery child who behaved before her debut as Fanny is now behaving; but the next season this suddenly dazzling creature conducted herself like an experienced prom-trotter. In another case, Tom complained, a young girl still in the nursery already behaved as though she had experienced her come-out, and she was dressed like a debutante.

Mary Crawford and Tom and Edmund Bertram all engage in lively condemnations of some consequences of the "come-out." In this scene, Mary continues to inquire whether Miss Price is in or out: "Does she go to balls? does she dine out every where, as well as at my sister's?" When Edmund replies that as far as he knows, Fanny has never been to a ball, Mary replies tartly: "Oh! then the point is clear. Miss Price is *not* out" (*MP*, 48–51). Edmund does not say that his foster-sister has never dined out anywhere before, let alone "every where."

The mercantile function of the dance is most pronounced and most ugly in *Mansfield Park*. When Sir Thomas Bertram gave a ball in honor of Fanny's visiting brother, she was shocked to be told "that *she* was to lead the way and open the ball." To make matters worse, "Miss Price had not been brought up to the trade of *coming out*; and had she known in what light this ball was, in general, considered respecting her, it would very much have lessened her comfort" (*MP*, 275, 267). Sir Thomas is a patriarchal tyrant who has planned to use his ballroom as though it were a breeding pen by marrying her to the rake Henry Crawford.

It is significant that Austen's last two novels create almost no chances for her heroines to feel even the "glorious anxieties of motion" that she describes in her earlier novels when she herself was younger and celebrating her first dancing seasons. Emma Woodhouse and Anne Elliot are trapped at home by fathers who are altogether indifferent to their dancing and mating desires, a crime of the heart that was especially pernicious in a society where marriage and motherhood were woman's only socially sanctioned roles. When Emma finally does wring permission from her father to attend her first country dance, she sees the public consequences of her self-serving conduct toward Harriet Smith. The Eltons superciliously snub this harmless illegitimate young woman, who is attending her own first ball, and whose feelings of sexual nakedness are at their most painful. At another ball, Emma colludes with the irresponsible Frank Churchill to humiliate Jane Fairfax. She has learned to handle the courtesies of the dance little better than Fitzwilliam Darcy, in some ways her male counterpart.

In *Persuasion*, Austen's last novel, the dance plays an even less important role that it had in *Emma*. Anne Elliot's sense of sexual guilt and shame are relatively muted, first because she thinks that her dancing days are over, just as her creator's were, and then because she has lived so long with two comic monsters that her feelings are under careful control. But it is not surprising that some residual erotic embarrassment should be aroused in her when she sits in a corner providing music for the spontaneous dancers at Uppercross, especially since Frederick Wentworth is among them. Frederick is playing two sisters against each other, and whenever Anne thinks how much and how genuinely she and he had loved each other, she feels hot with an almost penitential shame for both of them.

Elizabeth Elliot, on the other hand, is escorted to one London season after the other by her father, so that she will be seen by someone with a title and an estate at least approximating her father's. Anne is not considered worthy of the expense that her introduction to London society would entail. At the age of twenty-seven, Anne Elliot is still not officially out, whereas her sister Elizabeth, who is a mere two years older, has been going to balls for more than a decade (*P*, 7). Parents who refused their daughters the initiation of a debut, as Mr. Bennet, Mr. Woodhouse, and Sir Walter Elliot were guilty of doing, were, in Austen's judicious moral lexicon, just as chargeable with parental malfeasance as parents who rushed their daughters into premature public exposure, as Mrs. Bennet and Mrs. Dashwood did, with disastrous results.

But nowhere is Austen's treatment of the dance, as emblematic of her characters' social morality, more skillful than in her art of context. Two of her heroes, Darcy and Knightley, are reluctant dancers. When Darcy is asked to dance, so as to relieve a partnerless woman's embarrassment, he will not injure his own dignity by doing so. But when Knightley sees that Harriet Smith is without a partner, he steps forward to honor her, without any show of boredom in his mission of rescue. Emma teases him because he dislikes dancing, but as his creator's name for him suggests, both in irony and in great respect, he is a gentleman, with all the obtuseness to rebellious and therefore indelicate forms of suffering such as Emma's, which this breed of man so often displays. But he also demonstrates the fundamental kindness toward those whom social policy allows him to recompense as his inferiors, which so often characterizes members of the gentry.

The quality of Austenian joy breaks out throughout her fiction, even during its saddest moments. When Anne Elliot determines to allow the autumnal beauties to comfort her own bleak autumnal condition, Austen's oblique pleasure in the glorious scene she has created obviously comforts her own dying self. But Austenian joy is paradoxically most evident in one of her saddest books, her first published *Sense and Sensibility*, when she was fully advanced upon her dancing days: "But Sir John's satisfaction in society was much more real [than Lady Middleton's]; he delighted in collecting about him more young people than his house would hold, and the noisier they were, the better he was pleased. . . . and in winter his private balls were numerous enough for any young lady who was not suffering under the unsatiable appetite of fifteen."

Austen called Sir John "a blessing to all the juvenile part of the neighborhood." His hospitality is reminiscent of the genial habits of Austen's parents, who lavished entertainment upon the grateful neighborhood of Steventon when their boys were at home, although they did so with considerably more taste and discretion than anything that characterized Sir John's delightful vulgarity. Unfortunately, after Marianne Dashwood's ankle had mended, "the private balls at the park then began," and with them, the soft corruption of Marianne's heart (*SS*, 32–33, 53).

Throughout this part of *Sense and Sensibility*, readers are treated to fleeting pastoral scenes of innocent young people at play, on and off the dance floor, laughing, talking, eating, walking, dancing, sailing, arguing, by sunlight, moonlight, and firelight, while the utopian hopes of youth were high in them, and except for the watchful pair, Elinor Dashwood and Colonel Brandon, while they all expected nothing but benign happiness to come of their pleasures. Austen's apparent benediction for all this youthful felicity only resonates later, with mournful nostalgia, when the little band of Dashwood women, already exiled forever from their "beloved Norland," from which they had been driven almost as though they themselves had been the sinning Adam and Eve, ultimately comes to acknowledge that gardens and ballrooms anywhere may contain serpentine figures: "This was the season of happiness to Marianne. Her heart was devoted to Willoughby, and the fond attachment to Norland, which she brought with her from Sussex, and more likely to be softened than she had thought it possible before, by the charms which his society bestowed on her present home" (*SS*, 53).

On the subject of dancing, as on the subject of women's fleeting joys in general, Austen's satiric habit of creating ricocheting targets that become creators of counter-satire in their turn, possesses a fine, discreet, and tender irony. There can be no doubt that dancing and flirting had represented a season of happiness for her, as well as for her heroines, during those moments when youth, or love, or "happiness" was theirs. Lightly as she mocked Sir William Lucas, and clear as she was that in him she had produced another patriarch who shares Mr. Woodhouse's "habits of gentle selfishness" (*E*, 8), she obviously agreed with him that dancing is "a charming amusement for young people," and her nostalgia in her letters, when she was no longer acceptable as a dancing partner, suggests that she thought there never had been anything "like dancing after all."

6

Voices and Silences: The Province of the Drawing Room and the War of Debates

Readers interested in Austen's intellectual triumph over a mild but nonetheless restrictive verbal purdah seldom mentioned in Austenian studies should consult R. W. Chapman's "Appendix" in *Emma* (*E*, "The Manners of the Age," 499–516). Without further comment, Chapman observes that "Miss Austen's silence on public affairs" was mandatory for women (*E*, 501). One of her nephews thought to praise her by his comment that his famous aunt "was very careful not to meddle with matters which she did not thoroughly understand" and that therefore she "never touched upon politics, law or medicine, subjects which some [women] authors have ventured upon rather too boldly, and have treated perhaps with more brilliance than accuracy" (*Memoir*, 15–16). In short, Jane Austen, thank God, was not George Elliot.

Nonetheless, as an intelligent reader of sermons and Pope, who loved spirited dialogue as much as quiet and honest piety, Austen responded vigorously to two histories of women, the ancient orthodox and the recent revolutionary, when her fiction encompassed "the mixed discourse . . . of young persons of the two sexes" (Gisborne, *Duties of the Female Sex*, 110). The Shakespearean comedies she loved, and echoes of the ongoing debates about "the rights of woman" that she found among the moderate feminists and in Burney and Edgeworth, offered her examples of witty and thoughtful women as fond of talk to some purpose as her own heroines. And despite the usual bad-tempered attacks upon the salons of the Blue-stockings, their reputations had survived respectably enough so that they also obviously offered her useful models for her dialogues.

Austen replicates her own childhood shyness and her adult diffidence in discussing war and peace and other male preoccupations by creating the silent Fanny Price, who hardly ever talks when mixed groups are present, and then she often murmurs in Edmund's ear. Fanny may be a caricature of the ideal female, but by no means an outrageous one. Her responses to mixed conversation and to public affairs represent women's other past, their millennia-long silences, half-silences, denials, and evasions.

Austen's fictional debates between the sexes and between women themselves all testify to a great Austenian skill that is never critically stressed—her management of dialogues. The volatile and often confrontational conversations advance the plot, define the characters through the rhythms and contents of their speech, signify their conscious or unconscious assumptions about the place and kind of women's provinces, and altogether embody the particular tensions between the two sexes that reverberate so powerfully in each novel.

Sometimes these debates mark the painful beginnings of self-confidence and self-determination in the heroines. But in any case, the debating moments are designed to express themes already announced by the authorial voice or by the heroines' internal monologues, and they provide an ironic and often poignantly modern counterpoint to the traditional plots and the traditional outcomes. Above all, they create a forum where the characters reveal the particular feminine predicament of each heroine, which the anticipated outcomes cannot solve.

Austen's dialogues and formal conversations perform even more specific functions than the discreet and yet sometimes bitter reiteration of post-Enlightenment feminist themes. For almost without exception, each dialogue and each group conversation that includes characters of both sexes echoes not only two but sometimes three contemporary voices addressing "the women question," the radical or moderate, and the patriarchal.

Since speech articulates who we are and who we assume other people to be, one would expect to find women's speech to be a conduct-book subject that created as much anxiety as any other topic addressing the woman question. Fordyce had informed his women readers that female "modesty is often silent: female decorum is never bold. Both forbid young women to lead the conversation; and true religion dreads every thing that might look ostentatious" (*Sermons to Young Women*, II, 126). The adjectives *bold* and *ostentatious* are invariably code words for any reading and thinking woman who has "the misfortune of knowing any thing" and who has forgotten that she "should conceal it as well as she can" (*NA*, 111).

Burton assumed that rational debates would customarily take place between men only. His model of the civilized speaker "In all questions of debate" is "the Man of calmness"; this forensic paragon "will always have the advantage of him, who is hasty and impetuous." Burton's model of the woman debater is a creature overtaken by the "Anger" that "is justly called a sort of madness." He admitted that "these paroxysms of rage" can be found in either sex, but when they "are seen in female shape, who would not turn aside? In your Sex, they assume a more odious appearance." Burton tried to frighten his young women readers into avoiding temptation to engage in debates, since heated conversation tends to "encourage a Passion, which will so much contribute to deface the human form, and render even beauty disgusting." He assumes that women debaters are all female "Furies" who "are not formed for Society," and whose

> company will be shunned by both sexes: Would [young women], in such a situation, behold their form reflected in a Glass, I am sure they would be frightened at them. . . . The face is at once suffused with fiery redness; it puts on a fierce and menacing aspect; indignant flashes sparkle from the eyes; the countenance is disfigured; the Body is agitated by violent contortions; and a torrent of rancorous expressions proceed from the mouth. (Burton, *Female Education*, II, 107–108, 105)

Duff's model of women speaking to men assumes that confrontations will invariably occur: women require "weapons" when they try to deal with men; but his model disarms women and leaves men to respond only if they wish: "Tears, expostulations, and introitus, my lovely friends, are your proper weapons. By these, you may make an impression on . . . the susceptible and yielding heart of man. . . . To a dominion acquired and established by influence and persuasion, I have no objection" (*Character of Women*, 278–279).

Gisborne assumed that women of various ages and classes conversing together, or women conversing with men, would avoid conversations that "resemble the discussions of a board of philosophers" (*Duties of the Female Sex*, 109–110). Instead, talk between the sexes should be characterized by "ease and gaity, and laughter and wit," all moods likely to promote "delight," preserve "innocence" and prohibit "affectation" (*Duties of the Female Sex*, 109–110). Gisborne even went so far as to describe how much and what kind of wit he thought permissible in women. That he "permitted" any at all was obviously pleasing to one of his readers, already a mistress of wit, though hers went far beyond what he would have thought appropriate in women.

Gisborne's model young woman was considerably more mature than the ideal male model of the conduct-book woman, her eyes meekly downcast, her voice normally silent while her face signified approval of one speaker or another. This archetype infuriated feminists of both persuasions, for whether they believed that men's domination over women was divinely ordained or not, their arguments for women's right to the dignity of articulate speech also offered other and more enlightened archetypes upon which Austen drew. Feminists who one and all urged "the adoption of a more energetic model of [feminine] education," and who themselves engaged in a more energetic mode of philosophic discourse than was usually considered feminine, were living and writing examples of just that "cool unbiased judgment," unconfined by "the fetters of prejudice," which in women constituted a national need, they all thought, no matter how "contrary to established customs" it might be (Wakefield, *Present Condition of the Female Sex*, 73–75).

Maria Edgeworth's bitter "Essay on the Noble Art of Self-Justification" was a warning of what was likely to happen between the sexes if men mocked or raged at women who spoke cogently on any matter at all. And Mary Hays defined the meek and silent woman as a temptation to masculine contempt that all too often leads to verbal bullying, or worse. Expecting, as most men do, she said, that women would "suffer in silence and submission," the sound of a woman's articulated voice constituted a shock to them, and from women's trained "inability to do themselves justice," men then "not only bind them down, but talk them down, to this state of submission" (*Appeal to the Men of Great Britain*, 143).

Austen ironically attributed this masculine right of interrupting women to Mr. Knightley. When Emma denies that Knightley could possibly marry Jane Fairfax, because Jane's hysterically chattering aunt, Miss Bates, would be even more than he could bear, Mrs. Weston replies: "I do not think Mr. Knightley would be much disturbed by Miss Bates. Little things do not irritate him. She might talk on; and if he wanted to say any thing himself, he would only talk louder and drown her voice." Shortly thereafter Austen exploits her fictional technique of quiet contiguity by placing two scenes almost back to back; they both illustrate the same example of the relations between the sexes. Knightley has urged Emma to visit Miss Bates more often. During one of these visits, Emma is inside and Miss Bates is leaning out of her window gabbling incoherently at Knightley, who is riding by: "Mr. Knightley seemed determined to be heard in his turn, for most resolutely and commandingly did he" interrupt her with sentences that cut her off (*E*, 225–226, 244). He is bored with Miss Bates, and so he rides on, leaving Emma to her charitable visit.

Knightley invariably interrupts Emma with all the cool authority he exercises over Miss Bates and Mrs. Weston. On one such occasion, Emma makes an unusually exasperated retort: "You are very fond of bending little minds; but where little minds belong to rich people in authority . . . they have a knack of swelling out, till they are quite as unmanageable as great ones." Emma's comment itself has "a knack of swelling out" until it encompasses even the kind, complacent Knightley himself, as well as Emma's other target, her gently predatory father. But she hurls this accusation at Knightley during a debate when she is begging him to consider "the difficulties of dependence," the daily frustrations "of having tempers to manage," the impossibility for anyone "who has not been in the interior of a family" to "say what the difficulties of any individual of that family may be." She is ostensibly defending the conduct of Frank Churchill, although it is indefensible, as Knightley insists. But he is too deaf to anything she says, too used to dismissing her articulate speech as the petulant utterances of a spoiled child, and too used to playing the social arbiter in Highbury to hear the personal despair behind Emma's excuses for Frank. She reminds Knightley that he has "no habits of early obedience and long observance to break through," but for dependent people, including herself, "it might not be so easy to burst forth at once into perfect independence," and to "set all . . . claims . . . of gratitude and regard at naught. . . . Oh! The difference of situation and habit! I wish you would try to understand" (*E*, 146–148).

With Mrs. Weston, Emma can plead her own case, but still in discreet terms, since "the favouring blindness" or equally, the self-favoring deafness of everybody around her always forces her to cry futilely into a wind: "A young *woman*, if she fall into bad hands, may be teazed [*sic*], and kept at a distance from those she wants to be with, but one cannot comprehend a young *man's* being under such restraint, as not to be able to spend a week with his father, if he likes it" (*E*, 193, 122).

Readers whose experience has alerted them to small signs of patriarchal mentalities might well remember the authorial voice ironically preaching that a "woman, especially, if she have the *misfortune* of knowing any thing, should conceal it as well as she can" (*NA*, 111; emphasis mine). Such readers will almost automatically consider the association between this sardonic comment and Knightley's perfectly bland observation that at "ten years old, [Emma] had the *misfortune* of being able to answer questions which puzzled her sister at seventeen. She was always *quick* and *assured*; Isabella *slow* and *diffident*" (*E*, 37; emphasis mine). Knightley does not exactly say, with Bennett, that "confidence is a *horrid bore* in women." But he responds in a classically threatened way to "Emma's doctrines," because "they do not give any strength of mind," nor do they "make a girl adapt herself to the varieties of her situation in life" (*E*, 34).

This thirty-word portion of a long speech to Mrs. Weston contains four different code phrases, one of them oxymoronic, to describe the province of womanhood. "Doctrines" means "doctrines of woman's rights," but orthodox speakers such as Knightley always eliminated the words "woman" and "rights," while women of Emma's sort were now beginning to analyze the effects of their legal and domestic disenfranchisements upon themselves. But in women, the capacity to analyze was obviously dangerous, because it threatened what Knightley calls their "strength of mind," meaning its opposite, their willingness to endure any restraints that their families thought desirable. Again, when this phrase, "strength of mind," was assigned to women, it was always deceitful, since it did not mean politely yet confidently and clearly stated opinions, or the qualities of leadership, however tactful, as it did in men.

Knightley's saddest evasion of all Emma's grim truths occurs in his euphemistic phrase, "to make a girl adapt herself to the varieties of her situation in life." This stricture comes right out of the orthodox conduct-book literature. "Situations in life" always meant a woman's responses to the needs of her present guardian—the father, the husband, the son, or the closest dominant adult of either sex. The "varieties" of that "situation" required her to adapt to "a total change of conversation, opinion, or idea" (*P*, 42), from time to time, whether she is *fixed* in one place, as Emma is, or when she is shipped from one place to the other, according to male needs, or at least male initiatives, and according to the fictional pattern of the other five Austenian novels. But the responsibility to "adapt" to changing "situations" always lies with her. It is important to notice, although nobody yet has, that when Emma's irascible brother-in-law attacks her exasperating father, it is always Emma who gently urges John Knightley into safer conversational patterns, asking him tactful and appeasing questions about himself or about the Knightley estate, so as to keep the debates between John and her father as peaceable as possible between two touchy males.

Knightley's speech represents one of those microcosmic moments in Austen's fiction that reflect her complex combination of covert passions and their judicious modifications. If one believes, as the historical and fictional Knightleys all did, that women's provinces were generally benign, but that even when they were not benign, as he occasionally admits in Emma's case, they were socially necessary or at least inevitable, then his arguments are irrefutable. And there is considerable vocabulary in Austen's moral lexicon to suggest that sometimes she agrees with the Knightleys. But the Austen who suffered her own restraints and petty humiliating deprivations wants readers of her fiction to accept another perspective, as well. If so kind a man as Knightley could so willfully ignore such obvious misery as Emma's, what was the fate of women whose tutors were actively cruel and abusive? *Mansfield Park* answers that covertly stated question.

Knightley's speech is important to consider at length, because it packs into a few pages argument after argument favoring women's disenfranchisements, without actually admitting that it is doing so. It represents Austen's guerilla techniques of simultaneous revelation and concealment at their very finest. It offers "received opinions" in so sensible a way that no realistic person can altogether refute them. And then it undercuts them, before, during, and after Knightley has uttered them, but in such a way that they may easily be ignored, as they have been for almost two centuries.

One of the grimmest debates in all six novels occurs in *Mansfield Park*, after Fanny Price has refused Henry Crawford's offer of marriage, which he has only made because "he had so much delight in the idea of obliging her to love in a very short time, that her not loving him now was scarcely regretted." Crawford was one of those men who served as a warning to women in the conduct books of all three persuasions. The masculine literature stressed the threat to women's virginity in male predators of the Wickham-Willoughby-Crawford types. The feminists of both persuasions stressed as well the casually delivered insults of such men who believe that what they wanted was always best for the woman, since she was incapable of knowing her own mind. Crawford is a conduct-book example of a particularly insidious type: "He had vanity, which strongly inclined him, in the first place, to think she did love him, though she might not know it herself; and which, secondly, when constrained at last to admit that she did know her own present feelings, convinced him that he should be able in time to make those feelings what he wished."

Fanny's contempt had its origin in Crawford's previous callousness toward the Bertram sisters, which ought to have been plain for the entire Bertram and Crawford families to see. Underneath his sudden new tenderness, he is still "the clandestine, insidious, treacherous admirer" who had flirted with two women at once. It is only the challenge of Fanny's resistance that "made her affection appear of greater consequence, because it was withheld, and determined him to have the glory, as well as the felicity, of forcing her to love him." Crawford's verbs—"*force* her," "*make*" her "feelings what he wished"—are indeed the signifiers of a "treacherous lover." He is shocked that a woman so characterized by "diffidence, gratitude, and softness" should so thoroughly and persistently despise him (*MP*, 326–327).

These are the obvious facts that precede Sir Thomas Bertram's attack upon Fanny because she has refused this man whom Sir Thomas has chosen for her. Fanny has escaped from Crawford's polite sexual harassments and she is "growing very comfortable" in her cold, abandoned schoolroom at the top of the house, "when suddenly the sound of a step in regular approach was heard—a heavy step, an unusual step in this part of the house; it was her uncles's," and "the terror of his former occasional visits to that room seemed all renewed." Sir Thomas asks Fanny three times, with growing incredulity, whether she has actually refused so rich and charming a man as the libertine Henry Crawford. Fanny replies three times that she has. "In a voice of calm displeasure" signifying a demand for instant obedience rather than any search for understanding, Sir Thomas now asks what right she has to refuse a young man who can relieve the Bertrams of her care, who has been of service in getting her brother promoted, and whose sister was Fanny's "intimate friend"—another gross misjudgment of the facts.

Sir Thomas exhibits all the signs of a profoundly guilty conscience; Crawford had said that he wished to offer Fanny, the "dependent, helpless friendless, neglected niece," all the security and consequences, as *his* wife, which Sir Thomas, the "rich, superior, long-winded, arbitrary uncle" had hitherto denied her on principle, as a way of teaching this penniless and socially obscure girl-child her humble province. "What can Sir Thomas and Edmund together do, what *do* they do for her happiness, comfort, honour, and dignity in the world to what I *shall* do?" he asks his sister. Henry Crawford is another monstrous truth-teller, who artlessly demonstrates, without any conscience in the matter, that men and marriage alone give women consequence (*MP*, 312, 315–316, 297).

This ominous scene in Fanny's schoolroom represents the second time that Sir Thomas was prepared to sanction a morally disgraceful marriage of a young and reluctant woman because it "would bring him such an addition of respectability and influence." And as before, he was inclined only "to think any thing" . . . what was most favourable for the purpose," in common with the husband whom he wished to force upon his niece (*MP*, 201). As David Monaghan said about Fanny Price in another context, Austen's heroines had to learn that "in a society based on the cash ethic, those who have managed to accumulate excessive wealth do not commonly employ it" in honorable ways. "The rich value their money not because it enables them to be of service to others, but because it confers prestige on themselves."[1]

Now, in this second case where Sir Thomas wished to garner fresh prestige to embellish his wealth, his title, and his estate, Fanny sat crouching "in trembling wretchedness," while her looming, "arbitrary" uncle walked "toward the table where she sat . . . and with a good deal of cold sternness said":

> I had thought you peculiarly free from wilfulness of temper, self-conceit, and every tendency to that independence of spirit which prevails so much in modern days, even in young women, and which in young women is offensive and disgusting beyond all common offence. But you have now shewn me that you can be wilful and perverse, that you can and will decide for yourself, without any consideration or deference for those who have surely some right to guide you.

In case this charge that Fanny has been infected by the doctrines of the feminists does not frighten her into compliance, he next paradoxically attacks her in her vulnerable spot, her training in "diffidence, gratitude, softness," and in service to others: "The advantage or disadvantage of her family—of your parents—your brothers and sisters—never seems to have had a moment's share in your thoughts on this occasion. How *they* might be benefited, how *they* might rejoice in such an establishment for you—is nothing to *you*. . . . You do not owe me the duty of a child. But, Fanny, if your heart can acquit you of *ingratitude*" (*MP*, 318–319).

This example of blackmail is not only as cynical as Sir Thomas's manipulation of Fanny's pathologies always were, but it is foolish because it is inaccurate. Only William, the attractive eldest son in Fanny's otherwise rude, insensitive Portsmouth family, has ever paid her any attention during the ten years of her sojourn at Mansfield Park. The rest never responded to her letters, nor came to see her, nor sent her presents, nor asked her to visit. And her foster-parents ignored her desire to visit her birth-parents until Sir Thomas Bertram exiled her to Portsmouth as a punishment for her refusal to marry Henry Crawford.

Fanny Price's debate with Edmund Bertram over this whole sordid affair was even more insulting to her in its own way than the parental misconduct of his father. Edmund was "entirely on his father's side of the question," blind as he was to Henry's polite but perfectly public sexual harassment of Fanny. Lady Bertram, usually so indolent as to be incapable of any opinion on anything, had observed in a rarely decisive voice: "You must be aware, Fanny, that it is every young woman's duty to accept such a very unexceptionable offer as this." The authorial voice is bitter: "This was almost the only rule of conduct, the only piece of advice, which Fanny had ever received from her aunt in the course of eight years and a half.—It silenced her."

Edmund's opinion does not differ from his aunt's, for all his protestations to the contrary: "How could you imagine me an advocate for marriage without love?" he says, and spends a whole evening trying to avoid hearing her grave moral charges against Henry Crawford (*MP*, 335, 333, 346–347).

Edmund's gentle attempts to persuade Fanny through her "ready habits of submission," are prompted by his own needs to secure Crawford as an ally in his pursuit of Crawford's sister, and by his conduct-book attitudes about women and love: "I cannot suppose that you have not the *wish* to love him—the natural wish of gratitude." He echoes his father in saying that Fanny had done exactly right to refuse Crawford until she received Sir Thomas's permission to accept this flattering offer. He claims that he admires her refusal to be swayed by just such considerations that had prompted the marriages of his penniless mother and his two aunts: "You have proved yourself upright and disinterested, prove yourself grateful and tender-hearted; and then you will be the perfect model of a woman, which I have always believed you were born for."

In his quiet way, Edmund is also an example of Mary Hays's patriarchal men who try to "talk" women "down to this submission." Every argument that Fanny puts forward as to the total unseemliness of this match, he counters with a hasty denial, an equivocation, or a misunderstanding. When Fanny informs him that Crawford had behaved selfishly with both of Edmund's sisters, he brushes that argument aside. When she says about Crawford just what Elizabeth Bennet says about the irresponsible Lydia—"I am persuaded that he does not think as he ought, on serious subjects"—Edmund replies, with an unconscious reversal of sexual stereotypes, since any argument will do, that Henry had not been taught to think about principled conduct, but that Fanny is to be his teacher. She is now understandably saddened by Edmund's willful blindness.

He next tries to frighten her into accepting Crawford by telling her that everybody expects it and that Crawford's sister "is very angry" with her: "It is the regret and disappointment of a sister, who thinks her brother has a right to everything he may wish for, at the first moment. She is hurt, as you would be for William." Edmund's comparison between the sturdy and genial yet sensitive naval officer, William Price, and the professionally lethargic and sexually irresponsible Henry Crawford, is disgraceful, and worse is Edmund's charge that Fanny is behaving in a way "so very determined and positive!" as to be bereft of her "senses" and quite unlike her "rational self." In male conduct-book rhetoric, a "rational" woman is a woman who accepts male commands.

Fanny makes one feminist comment that Edmund again turns to his advantage, for as always he was in the habit of "scarcely hearing her to the end" of her arguments: In desperation, Fanny exerts herself to make the same observation which Emma makes to Knightley, and Elinor Dashwood makes to her callous half-brother:

> I *should* have thought . . . that every woman must have felt the possibility of a man's not being approved, not being loved by some one of her sex, at least, let them be every so agreeable. . . . I think it ought not to be set down as certain, that man must be acceptable to every woman he may happen to like himself. . . . How was I to have an attachment at his service, as soon as it was asked for?

Edmund's answer to this last plea leaves Fanny "oppressed" with feelings of "bitter aggravation," "weariness and distress." He says, "My dear Fanny, now I have the truth. . . . I thought I could understand you." She takes forever to become used to novel and startling ideas, he says, and he announces proudly that he has been explaining to the Crawfords just how timid Fanny is: "I told them . . . that you would tolerate nothing that you were not used to; and a great deal more to the same purpose, to give them a knowledge of your character" (*MP*, 347–355).

Edmund was another Austenian hero who assumes, as Darcy, Henry Tilney, and Knightley do, that he knows the heroine better than she knows herself. Austen had clearly been reading various types of conduct books with excellent fictional results. The male conduct books always described women as refusing to understand matters pertaining to their own good, and the heroes' reasoning is just as self-serving as the arguments of the official and historical tutors to women.

Sir Thomas's attack on Fanny could have come straight out of the horror stories about various parental atrocities against young women which so angered the radicals and so grieved the moderates. Furthermore, in Fanny Price's case, the double male charge, Sir Thomas's and Edmund's, that Fanny lacked automatic gratitude toward her suitor, and that she thought for herself in matters of conscience, is a polite duplication of assumptions so infuriating to the post-Enlightenment feminists.

Sir Thomas's horror that he is losing his previous control over Fanny—his utterly inappropriate condemnation that she is behaving in a manner as "offensive" and as "disgusting" as other unsexed females—is one more real travesty, considering the "creep-mouse" that the family at Mansfield Park have made of her. The adjectives *offensive* and *disgusting* are code words for women who have read too much in the works of Wollstonecraft and writers of her persuasion.

Anyone who has ever studied Dr. Johnson's pithy yet elegant prose or Boswell's comments on Johnson, as Austen had (*Letters*, Index V), will recognize one of the shapers of Elizabeth Bennet's anguished debate with Jane, after Charlotte Lucas had accepted Mr. Collins, and after Darcy has persuaded the whole casual Bingley crowd to desert the village of Longbourn. Elizabeth's cosmic despair would not customarily be considered Johnsonian, yet both debaters looked at cruel and foolish humanity through a complex yet candid lense. But as serious Christians, they both tried to look at the human species judiciously, although for Johnson, as for Boswell—*pace* Mrs. Thrale—men were human, whereas any woman was "better employed at her toilet than using her pen," and infinitely better giving a man "a good breakfast, like any other woman" than "whining about liberty," as these two pundits said about the feminist historian Catherine Macaulay.[2]

Elizabeth's debate with Jane was also clearly shaped by contemporary feminist indignation, even a principled horror, that any heirs of the age of reason, male or female, could treat rational women as irresponsibly as Collins, Bingley, and Darcy felt free to do. Elizabeth is arguing about many different issues to be found in the feminist conduct books: men may pay such marked attention to women as to raise all kinds of speculation and gossip, and then depart without declaring themselves. Women are so miserably placed, however, that often they will abandon all attention to their own legitimate rights and their Christian conscience, in order to conform to "the cash ethic" that constitutes their families' hidden agenda for them. Furthermore, women are placed in a social vice so that if they show a man the interest they feel in him, he may devalue them, but if they do not, he may feel free to appear to misunderstand them, and move with impunity toward a woman willing to flatter him more openly.

Elizabeth's primary distress was occasioned by Charlotte Lucas, who has decided to marry Collins against all orthodox strictures. Elizabeth's comment that Charlotte's marriage "is unaccountable! in every view it is unaccountable!" must be understood not only in its sexual perspective, that Collins is repulsive, but also in its theological perspective: Charlotte is blaspheming the sacrament of marriage. Jane's essential feminine diffidence, so carefully inculcated in her by her father's contempt for women, leaves her especially vulnerable to self-deceptions. Jane begs Elizabeth to remember "Mr. Collins' respectability and Charlotte's steady prudent character . . . that she is one of large family, that as to fortune, it is a most eligible match," and that therefore Elizabeth ought to "be ready to believe, for every body's sake, that [Charlotte] may feel something like regard and esteem for our cousin" (*PP*, 135). Jane's compassion is not the charitable yet seasoned wisdom of intellectual courage and experience; it is the pathetic naiveté of warped self-respect. She has been taught to accept all men and all men's champions at their own estimations of themselves. Although from time to time she is right, in the morally topsy-turvy Austenian world, nevertheless there is something pathetic in the way she forgives Charlotte, who has been made unprincipled through desperation, and the portentious, bombastic Collins, the arrogant Darcy, the craven Bingley, and his snide, badly educated, and sycophantic sisters.

Underneath Jane's apparent peace-keeping sentiments is an essentially defensive impulse to appease others and to avoid all sexual conflict. Her ridiculous encomia of Collins and of Charlotte, and her hope for the best, translated into less euphemistic terms, merely mean: "Mr. Collins is at least morally tolerable: he is neither a rake nor an infidel, and Charlotte does not have your principles; also, she must sell herself because her father has saved no more money for her dowry than our father has saved for ours. So please try to deceive yourself and let me deceive myself that she may have deceived *herself* enough to tolerate a barely tolerable husband." There is a mournful truth in what Jane says. Charlotte, regrettably clever, plain, poor, and cynical, does eventually find some genuine "charm" in "[h]er home and her housekeeping, her parish and her poultry, and all their dependent concerns," as Elizabeth's internal half-monologue tries to remind herself. Nonetheless, this ironic comment, with its alliterations, its artful parallel structures, and its emphasis on purely mundane and exterior comforts, is characteristic of the sad and occasionally cynical judiciousness of Austen's perspectives about dowerless women and marriage (*PP*, 216).

Charlotte shares with minor women characters in Austen's fiction, such as Lydia and Kitty Bennet, the wounds inflicted by grave parental failures. Despite her economic "prudence"—in fact, partly because of it—she is one more morally impaired Austenian character who "has never been taught to think on serious subjects," as Elizabeth complained to Mr. Bennet about Lydia Bennet (*PP*, 283). Serious subjects, in this context, is a polite Austenian way of saying that Lydia and Charlotte, each in her fashion, completely ignore the fact that marriage and the sexual congress that succeeds it is a Christian sacrament, a fact, nonetheless, that in doctrinaire syntax must never escape the lips of an Elizabeth Bennet or the pen of a Jane Austen. For Austen's beloved Dr. Johnson was hardly the only male she had encountered who shuddered at the bizarre spectacle of a woman preaching as he would at the equally bizarre spectacle of a dog walking on two hind legs.

Elizabeth is finally forced to exclaim that "no one else [but Jane] could be benefited by such a belief as this; for were I persuaded that Charlotte had any regard for [Mr. Collins], I should only think worse of her understanding, than I now do of her heart" (*PP*, 135).

In separating the understanding from the heart, and yet in recognizing that in women, just as in men, they are both essential but distinct talents for the gift of living well, Elizabeth speaks with the voices of the feminists. Readers have not recognized that she possesses the combinative and recombinative capacities to think, unthink, and then rethink, which Locke, Astell, and other Enlightenment figures recommended, because after all, Austen is really offering us little more than sophisticated love stories about mere marriageable young girls, or so many readers have largely assumed. But in demanding that the morally and intellectually self-indulgent Jane Bennet unthink and then re-think all her softly acquired conduct-book maxims, Elizabeth is trying to brace her sister not to make love to the spectacle of the wounding snobberies that Darcy, Collins, and the Bingley women represent, and to disabuse her of the idea that a heart in a woman is the same as a mind in a man. But if Charlotte thinks well of Collins, Elizabeth insists, then there is something wrong with her mind, her rational "understanding"; if she is marrying him under no delusion as to what he is, as indeed she is, then there is something wrong with her "heart."

In orthodox conduct-book terms, woman's "heart" meant her capacity to take almost all men on trust, as Jane does. In Elizabeth's modern terms, it means that women must learn to think both decombinatively and combinatively, that is, to combine such ideas as hearts and minds, and to separate any ideas that are pernicious when they are opportunistically riveted together. Each woman must function "as a rational creature, speaking the truth" from her mind and her own legitimate self-defense, as well as "from her heart" (*PP*, 109).

The most elegantly, yet passionately parliamentary of Elizabeth's condemnations of her beloved opponent Jane, are couched in a series of stern parallel structures, constantly mounting in intensity and in severity of arrangement:

> My dear Jane, Mr. Collins is a *conceited*, *pompous*, *narrow-minded*, *silly* man; *you know* he is *as well as I do*, and you *must feel*, *as well as I do*, that the woman who marries him, cannot have a proper way of *thinking*. You shall not defend her, though it is Charlotte Lucas. *You shall not*, for the sake of one individual, *change the meaning of principle* and *integrity*, *nor endeavour* to *persuade yourself* or *me*, that *selfishness is prudence*, and *insensitivity to danger*, *security for happiness*. (*PP*, 135–136; emphasis mine)

Generations of post-Freudian critics have called Elizabeth "pert," "impertinent," "strong-willed," "opinionated," or "self-opinionated," which I take to mean that she thinks for herself, instead of accepting "received opinions." Elizabeth's crime, in the eyes of these critics, is that like other reformers declaring independence before her and after her, she has "a decent regard for the opinions of mankind," and womankind as well, which forces her to explain what is honorable and of good report to *her*, whatever the cost may be, to *her*. Jane responds with the frightened heart only, rather than to Elizabeth's arguments: "I must think your language too strong" (*PP*, 136).

There is one sad little irony about Elizabeth's anger, splendidly accurate though it usually is. At the very moment she was begging Jane not to be a feminine dupe of Collins and of the Darcy-Bingley party, she herself had become Wickham's dupe. This is Elizabeth's only serious mistake, and as always when important characters make mistakes, Austen's authorial voice or some other fictional device explains the parental origins of failed judgment or conduct.

In this case, Elizabeth is "suffering from" the same "intellectual solitude" that afflicted Emma Woodhouse, Anne Elliot, and Fanny Price during Edmund Bertram's long absences. Elizabeth is surrounded by immature people—by parents who are morally irresponsible toward daughters, three sisters equally irresponsible toward the community, another sister who is afraid to make unflattering judgments, one intimate woman friend who is cynical about marriage, with good reasons, and close neighbors in the Lucas family, who are all governed entirely by the cash ethic and by the same lust for social prestige that corrupts her cousin, Mr. Collins. Now she is morally outraged over the damage inflicted by two visiting men who casually create havoc among the young women trapped in the village of Longbourn. Much as she and her uncle, Mr. Gardiner, admire each other, their relationship is hardly close, nor does she see him often, and it is symbolic that readers are treated to no dialogues between them, in stark contrast to the witty, affectionate, and sometimes serious debates between Elizabeth and her aunt, Mrs. Gardiner.

Elizabeth must largely teach herself the way of the masculine world, in common with all Austen's heroines, and Burney's and Edgeworth's for that matter. She must try to uncover truths, both bitter and liberating, and to distinguish between those truths and the myths and fictions of innate and earned worthiness, which people with many privileges to protect and lesser creatures to fend off, tend to weave around themselves. Eventually she does learn that Darcy is capable of stripping himself, at least in private, of his own myths about his right to arrogance, whereas Wickham is not capable of that moral learning. Eventually Elizabeth finds herself loved by a man who does not now treat her as a fool, as a marriage commodity for sale, and as an object of his sexual lust who is little better than a whore. The automatic masculine conduct-book association between articulate women and fornicating women does indeed partly explain Darcy's initial behavior, but nothing quite excuses it. He is intelligent enough to assume that Elizabeth can only be forced to provide him the sexual satisfaction he wants if he marries her; but he has assumed that her articulate self-confidence is nothing more than the sexual bait commonly claimed for it: "I believed you to be wishing, expecting my addresses," he later admits in shame (*PP*, 369).

Pride and Prejudice, the novel written just before *Mansfield Park*, explores the topic of two women urged to sell themselves in loveless marriages, both by their suitors and their families. Although the topic is not altogether in the foreground, as it is in the *Mansfield Park* volumes describing Fanny Price's coming of age, nonetheless the sad case of Charlotte Lucas functions as a deliberate contrast to Elizabeth. Neither woman has had any masculine examples before her that would encourage her to think "highly either of men or of matrimony" (*PP*, 122), but Charlotte does not have the intellectual resources to abide by a principled distaste for the prevailing matrimonial arrangements in the world of this fiction, at least, whereas Elizabeth does. But in each case, as in the case of Fanny Price, the heroine in the next novel, a young woman is urged to marry so as to benefit various members of her family, who are willing to accept her sacrifice without a single thought for her welfare. Sir Williams Lucas makes plans to be presented at court, "the younger girls formed hopes of *coming out* a year or two sooner than they might otherwise have done, and the boys were relieved from their apprehension of Charlotte's dying an old maid . . . . The whole family in short were properly overjoyed" at this disgraceful event (*PP*, 122).

Sense and Sensibility has some interesting dialogues on how women are stereotyped, or sometimes stereotype themselves. Marianne Dashwood's "sensibility" and its unfortunate results emerge right out of all three conduct-book types. Burton, Duff, Hamilton, and More all remarked, justly enough as far as it went, that women afflicted with hyperbolic sensibilities are usually not deeply feeling women, that they are often merely assuming an affectation, and in any case, that they are hardly ever concerned with the people nearest them, but on the contrary, that they are far more impressed with themselves and their own sensations than with what they owe their social community. The radicals, as always, described the feminist issues: they perceived affectations of extreme sensibility as simply gross perversions of perversions. They understood the psychological dynamics of dammed-up energies, both physical and mental, and so they accepted the fact that these energies are bound to erupt in violent and inappropriate ways, for lack of legitimate outlets. The moderates, as usual, mediated between the radical and the orthodox writers, and as usual, they offered sound advice: let mothers—and fathers too—keep young female minds solidly occupied on prayer and on tougher intellectual fare than that usually permitted them.

When Colonel Brandon asks Elinor Dashwood whether Marianne Dashwood may ever be cured of her "romantic" assumptions that "second attachments" are erotically impossible, Elinor replies that she certainly hopes so. Brandon himself is an incurable romantic who had cherished a hopeless attachment to his married cousin, who had fought a duel, and who places women on pedestals, which is just where Marianne wants to be placed. Brandon remarks wistfully: "there is something so amiable in the prejudices of a young mind, that one is sorry to see them give way to the reception of more general opinions." Elinor, understandably irritated at the "inconveniences attending such feelings as Marianne's, which all the charms of enthusiasm and ignorance of the world cannot atone for," worries, as Marianne's surrogate mother and surrogate conscience, that "her systems have all the unfortunate tendency of setting propriety at nought" (*SS*, 55–56) and rendering her vulnerable to the predatory Willoughby.

Elinor rightly worries about Marianne, whom she rightly describes to Edward Ferrars, as "hardly . . . a lively girl—she is very earnest, very eager in all she does—sometimes talks a great deal and always with animation—but she is not often really merry." When Edward wonders how he could have supposed Marianne to be "a lively girl," Elinor responds that she, too, often fancies people to be "so much more gay or grave, or ingenious or stupid than they really are," and that she can "hardly tell why, or in what the deception originated. Sometimes one is guided by what they say of themselves, and very frequently by what other people say of them, without giving oneself time to deliberate and judge." When Marianne cries out: "But I thought it was right, Elinor . . . to be guided wholly by the opinions of other people. I thought our judgments were given us merely to be subservient to those of our neighbors. This has always been your doctrine, I am sure." Elinor's stern response is a classical example of the moderate feminists' kind of advice, in fact, of Elizabeth Hamilton's advice. Elinor, who has the capacity to separate one idea from another, tries to explain to Marianne, who is pretending far more innocence here than she actually possesses:

> No, Marianne, never. My doctrine has never aimed at the subjection of the understanding. All I have ever attempted to influence has been the behaviour. You must not confound my meaning, I am guilty, I confess, of having often wished you to treat our acquaintance in general with greater attention; but when have I advised you to adopt their sentiments or conform to their judgment in serious matters? (*SS*, 93–94)

There, once again, is Austen's phrase, "serious matters," a code word for Christian values that transcend both orthodox male hostility to women and radical hostility to the Anglican faith, the very faith in whose name orthodoxy all too often aimed at the subjection of feminine understanding. Hamilton's assessment of a problem that faces us all, in and out of public life, is as judicious as Elinor Dashwood's:

> We have no right to shock or to offend those who have given us no moral cause of offence. Nor do we sin against truth by refraining, on such occasions, to express our feelings. But if we *pretend* to regard those for whom we have no regard, to respect those for whom we have no respect, and *gladly* to receive those whom we in reality are vexed to see, we then sin against truth and against our own souls. (*Letters to the Daughter of a Nobleman*, 1, 92)

Elinor Dashwood has thought her way through to principles of conduct, in the way that Elizabeth Bennet has done. And though she is habitually graver than Elizabeth, she is not dour. Her creator has even bestowed upon her a delightful dry wit. When Marianne, with a fine, adolescent romantic flourish, denies that "wealth or grandeur" can ever have anything "to do with happiness," Elinor, who is suffering the classical Austenian fate of the dowerless woman unable to marry the man she very much loves and respects, now has the wit to reply: "Grandeur has but little . . . but wealth has much to do with it" (*SS*, 91). The two dowerless young women then bandy back and forth various ideas they have harbored as to the difference between wealth and grandeur. It is ironic, as the implications of these debates almost invariably are, that Elinor merely wants simple wealth, so as to give her an independence in her choice of marriage partner—or whether to marry or not—which is now denied her. Marianne, despite her disclaimers to the contrary, wants grandeur. She want "Two thousand a year," "a proper establishment" of servants, and "a carriage, perhaps two, and hunters," everything, in short, that she has seen at Combe Magna, the estate of Willoughby's aunt, whose heir he is (*SS*, 91). The sad irony is this debate only emerges later. Wealth does indeed have much to do with what Marianne now perceives to be her happiness: Willoughby refuses to marry her because she has no dowry.

Elinor's rueful wit emerges only in these dialogues, which create the impression of young people working out their moral and marital destinies in each other's presence, articulating what they think and what they feel, and sometimes in Marianne's case, what they think they ought to feel. Edward Ferrars has joined this debate: it takes place around a fire that is comforting them all after dinner.

Edward loves to tease Marianne; and his own quiet wit makes him an ideal husband for Elinor. He will not pander to Marianne's hysterical ardors. To him, as he says during a debate on Marianne's sensibility, a dirty lane is merely a dirty lane, and dry autumn leaves are merely dry autumn leaves. He is the only Austenian hero who is also an heir but who has been exiled from his own home and stripped of an inheritance. Perhaps for that very reason he is the only hero of the seven unwilling to condescend to women.

Elinor, who deplores Marianne's breathless affectations of sensibility, nonetheless understands them and their tragic undercurrent. Marianne's feminine liveliness is a mask for desperation. She is suspiciously like a young heroine who has read everything from Fordyce to Wollstonecraft and Hamilton, as Emma Woodhouse is covertly described as having done, and whose inexperience has made her thoroughly confused. Elizabeth Bennet's defense against feminine tragedies is classically articulate and fervently rebellious. Marianne Dashwood's is inchoate and ultimately useless, as Elinor knows. Elinor's resignation has some of the sad patience that the moderate feminists usually advised and that readers will later encounter in Anne Elliot and, in a less mature and less attractive form, in Fanny Price.

One of Austen's most ironic debates about the man and woman question and the contemporary condition of marriage takes place in

Mansfield Park, between the Crawford sister and brother and their half-sister, Mrs. Grant. It represents one of those Austenian moments when Austen places truths that hardly anybody wants to hear in the mouths of characters whom hardly anybody is expected to like. Austen employed the same guerrilla techniques when Emma repeatedly debates with Knightley and with Mrs. Weston, hoping vainly that these two genial but orthodox tutors to women of the Gisborne kind, would notice her imprisonment. It appears with equal pertinence, even if more fleetingly, in Mrs. Bennet's whining litanty about the inequities of male entail, which is duplicated by Lady Catherine de Bourgh's crisp and authoritative observations that fathers have no use for daughters, and that male entail was a pernicious custom.

In the debates between Mary Crawford, Henry Crawford, and Mrs. Grant, Austen demonstrates an attractive moral suaveté with which she is hardly ever credited. Mrs. Grant is married to the rector of Mansfield, and she knows perfectly well that he is a glutton far more interested in his food than in his heavenly father, to say nothing of his earthly family. Yet she has maintained a sweet and affectionate temper, a nice sense of wit, and a legitimate sophistication about the ways of the world. She knows that her younger half-sister and half-brother are corrupt, but she loves them for their undeniable wit and charm. She is even more generous in that she is plain compared to her half-sister Mary, yet she exhibits no jealousy; in fact, to show off her sister Mary and get this heiress a husband more affectionate than hers is her avowed aim. She also knows the source of these two young people's cynicism, for they are orphans and their widowed uncle has taken his mistress into his house, thus exiling Mary from her second home, as her parents' death has already exiled her from her first. Furthermore, Mrs. Grant knows that each of the Crawford children was symbolically half-orphaned, even after their actual orphanage, for the uncle, Admiral Crawford, "delighted in the boy," and "Mrs. Crawford doted on the girl" (*MP*, 40). So Mary Crawford was stripped of a caring male guardian, and Henry of a mature female model worthy of respect.

In this debate, Mary charges Henry with the cold habit of enticing women to fall in love with him. Henry quips that according to Milton, woman is "Heaven's *last* best gift," and that he can do without such gifts for the foreseeable future.

Mary Crawford has been left particularly bereft by her uncle's indifference to decent discretion, since she is now homeless. She agrees quite heartily with Henry, but from a woman's perspective, that marriage is "a take-in," even as it is for the man, "for there is not one in a hundred of either sex, who is not taken in when they marry." Mary's reasoning would do justice to modern marriage counselors: "Look where I will, I see that it is so; and I feel that it must be so, when I consider that it is, of all transactions, the one in which people expect most from others, and are least honest themselves."

Mrs. Grant replies very sanely, in imitation of the more urbane and less bitter moments, perhaps, of Jane West, Elizabeth Hamilton, or of Austen, Burney, or Edgeworth, that "we are all apt to expect too much," and that if the marriage is considerably less than ideal, as hers obviously was, "we find comfort somewhere, for if one scheme of happiness fails, human nature turns to another" (*MP*, 43, 46).

This kind of frankness even between brothers and sisters would have horrified the orthodox thinkers, who would condemn Henry Crawford and Mrs. Grant for pandering to Mary Crawford's "unreasonable desire," in a woman,"to influence the opinion of others" (Edgeworth, "Letter upon the Birth of a Daughter," 55). And Mary's italicized vehemence against marriage as she had observed it comes perilously close to the angry engorgement of the mind and heart, as women express wrongs, which Duff, Burton, Fordyce, and even the genial Gisborne condemned in women, as a self-induced mental orgasm. Burton's description of fiery, menacing female furies was particularly guaranteed to frighten any woman less candid and intrepid than Mary Crawford.

The question of what orthodox patriarchs would have thought of Sophia Croft, in *Persuasion*, who has lived on board ship for decades, and who keeps excellent company with her husband's officers, all the while giving as good as she gets, must have caused Austen a great deal of silent ironic pleasure. Mrs. Croft loves her brother, Captain Frederick Wentworth, even while with wry amusement she watches him trying to make both Musgrove sisters fall in love with him. But when he says that he does not like to see women on board any ship under his command, that one simply cannot make feminine women as comfortable on board as they ought to be, and as true women ought to want to be, that a woman on board, is "an evil in itself," and that "women and children have no *right* to be comfortable" on board, "particularly in large numbers," Mrs. Croft explodes:

> Oh Frederick!—But I cannot believe it of you—. All idle refinement!—Women may be as comfortable on board, as in the best house in England. . . . I know nothing superior to the accommodations of a man of war. . . . I hate to hear you talking so, like a fine gentleman, and as if women were all fine ladies, instead of rational creatures. We none of us expect to be in smooth water all our days.

There is considerable bad faith in Frederick's highly revealing response to his sister's expostulations. He says that he "might not like" women "any the better" who were unfeminine enough to make themselves comfortable on board ship (*P*, 70). His hostility toward his sister, who has done just that all her life, is odd, indeed, in a man who has condemned Anne Elliot for her craven feminine submission to family wishes in refusing to marry him. He is so imperiously constituted as a ship's commander that he cannot distinguish between Anne's youthful deference to her surrogate mother's warnings about a penniless sailor, as he then was, and his sister's ingenious capacity to adapt to the life her husband created for her. He condemns both the diffident young woman and the woman practicing classical feminine flexibility, as female intruders, or spoilers of male desires, usurping male control, invading male territory, or refusing to bow at once to male wishes.

Frederick's logical confusion and his tendency to argue in circular bad faith whenever it suits him emerge later when he tells Louisa Musgrove that he likes intrepid women. The truth is that he likes them to be intrepid in responding to his need for their attention and their praise, but once he had got their attention, he wants them to be thoroughly aware only of "the relation they bear to the other sex" (Duff, *Character of Women*, 19). His sister is quite used to him, however irritating she sometimes finds him, and she merely tells him good-naturedly that he is talking nonsense.

Since Anne Elliot's haunting debate with Captain Harville is the queen of all Austenian dialogues and other verbal confrontations, we might expect it to contain elements of all three conduct-book persuasions. And so it does in an ironic fashion. The peripatetic Hannah More had described women's English-style purdah as a blessing: "Women are . . . secured from those difficulties and temptations to which men are exposed in the tumult of a bustling world. Their lives are more uniform, less agitated by the passions, the business, the contentions, the shock of opinions, and of interests which convulse the world" (*Female Education*, II, 35).

Fordyce also praises the way that women's needs and desires tended to be fixated upon others: "It has been said of women . . . that they are remarkably steady to their purpose. Let it be seen that you are so on what is good" (*Sermons to Young Women*, II, 42). Gisborne lovingly described "the widely differing professions and employments into which private advantage and public require that men should be distributed. The barrister and the physician have their respective duties and their respective trials . . . . But the wife and the daughter . . . are scarcely . . . distinguished as such, by any peculiarities of moral obligation" (*Duties of the Female Sex*, 2–3).

The radical feminists, on the other hand, thought about this matter as radicals always do. They described again and again in the exact terms that Anne Elliot was to offer the befuddled and bewildered yet kind Captain Harville, what it was like to be members of the sex that throughout history had hardly ever been permitted or trained to have the pen in their hands, or to describe their constrained universe for themselves. Wollstonecraft observed sternly what Anne Elliot was later to observe more discreetly but nonetheless fully as persuasively, that "the character of every man, is, in some degree, formed by his profession":

> In the middle rank of life . . . men, in their youth, are prepared for professions, and marriage is not considered as the grand feature in their lives, while women, on the contrary, have no other scheme to sharpen their faculties. It is not business, extensive plans, or any of the excursive flights of ambition, that engross their attention; no, their thoughts are not employed in rearing such noble structures. . . . A man when he enters any profession has his eye steadily fixed on some future advantage direct to one point. (*Vindication*, 18, 60)

Throughout the radicals' lengthy essays on how women's minds and tongues have been corrupted and their hearts artificially bloated, the radical logic, the syntax, and even the metaphors all anticipated Anne's arguments as they inform Wollstonecraft's and Hays's. When men are faithful to women, Wollstonecraft says, as Anne says, they are so accidentally; when women are faithful to dead or absent men, they are so because their social environment and their only permissible preoccupations offer them no other ideas and professions to replace this humiliating and useless suffering.

Anne turns upside down the whole conduct-book conservative argument about women's weak minds, and their weak bodies and clinging, yet inconstant natures. Women's bodies may be softer than men's, says Anne, but they live longer than men, and so, by analogy, their affections are more trustworthy and persistent than men's. Anne refuses to accept the solipsistic impulse of orthodox men that women's suffering is imaginary, yet benign and providentially ordered: "It is, perhaps, our fate rather than our merit . . . our feelings prey upon us. . . . You have difficulties, and privations, and dangers enough to struggle with" (*P*, 232–233).

Anne offers a gentle reminder to Captain Harville that each sex has its own perspective, which touches the other sex only where experience has been the same; and under patriarchal arrangements, the experience of the two sexes is hardly ever the same: "We each being probably with a little bias towards our own sex, and upon that bias build every circumstance in favour of it which has occurred in our circle" (*P*, 234).

Captain Harville's response is most heart-warming, although he answers her tone rather than her logic: " 'You are a good soul,' cried Captain Harville, putting his hand on her arm quite affectionately" (*P*, 235). That single gesture, that one moment in Austen's fiction, when an older married man reaches out to touch a young unmarried women, is laden with symbolic meaning: for even declared Austenian lovers can seldom embrace.[3] The spontaneous and affectionate gesture from this kind, domesticated husband, which transcends all sexual decorum, and which neither party misunderstands, is a fitting end to a debate brought to its conclusion by Harville's conciliatory, almost benedictory response: "There is no quarreling with you.—And when I think of Benwick, my tongue is tied" (*P*, 235–236).

7

Reconciliation in the Province of the Garden

Because orthodox writers on "the woman question" were obsessed with Milton's Eve and with the archetypal female sinner in Genesis, they were equally obsessed with contemporary women in gardens. The garden symbolized the utmost theoretical extension of a young unmarried woman's province, where she could be alone outdoors with no loss of safety or propriety, as Eve was considered safe from contamination as long as she remained close to Adam, but functionally quite separated from him. When Fanny Price exhibited the distinct signs of the agoraphobia that occurs in some people who are psychologically and spatially confined, she was behaving according to the neo-orthodox dictates of women's proper responses to their proper limitations of confidence and of movement.

Austen's primary responses to gardens and pastoral scenes in her fiction and her letters differed profoundly from those of orthodox males. She simply loved them for themselves, for their beauty and the invigorating support that they offered to people under stress, and for the archetypal reassurances they provided, as budding, blooming, or falling leaves and flowers responded to the cycle of the seasons.

But discreet symbolist that Austen was, she also loved pastoral scenes for patriotic reasons. Napoleon had been threatening to make England's gardens and pastures his property, as though the country for which Austen's naval brothers were fighting was a mere woman, ripe for his exploitation. Austen had seen and suffered enough casual exploitation so that she took the pastoral world under her tender but unobtrusive fictional protection, just as she felt protective toward human figures under threat of abuse or neglect. Her loving descriptions of Donwell Abbey's plantations as typical of English verdure and therefore of English moral values, and of Knightley as well, suggest, as Alistair Duckworth's *The Improvement of the Estate* has spelled out, how highly symbolic her treatment of pastoral scenes invariably was.

Austen was very well aware, as well, that gardens symbolized not only those pastoral pleasures that could unite men and women on plantations, but also all the patriarchal arrangements that divided the two sexes. Marion Morrison has drawn a delightful picture of the proprietorial male's pleasure in his gardens as it appears in Austen's fiction. Although the plantation gardens signify in part all the privileges that supported men's dominion over women, the more admirable male characters knew that women's welfare on an estate depended entirely on the managerial efficiency of its owner, and on his willingness to let her share in its benefits without crippling restrictions.

> We watch the country gentlemen and their visitors surveying happily their groves and coppices, their lime walk, their stretch of water, their ha-ha, their prospects and vistas, dovecotes, stewponds, and succession houses. Mr. Bennet escapes to the little copse at Longbourn; Mr. Woodhouse, warmly wrapped, walks in the shrubbery at Harfield; Colonel Brandon, in his flannel waistcoat, is ensconced in the yew arbor at Delaford; the Musgrove children play on the lawn at Uppercross. Familiar "props" appear again and again; the plantation, the summer house or arbor or bower (sometimes damp), the gravel walk, the sweep, the paddock, and above all, the shrubbery.[1]

The shrubbery was important because young unmarried women—the elder Bennet sisters and Fanny Price, for instance—often escape there for privacy. But Morrison's charming paragraph and her whole short essay unconsciously dwells more upon the master's pride and ownership in each heroine's outdoor province, than in her welcome and comfortable presence there.

Chapman's appendix in *Emma*, called "Manners of the Age," also describes provinces within provinces which monitored women's spatial and occupational freedoms both indoors and outdoors. The system of male entail customarily insured that the whole plantation of a gentleman's county estate belonged to the master of the house, "except," by a kind of matrimonial courtesy, "the flower garden and (sometimes) the shrubbery." But even on the estate grounds, "the concern of the male . . . [was] with game, horses, dogs, and newspapers," whereas "ladies did not take part" in "sports" such as hunting (*E*, 509, 507). In less affluent country homes such as Austen's, which belonged to the minor gentry, women did not even ride. The prevailing masculine obsession with scarcities—of privileges as well as goods and funds—and the consequent systems of female triage, all ensured that many women would be trained very early to recognize no desire for these masculine occupations. But in any case, whether the family were affluent or politely poor, the refusal to provide chances for women to ride or hunt functioned as one more symbol of their penitential status. The Bertrams' insistence that Fanny Price did not need a horse of her own, despite their obvious wealth, signified her humble origins and her training for permanent poverty and domestic utility. Fanny's symbolic occupation was to be fetching and carrying, knitting and tatting, not galloping zestfully over the countryside.

Austen's heroines do not characteristically ride or hunt. The complete absence of any indication that Emma Woodhouse's wealthy father allowed her to keep a horse of her own is as resonant with significance as all of Austen's silences. Her epistolary jokes on the subject of male game-hunting is another example of her implicit contrasts between *HIS* privileges and *her* deprivations. But her irony on the subject of brothers who relished game-hunting would have cheered the theoretical feminists of both persuasions; they all associated the killing of defenseless game for mere sport with men's legal and social permission to abuse defenseless women.

Austen's heroines are unusually casual about leaving the estate alone, as provincial gentlewomen went—or ideally, were not supposed to go. Catherine Morland, the Bennet sisters, the Dashwood sisters, and Anne Elliot roam by themselves all over the countryside, yet they were not supposed to discuss the weather: Chapman observes blandly that "the weather was another subject on which only masculine opinion was valued" (*E*, 510). And readers are all subliminally or otherwise aware that Austen was forced to tether all her heroines fairly close to the province of the home: she could never have allowed them the peripatetic freedom of a Lazarillo de Tormes, a Don Quixote, a Tom Jones, a Huckleberry Finn, or a Wilhelm Meister, to say nothing of a Darcy, a Knightley, or even those dutiful sons, Edmund Bertram and Edward Ferrars.

When Emma Woodhouse's governess is about to be married, this tender but conventional woman is delighted that her new home will be "only half a mile" from Mr. Woodhouse's estate, "so convenient" a distance "for even solitary female walking" (*E*, 7, 18), and thus for Emma's occasional escape from her paternal jailor. Miss Taylor's orthodox assumption that Emma was only safe within half a mile of Hartfield, in a village where everybody knew her, is a casual example of that persistent denial in Emma's elders that her entrapment required any solution. That this denial is encapsulated in the half-monologue of a mother-surrogate, the concerned and affectionate Miss Taylor, signifies in Austen's typical oblique fashion that the frustrations of her heroines were causes of radical concern only to themselves.

Bennett was one of several orthodox tutors to women who recreated prelapsarian feminine provinces within provinces. The husband's garden was indeed his "retirement Paradise," where his wife and his gardeners were expected to "have delicious pleasures spread around" so as to embellish his sense of ownership. But for the woman, the garden was almost as equivocal a province as the forbidden wilds beyond it. In this place of confinement, she was permitted to act as "preceptress" to her "well nurtured sons," but she must raise her daughters to expect to become mere modest flowers on the borders of the pathways, and "polished corners in the temple" of the summer house (*Female Education*, 17, 78, 115).

Hannah More classified women with "some timid animals," providentially equipped with "sensitive and tender organs" that function "as a natural guard, to warn of the approach of danger." But she stressed that gardens were healthy symbols of prelapsarian innocence, where young girls should be "bounding with the unrestrained freedom of little wood-nymphs, over hill and dales, their cheecks flushed with health, and their hearts overflowing with happiness." For a child in "her natural state" of "simplicity" will be delighted with "every little change," such as "a ride or a walk." All these preoccupations will promote the health of women, "quicken their activity, enliven their spirits, whet their ingenuity, and qualify them for their mental work" (*Female Education*, II, 26; I, 86–89).

But More's Edenic vision of women outdoors suffered from some familiar logical and psychological confusions. Her active, liberating verbs and phrases such as "*quicken*," "*enliven* their *own spirits*," "*activity*," "*whet* their *ingenuity*," "*bounding with unrestrained freedom*," and her extraordinary subversive suggestion that young girls should be trained to "*qualify* for . . . *mental work*," indicate her ambivalence about the English purdah from which she had suffered as a child. Yet her garden symbolism was all too frequently shaped by false assumptions of innate gender differences: "A woman sees the world . . . from a little elevation in her own garden, when she takes an exact survey of home scenes." More's metaphors often associate women's spatial confinements with their intellectual and psychological deficiencies, as though all three were inevitable: A women "takes not in that wider range of distant prospects, which he who stands on a loftier eminence commands" (*Female Education*, II, 25). More makes no attempt here to reason from causes and effects, or ends and means, although she is most ingenious in doing so when she argues for women's intellectual confinement. But her visions of young women bounding over hills and dales like young nymphs foreshadow Austen's equally delightful vision of Catherine Morland playing cricket and rolling down hills, before the prison house of young adulthood closed over her, of Elizabeth Bennet jumping playfully over stiles, and of Marianne and Margaret Dashwood enjoying the Devon dales while they buffet a vigorous wind.

It was not the purpose of orthodox men and their female imitators to investigate how provincial gentlewomen fared on family estates, as wives, young daughters, or marriageable and unmarriageable spinsters. Instead, they merely dictated the protocol of women's deportment. Fordyce had warned women readers "that in your sex, manly exercises are never graceful, that in [women] a tone and figure as well as an air and deportment of the masculine kind, are always forbidding; and that men of sensibility desire in every woman soft features, and a flowing voice, a form not robust, and a demeanour delicate and gentle" (*Sermons to Young Women*, II, 163).

Dr. Gregory exhibited the same confusions as Fordyce and More, between genetics and fashion, that is, between innate feminine debilitation and the same condition artificially produced. Yet he must have accumulated some wealth or else have lived among people who did not think it necessary to deny women the pleasures of riding. He "particularly" recommended "those exercises that obliged" his daughters "to be much abroad in the open air, such as walking and riding on horseback." These activities would "give vigor to [their] constitutions, and a bloom to [their] complexions" (*Legacy to his Daughters*, 48–49).

Burton would permit open-air perambulations as an "agreeable amusement" because they promoted "that gentle exercise" presumably so well "adapted to the female constitution." But any woman moving even with slow female decorum outdoors, inevitably led his presuppositions to the primary Edenic scene and its connection with modern restless women: "A garden," he said, quoting Addison, "was the habituation of our First Parents before the Fall." As long as women moved quietly in a garden, it was "naturally apt to fill the mind with calmness and tranquility; and to lay all turbulent Passions at rest." Furthermore, gardens "give us a great insight into the contrivance and wisdom of Providence." In order to be sure that women were tranquilized enough to accept "the contrivance and wisdom of Providence," he advised them to "raise the tender Plants, to observe the variegated flowers and to mark the progress of vegitation." Once again Burton utters the cliché about the automatic connection between women's physical and mental structures: these occupations are not only "grateful amusements particularly adapted" to the "female constitution," but "to the female mind" (*Female Education*, II, 41–42).

Fordyce and Burton both urged young women not to *be* robust, since they were *not* robust. Gregory added confusion upon confusion when he urged them not to *appear* robust: "good health," he had to admit, is "one of the greatest blessings of life." But because men "so naturally associate the idea of feminine softness and delicacy with a correspondent delicacy of constitution," he urged women of "great strength," vigorous "appetite," and a tireless physique to hide one of the greatest blessings of life, since men "recoil" at women's attribution of these blessings to themselves, "in ways [they are] little aware of"

(Gregory, *Legacy to his Daughters*, 50–51). On this advice too, orthodox men confused "What men would have women to be," and how they had contrived to arrange that this is "What women are," and to assume that this is "what women ought to be.———All of which, as they at present stand," Mary Hays took "to be essentially and necessarily different from each other" (*Appeal to the Men of Great Britain*, 30).

Both radical and moderate feminists condemned orthodox attempts to create women with sluggish minds and quiescent bodies. Macaulay insisted that "No human enjoyment can be great, without a robust habit of body" (*Letters on Education*, 24). Hays stressed that "No amusement which contributes to health of body and mind . . . can possibly have any moral turpitude whatever." And in a phrase about universal acknowledgments of verifiable truths, which frequently functioned as feminist code words refuting masculine wisdom, Hays said firmly: "And it must be acknowledged a truth equally infallible, that any class so held in subjection and dependence [as women are], will degenerate both in body and mind" (*Appeal to the Men of Great Britain*, 186, 69).

Wollstonecraft, the feminist governess to small girls, foreshadowed Catherine Morland's girlhood with the observation that any young girl "whose spirits have not been dampened by inactivity, or innocence tainted by false shame, will always be a romp." Wollstonecraft next described a young girl treated, as Catherine Morland was initially treated, with a neglect that may indeed have been more benign than orthodox supervision: "dolls will never excite attention unless confinement offers her no alternative." Wollstonecraft then identifies a social phenomenon that has only recently become acceptable wisdom to members of the health profession who supervise the growth of young girls: "most of the women in the circle of my observation, who have acted like rational creatures, or shewn any vigor of intellect, have accidently been allowed to run wild" (*Vindication*, 43). This description of women who behave like "rational creatures" fits Elizabeth Bennet and Anne Elliot much more aptly than Catherine Morland. But Elizabeth and Anne suffered or enjoyed permanent family neglect, whereas Catherine was sent to Bath to become a decorous woman.

Austen's description of Catherine's healthy outdoor girlhood sounds suspiciously like Wollstonecraft's. Catherine was also "accidently allowed to run wild," as the fourth child and first daughter of a brood of ten children. Until she was fourteen, she "was fond of all boy's play and greatly preferred cricket not merely to dolls but to the more heroic enjoyment of infancy, nursing a doormouse, feeding a canary-bird, or watering a rose bush. . . . Indeed, she had no taste for a garden." The activities of nursing dolls, doormice, and canaries were all archetypal female tasks of the girl being trained for maternity. Instead, Catherine occupied herself with "baseball," and she "loved nothing so well in the world as rolling down the green slope at the back of the house." But by the time her parents had looked at their firstborn daughter long enough to notice that she was "almost pretty," they began to stress the exclusively superficial and exterior characteristics of the growing girl, and the confinement of Catherine's artlessly independent limbs and interests had begun. The artless mind, which was calculated to follow the spatial limitations and the prohibitions against bodily vigor, did indeed follow in consequence (*NA*, 13–15).

Gisborne, who was perhaps as good an ecclesiastical friend to women as the age, combined with the masculine conduct-book sensibility, could have produced, wanted girls brought up to acquire "a healthful constitution, steady spirits, and a strong, alert mind." Any other system, he said, resulted in "Pale cheeks, a languid spirit, and a feeble frame," and he feared that these signs of artificially produced debilitation afflicting generations of women would "prognosticate the long train of nervous maladies which lie in wait for future years," and thus unfit women to produce healthy heirs. He denied women the right to "contend in the hardy amusements which benefit the young of the other sex," but for once he reasoned both scientifically and morally that languid mothers produce languid babies, and that languid mothers are produced by languid policies unfit for a vigorous people. He recommended that parents "let active exercise in the open air be one of [young women's] daily occupations." He even offered the sexually daring comment that "a few dagged frocks and dirtied gloves" were a small price to pay for "the healthiness of the employment," when young girls tended "little gardens of their own," in which they might salubriously "amuse themselves with the lighter offices of cultivation."[2]

Gisborne's refusal to make the usual false associations between women soiled with garden dirt or any other kind of dirt and women soiled by sexual license is heart-warming. He was one of the rare conduct-book men to condemn the system, now gradually becoming obsolete, of deforming women's bodies by tight stays, purges, debilitating diets, and enforced passivity indoors. Lawrence Stone, Phyllis Stock, Josephine Kamm, and Muriel Jaeger, among other social historians, have stressed the morbid and sometimes even lethal consequences of the attempt to force upon growing girls the look of innate feebleness. Girls were starved and purged in order to reproduce a characteristic pale, feminine languor and a quiet passivity that paradoxically enough were traits totally at variance with other traits also presumed to be innate, such as sprightliness, a restless, imaginative vivacity, quickness of intuition to male needs, and a constant and vigorous attention to their Christian duties to others. Young girls were swung by the neck, with their feet off the ground, so as to produce swanlike necks. "One Mary Butt," says Stock, "did her lessons around 1789 standing in stocks with a backboard strapped over her shoulders and an iron collar. In the same period, Mary Fairfax, age ten, wore stays, a steel busk, bands that forced the shoulder blades to meet, and a steel rod up the back, attached to a semicircle under her shin." The most tragic case concerns a young girl whose internal organs were eventually crushed, as an autopsy disclosed after her early death. Her mother forced the maid to lace her stays so tightly that her eyes were dimmed by helpless tears every time this torture was inflicted upon her. To these draconian measures, undertaken so as to make masculine myths of femininity appear to be both natural and scriptural designs, Wollstonecraft and other feminists expressed understandable horror: "To preserve personal beauty, woman's glory! the limbs and faculties are cramped with worse than Chinese bands [upon the feet], and the sedentary life which [girls] are condemned to live, whilst boys frolic in the open air, weakens the muscles and relaxes the nerves" (*Vindication*, 41). Lawrence Stone describes a pathetic case that was by no means altogether atypical: "When Arthur Young's beloved daughter Bobbin caught tuberculosis in 1797, he blamed in part the school regime of inadequate food, no fresh air, and the forbidding of all running about or quick motions."[3]

Such atrocities horrified feminists of both persuasions as they must have horrified many compassionate and sensible parents, even the most orthodox. Wollstonecraft and Hays both associated the deformation of English women's bodies with the barbarous binding of Chinese women's feet. Priscilla Wakefield admitted that "instances of deformity" were now relatively "rare." But she nonetheless remarked categorically:

"every restraint [imposed upon girls] that tends to distort and compress any part of the body is as injurious to grace and proportion, as to health. Steel collars, braces, backboards, and feet-stocks, may be carried to a very dangerous excess, and cause that deformity which they are intended to prevent." Wakefield urgently recommended exercises that were much more strenuous than sedate walks and gentle female gardening. She insisted that "running races, trundling a hoop, skipping with a rope, battledore and shuttle-cock, ball, jumping, dumbbells, swinging, and many other amusement . . . may with propriety be practiced by both sexes" (*Present Condition of the Female Sex*, 24–25, 22).

Since for Austen, all orthodox prescriptions against healthy occupations smacked of that "Evangelical" temper that she had told Cassandra she disliked, her heroines' conduct in gardens symbolized the extent to which they had or had not been mentally deformed by feminine protocols. Elizabeth Bennet and Jane not only dance with verve and pleasure, but they run eagerly toward each other after they have been separated, or run anxiously toward their lazy and irresponsible father, so as to quicken his lethargic disinclination to rescue the eloping Lydia. There is no false bodily languor in either of them, despite Jane's habit of psychological denials. Elizabeth's spontaneous act of leaping over stiles so as to arrive quickly at her sick sister's bedside eventually receives Darcy's warm praise.

Sometimes whole sections of Austen's novels seem to dwell lovingly on pastoral scenes. In summer, the hospitable Sir John Middleton "was for ever forming parties to eat cold ham and chicken out of doors," and he made dazzling plans to visit "a noble piece of water; a sail on which was to form a great part of the morning's amusement, cold provisions were to be taken, open carriages only to be employed, and everything conducted in the usual style of a complete party of pleasure" (*SS*, 33, 62).

None of the conduct-book conservatives thought to forbid a woman writer to say anything about nature—that is, to paint nature with her pen and her imagination, if she should have the audacity to write for publication in the first place. She ought not to gush over nature, as Marianne Dashwood does, and as Austen does not. But Austen knew that when a young woman lavishes affection over nature, however discreetly, as Fanny Price lavishes affection over the great panoply of the stars, and does so in Edmund Bertram's presence, she may continue to do so, as long as this topic meets with the man's approval, since to praise nature discreetly is to indicate to a lover that a woman understands her utterly subordinate place in it. For a woman to praise nature is thus a very discreet form of courtship.

Gardens symbolized women in multiple conflicting ways. The neat rows of obedient vegetation represented women as the compliant creature over whom the man had total authority, in whom he planted his seed, yet who paradoxically planted seeds in his gardens, in patient and modest prelapsarian fashion. Yet the orthodox writers emphasized her *nourishment* of these seeds, not the *planting* of them, just as she nourished him and his heirs indoors. But most symbolically to the thoroughly orthodox man, she represented a Ceres figure—a creature whose mind and body, like the minds and bodies of all similar animal or vegetable kinds, moved at slow, predictable rates, depending largely upon the husband's tillage or his pastoral care of her; and eventually, in the fullness of time, his child in her womb—usually described as a son—emerged.

We have difficulty understanding Mrs. Bennet's muffled anguish, which she displays only as inchoate feminine hysteria, unless we realize the crime she has committed. With Mr. Bennet's tillage, they had both intended her to produce a son. Her very crop—five daughters—was imperfect, and her peevish temper symbolizes how worthless she feels. The extended pastoral implications here are both sardonic and tragic.

The garden thus represented orthodox ideas of women's four functions: to be an incubator for the heir; to be ornamental and beautiful, as flowers are; and to make herself so without knowing she was making herself so, in case nature had not performed that nourishing function for her; to be as passive and receptive as flowers are; and to be as domestically useful as vegetables are. But just as flowers will appear to be "lively," an orthodox epithet for flowers when they are vigorously moved by the gale of a robust wind, so will women appear "lively," even witty themselves for a moment, they were told, when they respond actively and appreciatively to the robust gales of male wit or brilliance.

The figure of a woman as the symbol of the fallen pastoral world, not the manager of it, and always the potential victim of violation, emerges most satirically in Austen's *Sanditon*, the last unfinished novel, which Elizabeth Jenkins called "that glittering fragment" (*Jane Austen*, 197). *Sanditon* mockingly reproduces the whole myth of woman "doing

Penance" as a generic social sacrifice for some unnamed offense. Clara Bereton's tormentor considers her to be a young woman whose "Poverty and dependence" had "placed" her in the world, "on purpose to be ill-used." The repetitive vignettes of Sir Edward Denham, trying to tempt the impoverished, dependent, and sycophantic orphan, Clara Bereton, into the farthest reaches of the garden spaces, so as to seduce her with fatuous quotations from *Marmion* and *The Lady of the Lake*, are "very amusing, or very melancholy, just as Satire or Morality might prevail." Sir Edward's "great object in life was to be seductive," a serpentine quality that he shares with four other Austenian antiheroes, Willoughby, Wickham, Crawford, and Frank Churchill. As for Sir Edward, himself penniless and dependent upon his aunt, Lady Denham, and also shallow and therefore bored with life, "it was Clara alone on whom he had serious designs; it was Clara whom he meant to seduce.—Her seduction was quite determined on. Her situation in every way called for it." For after all, was it not "Woman in our Hours of Ease—" whom we may require to satisfy all our demands (*MW*, 396, 391, 405, 397), whatever those demands may be.

Despite the fact that Austen was dying and in considerable discomfort and weakness when she began *Sanditon*, her spoofing allusions to *Paradise Lost* are delightful, as Austen so often was when she experienced a respite from loneliness, depression, or illness. Mr. and Mrs. Parker leave their own inland estate to take up residence in the trashy seaside resort of Sanditon, which Lady Denham was attempting to create overnight by exploiting her wealth and social dominance, both so rare in a woman. In this new town, the word was Lady Denham, and the word was with Lady Denham, and lo! there was Sanditon!

As the Parkers journey toward this spurious seaside paradise, Mrs. Parker, the more sensible of the two, looks nostalgically through the back carriage window at the fine inland "garden, orchard and Meadows" which she has left behind her, mournfully calling it "such an excellent Garden"; she prophesies correctly that she and her husband will not be able to reproduce anything like it in Sanditon (*MW*, 379, 380). All the world before her does not tempt her as it does her foolish husband, who abandons his own estate for pastures new, and thereby loses more than he can ever comprehend. Mrs. Parker understands what the loss will be before she ever sees Sanditon—before she even starts to pack her household goods.

In the meanwhile, as the Parkers approach Sanditon, they are gratified by a vision of "a Hill, whose side was covered with the Woods & Enclosures of Sanditon House," and by the various valleys, heights, downs, and groves of old trees and "very young plantation[s]" that characterize this tarnished new paradise by the sea. And in it, ready to begin the mythical male practice of seducing vulnerable women without experience and without visible male guardians, is Sir Edward Denham, who intends to initiate "the quietest sort of ruin & Disgrace for the object of his Affections" beyond the "Park paling," where "there were vacant spaces . . . in the field on the other side" (*MW*, 382–384, 406, 426).

Austen treats gardens both mockingly and seriously, and the pastoral world as places both of feminine privacy and of crises in the young woman's life: women could sometimes command privacy in gardens, as they could not usually do indoors, and they sometimes found males there, either predators or well-wishers, and therefore they came to know themselves in the male world in ways that were not always possible indoors.

For Austen, gardens also symbolized an androgynous space, halfway between the man's absolute freedom to travel all over England at will, and the woman's small, restricted, domestic boundaries. But first Austen had to disabuse herself and her readers of the bizarre sexual equations between the noun *gardens* and the nouns *female*, *sin*, *temptation*, *dependency*, *debilitation*, *idiocy*, and *stain* or *dirt*, for if gardens symbolized the original place of sin, woman was sin itself.

Northanger Abbey is fully as much an irreverent mockery of the conduct-book orthodoxies about women's confined spaces, such as ballrooms, schoolrooms, and drawing rooms indoors, and gardens outdoors as it is a mockery of the Gothic novel. The contrast between Catherine Morland's preadolescent freedom to romp at will and her later confinement does not become clear until she meets Henry Tilney at a Bath assembly. This contrast becomes even more clear when Henry sedately chaperones his sister and his potential bride to the famous beauties of Beechen Cliff, "that noble hill, whose beautiful verdure and hanging coppice render it so striking an object from almost every opening in Bath" (*NA*, 106). Catherine and the young Tilneys are free of middle-aged adults, and they begin the guarded but distinct moves in the game of courtship. Henry displays his intellectual attainments, mocks the young women because they have not gone to Oxford, and assumes that

Catherine is going to find him irresistible, as of course she does. But the authorial praise of this particularly striking Bath scene, and two of the young people's muffled sexual interest in each other, while Eleanor Tilney, the third, already herself in love with an absent lover, looks on with complacent, even witty approval, symbolizes Austen's silent awareness of the aphrodisiac quality that arresting outdoor scenes can create for a couple testing each other's hidden intentions.

Northanger Abbey, the home of General Tilney, offers many symbolic pastoral moments. General Tilney is himself a gardener, and he forces his plants into the rigidly obedient rows that the orthodox writers prescribe for feminine discipline. The general's treatment of his plants characterizes his treatment of his children. The hyacinth scene also harbors symbolic meanings that both buttress and mock Gisborne's opinion on women and gardens. Catherine artlessly says that now she has "just learnt to love a hyacinth." Henry's Oxonian training is at work here. He wants to know whether Catherine learnt this healthy love accidentally or by "argument." Catherine replies that Eleanor has taught her just a few weeks ago, whereas Mrs. Allen had failed to interest her in them, "year after year." Henry replies in his usually condescending fashion, that "a taste for flowers is always desirable in [Catherine's] sex," just as the conduct-book conservatives had been telling her sex for decades. Henry, who claims that he knows everything about Catherine, says that gardening is good for women because it offers them fresh air and exercise, which most women find unappealing. Catherine tries to tell Henry that he does not know her as well as he thinks he does: "But I do not want any such pursuit to get me out of doors. The pleasure of walking and breathing fresh air is enough for me, and in fine weather I am out more than half my time.—Mama says, I am never within." Henry's reply is predictable: "At any rate, however, I am pleased that you have learnt to love a hyacinth. The mere habit of learning to love is the thing; and a teachableness of disposition in a young lady is a great blessing. Has my sister a pleasant mode of instruction?" (*NA*, 174).

Henry's repartee is full of sexual allusions to courtship, love, traditional marriage, and the presumed nature of women, who must have everything taught them in an easy and pleasant fashion. Catherine is understandably embarrassed, for Henry talks as Marianne's Willoughby talks, by insinuation rather than by open and undefensive conversation, so that he can withdraw at any time, if he wishes. He is courting her, and she knows that he is, but in so general a fashion here and elsewhere, with so many remarks about women in general, that nobody could accuse him of outright fraud. Yet his caution is understandable; readers later learn that his father has ordered him to marry Catherine; he is merely trying to discover whether this command is in his best interest or not. He is testing Catherine while they both look out of the window at the attractive garden scene outside. The very sight of the hyacinth has moved them in closer accord, for all their vast differences in sex, age, training, occupations, and privileges.

Barbara Hardy made some brilliant suggestions about the symbolic content of this hyacinth:

> It seems significant that the single object in the Abbey which is in no way associated with General Tilney is a hyacinth, the only sign of spring and natural growth at Northanger Abbey. One of those small indexes of the advancing year which Jane Austen places so discreetly in to the action, it is mentioned briefly but is not visually present. The hyacinth is part of Catherine's advance in appreciation, and is associated with Eleanor's nature.[4]

Although Hardy does not say so, this scene is even more closely associated with Henry's orthodoxies. When Henry comes to propose to Catherine at Fullerton, the proposal takes place outdoors, while the couple is alone and now free to become reconciled to one another. Of Austen's seven heroines, all but the Dashwood sisters get engaged in gardens or outdoor spaces.

In *Northanger Abbey*, as in all Austen's completed novels, the garden ultimately becomes a place of earthly redemption for the heroine, as it had earlier functioned as a place of play, of solitude, of trial, and sometimes of danger. Austen's couples are indeed seeking pastures new, once they learn to trust each other.

When Henry leaves Catherine at Fullerton, having proposed to her near "Mr. Allen's grounds" and extracted permission to court her if he can get his father's grudging approval, he remembers the lecture he had given Catherine about the therapeutic properties of gardens and gardening, and he elects to act upon his own advice. Since he has earned his father's displeasure, he had been temporarily exiled from Northanger Abbey, and so he returns to Woodstone, his rectory, "and now his only home, to watch over his young plantations, and extend his improvements for her sake, to whose share in them he looked anxiously forward; and Catherine remained at Fullerton to cry." To be sure, until Henry finally wrings reluctant permission to marry Catherine from the comic monster, General Tilney, "the young people . . . must have had a sad time of it," as the sympathetic Mrs. Morland said earlier of Henry and Eleanor Tilney. But Henry will not restrict his wife to one part of his plantation only, as his father had done, and the authorial voice manages to suggest that while he waits for Catherine, he may plant a few hyacinths himself (*NA*, 250, 234).

In *Sense and Sensibility*, as in all of Austen's novels, her plots, her character drawings, her ruthless social anatomies, and her elusive symbolism are all so tightly linked that they function as interchangeable analogies for each other. *Sense and Sensibility* is an account of an archetypally double feminine expulsion. First the Dashwood family of women, the mother and three daughters, are expelled from the gardens of "dear, dear Norland" (*SS*, 87), economically naked, for they have very little "pewter," as Austen called money, and they lack even the remote possibility of comfort and pecuniary support from any Adam of their own. In Devonshire, Marianne undergoes a more devastating expulsion, this time from her "season of happiness" (*SS*, 54). Her second expulsion is permanent.

Marianne's hysterical adoration of the pastoral world, the wilder the better, was a contemporary affectation that she shared with "sensibility" experts of both sexes. It is also a perennially feminine way of coping with oppression and insecurity. If a woman is forbidden to think that she has the capacity to like or do ninety-nine things, or any need to like or do them, and if she is told that she may like or do the hundredth, and in fact that she is not quite feminine if she does not, any exaggeration she then demonstrates in liking what she is bidden to like ought to be understandable. And for Marianne especially, the pastoral world is an unconscious symbol of a lover, and of the security, as well as the sexual comfort and reassurance such a lover might bring.

Annis Pratt's analysis of "The Green-World Archetype," which she has observed in Simone de Beauvoir's *The Second Sex* and elsewhere, brilliantly fits Austen's novels, although Austen symbolized the green world and the green-world lover as obliquely as she always symbolized anything. For Pratt, as for Austen, too,

> The patterns of pain in the female *bildungsroman* are embedded in image, leitmotif, and larger narrative patterns; their antitheses are images of desire for authentic selfhood. These images so often involve a special world of nature that they describe a green-world-archetype, and the figure of Eros who inhabits this world we have correspondly identified as the green-world lover. Conversely, the villain/rapist assault symbolizes the fulcrum of a world of enclosure and atrophy opposite the freedom of the green world, and we call it the rape-trauma archetype. . . . At the adolescent stage, however, [the young girl's] appreciation of nature is retrospective, a look backwards over her shoulder as she confronts her present placelessness and her future submission within a male culture. Visions of her own world within the natural world, or naturalistic epiphanies, channel the young girls's protests into a fantasy where her imprisoned energies can be released.[5]

Pratt implies, as de Beauvior does also, that young women never find their green-world lover in the actual world. One of Austen's great gifts is her capacity to cope symbolically and realistically with the green-world archetype and its lover, and she describes him either as metaphorical rapist or as the eventual husband, and sometimes a husband as undestructive of the heroines' needs as a post-Enlightenment man could be. Sometimes she places both the symbolic rapist and the eventual husband in urban sites, so that she offers both the best and the worst of both worlds and both masculine types.

It is not surprising then, that *Sense and Sensibility*, a novel with two heroines, two heroes, and a double feminine expulsion from two worlds, should be characterized by haunting imaginary fragrances of downs, hills, valleys, woods, lakes, and parklands. Nor is it surprising that the expulsion of the Dashwood women from the Norland parklands in Sussex to Barton Cottage in Devonshire deliberately invokes the expulsion from *Paradise Lost*:

> The first part of their journey was performed in too melancholy a disposition to be otherwise than tedious and unpleasant. But as they drew towards the end of it, their interest in the appearance of a country which they were to inhabit overcame their dejection, and a view of Barton Valley as they entered it gave them cheerfulness. It was a pleasant, fertile spot, well wooded, and rich in pasture. After winding along it for more than a mile, they reached their own house. A small green court was the whole of its demesne in front; and a neat wicket gate admitted them into it. (*SS*, 28)

Readers have only to remember where and under what circumstances Marianne meets Willoughby to understand how complex and ironic is Austen's vision of innocent paradise, briefly glimpsed and ultimately lost.

> The whole country about them abounded in beautiful walks. The high downs . . . invited them from almost every window of the cottage to seek the exquisite enjoyment of air on their summits . . . and towards one of these hills did Marianne and Margaret one memorable morning direct their steps, attracted by the partial sunshine of a showery sky, and unable longer to bear the confinement which the settled rain of the two preceding days had occasioned.

The two young girls, seventeen and thirteen, behave like Hannah More's innocent and frolicsome wood nymphs, laughing uproariously as they run into a "south-westerly wind," when a sudden assault from a "driving rain set full in their face," instead of the bracing and virile wind, which they had greeted with such exuberance. They decided to run "with all possible speed down the steep side of the hill which led immediately to their garden gate." All would have gone well, "but a sudden false step brought [Marianne] to the ground," spraining her ankle, so that Willoughby, who was passing by, "took her up in his arms without farther delay, and carried her down the hill" (*SS*, 40–42).

Marianne's "sudden false step" was very costly: Willoughby's rescue is harmless, on the surface, for he does what any gentleman would do. Nevertheless, he stimulates Marianne's sexual interest in him, and his gesture in rescuing her eventually brings her no greater joy nor security than his later flirtations with her.

Readers need to remember the onset of Marianne's almost mortal illness at Cleveland, as well as its cause. Medical scholars of all sorts are now beginning to acknowledge the role that prolonged and irredeemable stress followed by severe shock plays in mortal or near mortal illnesses, as they have now acknowledged in Austen's case. At Cleveland, Elinor Dashwood was merely left to the irritating spectacle of her host, Mr. Palmer, who possessed "no traits at all unusual in his sex and time of life," such as his "too great aptitude to fancy himself . . . superior to people in general," his casual disdain for domestic timetables and the convenience of his wife and her staff, his "Epicurism, his selfishness, and his conceit." Marianne, in the meanwhile, was trying to confront the shock and mourning of Willoughby's betrayal, as well as "the beginning of a heavy cold," by just such behavior as was bound to turn the cold into severe pneumonia. She insisted upon taking "twilight walks . . . not merely on the dry gravel of the shrubbery, but all over the grounds, and especially in the most distant parts of them, where there was something more of wildness than in the rest." In the violence of her grief, she sought those distant places on the Cleveland plantation "where the trees were the oldest, and the grass was the longest," so that "assisted by the still greater imprudence of sitting in her wet shoes and stockings" (*SS*, 304–306) she became gravely ill.

Just as Marianne's first and second fall from innocence occur in wild, free, unconstraining places, her struggles for earthly redemption also take place out of doors. She is now fittingly less wild, less impetuous, less trusting than she had been. She and Elinor take many gentle convalescent walks together, while they repeatedly review Willoughby's perfidy and Marianne's responsibility in permitting it—even in naively courting it.

The novel ends with a series of benedictory pastoral scenes or leitmotifs that characterize all of Austen's fictional closures, and that work symbolically, aesthetically, and rhetorically, though never altogether realistically. Colonel Brandon's estate turns out to be twice or three times as commodious and as blessed in its lands as the estate to which Willoughby is heir. Delaford, to which Marianne eventually comes as mistress, is so impressive that it evokes the spiteful envy of Marianne's brutish half-brother, who now wants "to call Colonel Brandon brother," although he has never had any inclination to call Marianne sister. "His property here, his place, his house, everything in such respectable condition!—and his woods!—I have not seen such timber anywhere in Dorsetshire as there is now standing in Delaford Hanger!" (*SS*, 375). If Marianne still feels the constraints of the feminine predicament after she is married to Brandon, as she will be bound to do, she will have plenty of wild places on the Delaford estate to which to repair. Colonel Brandon will not be the husband to try to stop her.

Elinor Dashwood also acquires her pastoral reward for suffering and patience, although in keeping with her temperament and her desires, it is less impressive than Marianne's. She and Edward lack the exaggerated *panache* that characterizes her sister and Colonel Brandon. Brandon glories in Marianne's sensibilities, of which he has his share, and he grieves for her past suffering, so like his own.

Elinor's paradise regained is as satisfying to herself as to her modest clergyman husband: "The first month after their marriage was spent with [Colonel Brandon] at the Mansion-house, from whence they could superintend the progress of the Parsonage, and direct everything they liked on the spot;—could chuse [*sic*] papers, project shrubberies, and invent a sweep [up to the front door]" (*SS*, 374).

The Barton Cottage section of this novel had begun with a description of separate male and female territories, of Sir John Middleton, the archetypal sportsman, and Lady Middleton, the bored mother. The novel closes with a young couple occupying the same territories, as far as their domestic interests are concerned. They are both busy with indoor and outdoor details, with wallpaper, shrubberies, and the new sweep for the carriage.

Austen has arranged a quietly satisfactory comic circle of felicity, for between "Barton" in Devonshire and "Delaford" in Dorsetshire, that is, between their affectionate mother in their old home and their husbands in their married residences, "there was that constant communication which strong family affection would naturally dictate," but the family affection is no stronger between Barton and Delaford than between Delaford mansion and Delaford parsonage, or between the squire and his young wife, and the clerical incumbent and his slightly older one (*SS*, 380). Brandon, Elinor, and Edmund are cultivators of pastoral inheritances or properties, as Marianne will soon be. They do not manipulate or spoil the land merely for their own sporting pleasure. These two couples are preservers of lands and of domestic serenity alike.

In *Sense and Sensibility*, Austen was to inaugurate a contrast between the false green-world lover, who exemplifies Pratt's "rape-trauma," in this case metaphorically, and the genuine green-world lover, who usually enters the novel as a socially uncouth or prosaic male. The genuine Austenian green-world lover stands in sharp contrast to the ingratiating and usually socially iconoclastic false green-world lover, who exploits women's predicament for his own narcissistic purposes.

John Willoughby cynically exploits Marianne's deep need for freedom, even as she seeks the masculine approval that she has never experienced since her father died. The pastoral scene of their first encounter was profoundly useful for his purposes. But he encourages and then manipulates her own rebellions against feminine protocols, in fact, against all social restraints. He agrees with all her hyperbolic adoration for the green world and all her contempt for women's enclosed domestic provinces, for it is only in the freedom of the green world that he can woo her without becoming engaged to her.

The quiet joke, a joke that is all the more tender because it seems so inappropriate, is that Colonel Brandon should become "Marianne's preserver," and that the fine expanse of his estate, which one can appropriately imagine them improving together, will not incarcerate her. Brandon's loving tolerance of her postadolescent excrescences will allow her to shed them when she is ready. She will soon discover that to be mistress of Delaford represents a very different future from the role of mere grudging pensioner at "dear, dear Norland," or even a welcome guest at Barton Cottage, where, as she rightly complained, she and her abandoned mother and sisters were looked upon, however kindly, at least by Sir John Middleton, as one source of his country amusements, and by his wife and as a bait to keep him happy at home.

To suggest that Austen's Darcy, as the "preserver" of Pemberley, is a genuine green-world lover, may seem at first to compound the difficulties inherent in the implausibly double-natured character of Darcy, the haughty masculine snob, and Darcy, the benevolent feudal squire, stereotypically redeemed by a good woman's love. Darcy is a product of the female imagination as it responds to its predicament in the easiest subconscious way it knows how—through wishfulfillment. He anticipates not only Charlotte Bronte's Rochester, no matter how vehemently Bronte would have denied that fact, but also the heroes of the Harlequin Romances, which sell in the millions yearly. This tall, rich, handsome aristocrat is also what every man envies; he stalks through the land, legally beholden to nobody—he is an orphan and he has therefore already stepped into "Dead men's Shoes" (*Letters*, 18), as Pemberley's Henry V. Abroad, he acknowledges no social superiors and he submits to no constraints of courtesy or charity. His intellectual and social judgments are fallible, because he is too consumed with himself to judge reliably about others or for others, even assuming that he has the right to judge for others in the first place.

Darcy appeals to women because the fantasy of taming the male beast who is brutal or indifferent to woman's dignity is as old a fantasy as it is in vulnerable, dependent children, whose dreams and fantasies of psychic wounds miraculously healed, parents reconciled, and paradise otherwise regained, are now acknowledged archetypes.

How, then, does Austen make this impossible man palatable, and even aesthetically, or symbolically at least, believable to those who struggle along with the unredeemable Darcys every day of their lives? The answer is that he is really more comfortable outdoors, with horse and hounds, with rod and gun through brightest Pemberley, and with taxes and tenants, and in his free moments from administering the estate, he is much happier in his library than he is in the confines of female provinces, such as ballrooms and the drawing rooms, with their predictable shallow mothers and daughters on the prowl to ensnare him into a disastrous marriage. On his own estate he is legally and socially lord of all he surveys, and these series of reassuring patriarchal surroundings all allow him to function there as a sensible, responsible, serious, benevolent despot of the Hobbsian kind, who will engage Elizabeth's affectionate humor, as well as her ardent respect.

The Pemberley scenes, which have transfixed generations of critics, accomplish Austen's aesthetic and ethical miracles, even though they perilously skirt stereotypes, and they do so triumphantly. Austen's alchemy is primarily mythical and symbolic. First, she invokes the spacious beauties of Pemberley, both the internal and external, which are to be her heroine's vastly extended spatial and mental provinces in the future, and then she deftly connects them not only with the present owner's inherited and authoritative male role, but she also invokes his *pastoral* forbearance, in both senses of the reverberative adjective *pastoral*. He is the proverbial biblical "good steward," a good father, or a good shepherd or secular pastor to his inheritance under his care. And as his housekeeper implies, he is as good a secular shepherd to his tenants, his servants, and his surrogate-daughter, who is really his sister, the terrified young woman "*en Penitence*," Georgiana Darcy. He is even singularly generous where Georgiana Darcy is concerned, for he knows that his treatment of her has been heavy-handed, especially since their father left him as her guardian. He welcomes the partnership of Elizabeth, who will be to Georgiana, indoors and out, a careful mentor of Georgiana's fullest possible autonomous development.

Austen's secondary magical techniques are rhetorical, even grammatical, as well as symbolical and mythical. For as Elizabeth moves about Pemberley, looking at the fine scenes and vistas from the spacious interior as well as from the almost limitless plantations, and as she acknowledges with longing what she now supposes she has lost, Austen's indirectly authorial voice—half hers and half Elizabeth's, which extols Pemberley's domestic beauties and its woods, fields, hills, valleys, pastures, and trout streams—moves from the mere positive grammatical degree, in which beautiful scenes and their accompanying fine ethical values appear merely *very* beautiful indeed, and then later to the comparative degree, where they appear even *more beautiful yet*. But about the owner of this earthly paradise, only the superlative degree will do: he is the *finest* landlord imaginable.

> First, every disposition of the ground was good; and she looked on the whole scene, the river, the trees scattered on its bands, and the winding of the valley as far as she could trace it, with delight. As they passed into the other rooms, these objects were taking different positions; but from every window there were beauties to be seen. The rooms were lofty and handsome, and their furniture suitable to the fortune of their proprietor; but Elizabeth saw, with the admiration of his taste, that it was neither gaudy nor uselessly fine; with less of splendor, and more of real elegance, than the furniture of Rosings.

Darcy's housekeeper speaks of him in the superlative; "He is the best landlord, and the best master . . . that ever lived. Not like the wild young men now-a-days, who think of nothing but themselves." Readers' minds will inevitably contrast this patriarchal paragon with John Dashwood, the reckless hacker of his father's fine timber, or Tom Bertram, the prodigal son, wasting his father's substance on England's racecourses, or Sir Walter Elliot, who thinks only of the social prestige that his estate bestows upon him, and not what he owes to it and to its dependent female residents.

When Elizabeth has had her fill of all these domestic and pastoral beauties, "they walked across the lawn towards the river," and she "turned back to look again; her uncle and aunt stopped also, and while the former was conjecturing as to the date of the building, the owner of it himself suddenly came forward from the road, which led behind it to the stables" (*PP*, 246, 249, 251). This abrupt arrival of "the owner himself" might well suggest something of the providential about it. In any case, there is something profoundly moving in the fact that Elizabeth has courageously allowed herself to spend time mourning what she supposed herself to have lost; she does so now without any sycophantic gratitude to Darcy, merely a frank and honest acknowledgment of the serious and important role she could have played as Pemberley's mistress.

Elizabeth's mourning is fully as much ethical as economic and aesthetic. Expanded ethical and functional opportunities would indeed, she assumes, have been hers. Instead of having to pander to a contemptuous father and a neurotic mother, she would have been offered an administrative post worthy of her conscience and her talents. But because she is willing to go through a painful process, which in modern psychology is beginning to be known as "the work of mourning," and to endure the final pain of her last look at her lost paradise, she gains it. The owner returns, and paradise may yet be hers.

After Darcy has spoken most courteously to her and to her beloved aunt and uncle, despite his embarrassment, and after he has engaged them for visits the next day, Elizabeth and the Gardiners tactfully leave "the present owner" to his magnificent estate. But now it is not merely beautiful in every way to Elizabeth; it is even *more* beautiful than she had previously thought, since shock has quickened her perceptions: "They had now entered a beautiful walk by the side of the water, and every step was bringing forward a *nobler* fall of ground, or a *finer* reach of the woods to which they were approaching; but it was some time before Elizabeth was sensible of any of it" (*PP*, 253; emphasis mine).

Elizabeth's mind is only intermittently upon these beauties so glowingly described in this monologue, half hers and half authorial. The other half of Elizabeth's mind yearns to know exactly what spot inside Pemberley its owner now graces. This scene represents one of those rare moments in Austen's fiction when a woman is actually observed standing outside, in her exile, debarred now from entering a privileged house of beauty and plenty, and condemned, she supposes, to return to a house of resentful parents and three shallow, bad-tempered sisters. Austen's scenic recognition of women's double jeopardy, incarceration or exile, is more likely to occur in scenes where women watch the men from garden plots or from windows, while these emancipated creatures come and go on foot or on horseback, upon their own freely chosen pursuits.

Austen's subtle grammatical distinctions between the positive degree—"large, handsome stone building" flanked by the "natural beauty of the setting"—and the superlative degree, with it sensation of a crescendo at its height, as the housekeeper describes the master of all these beauties in the superlative degree—"the best landlord, the finest master"—and then the falling sense of tumescence, in the mere comparative degree of exterior beauties, as in "a nobler fall of ground or a finer reach of woods," all suggest the symbolic postcoital *tristesse* that Elizabeth is now enduring. Austen's skillful management of grammatical forms symbolizing emotions that she was not allowed to express or even to know about as an unmarried woman, should have prevented all critical stereotypes about the sexless Miss Austen.

There is another fine pastoral scene, or rather two of them, when Elizabeth and Darcy achieve the reconciliation of lovers that is comparable to no other. Darcy, now free of all his false pride and prejudices, and Elizabeth now quickly freeing herself of the prickly defensiveness into which his insults have driven her, wander together over and beyond the boundaries of Longbourn plantation, having no idea how far they have gone or how long they have been out together. During both these scenes, Darcy does penance in a manner customarily thought necessary only for the female sex:

> As a child I was taught what was *right*, but left to follow right conduct in pride and conceit. Unfortunately an only son, (for many years an only *child*), I was spoilt by my parents, who though good in themselves . . . allowed, encouraged, even taught me to be selfish and overbearing, to care for none beyond my own family circle, to think meanly of all the rest of the world, to *wish* at least to think meanly of their sense and worth compared to my own. (*PP*, 369)

Darcy's monologue to Elizabeth, which goes on for one whole page, contains many phrases by which feminists had earlier made their charges against the male sex: "spoilt," "selfish," "overbearing," "taught to think meanly of [women's] sense and worth compared to [their] own" are accusations that could be found in almost any radical or moderate feminist tract. Elizabeth then comforts Darcy by reminding him that the "conduct of neither, if strictly examined, will be irreproachable," as indeed, hers has not been according either to contemporary or to modern orthodoxies about proper conduct in women. She is now too tactful to remind him that he had earlier provided her with endless "provocations" and that she had "some excuse for incivility if [she] *was* uncivil" (*PP*, 191). Now she acknowledges her mistake about Wickham, but she will not grovel even before the man she has won, and even as she earlier had grovelled in private, according to orthodox dictates about the immense and life-long gratitude that a woman in love owed to the man who had stooped to make her his wife.

Now the lovers' reconciliation is complete; and Elizabeth can lighten Darcy's profound sense of guilt with gentle wit—but not at his expense. They now wander on together, discussing the best ways to smooth over the relations between their adversarial families. As Austen said in another connection with another pair of reconciling lovers, most of us know where we are and what time it is during the passing hours, "yet with lovers it is different. Between *them* no subject is finished, no communication is even made, till it had been made at least twenty times over" (*SS*, 364).

Nowhere is the sense of Austenian context sharper than in Austen's pastoral scenes. In *Northanger Abbey*, the Beechen Cliff scene is more or less benevolent and it is distinctly understated. In *Sense and Sensibility*, Marianne's pastoral "season of love" is poignant and retrospectively haunting, as all lost hopes are. In *Pride and Prejudice*, they are triumphant. In *Mansfield Park*, the fine pastoral scenes at Sotherton are first disquieting, then ominous, and ultimately tragic in their social consequences for four different families, the Bertrams, the Rushworths, the Crawfords, and the Grants. In describing Sotherton plantations, Austen or her characters keep repeating the landscape gardening noun *wilderness* half a dozen times. Once it is called "serpentine" (*MP*, 94).

The Sotherton wilderness, a shady wood beyond the house palings, is ominous and yet rigidly landscaped, as an analogue for the rigidly stereotyped adultery that it is to produce. Yet even in these scenes, which create a midsummer day's dream and ultimately a nightmare, Austen provides her quiet pastoral magic. Mrs. Rushworth, of the stately simper and Mrs. Norris, the stereotypic witch-mother, argue about "the question of surveying the grounds, with the who and the how . . . by what junction of carriages and horses most could be done, when the young people, meeting with an outward door, temptingly open on a flight of steps which led immediately to turf and shrubs, and all the sweets of pleasure-grounds, as by one impulse, one wish for air and liberty, all walked out" (*MP*, 89–90). Even the grave and pompous Fanny Price and Edmund Bertram feel the same desire for air and liberty and for pastoral sweets as the scandal-makers, Henry Crawford and Maria Bertram.

Maria's conversation with Henry, while he tempts her to walk around a locked gate rather than to wait for Rushworth's "key" and "Rushworth's permission," is painful in the extreme. Henry does his best to get Maria to admit that she loves him, without declaring himself. Her response is tragic, not for herself alone, although it is that, but because it microcosmically expresses the feminine predicament: "I cannot get out, as the starling said" (*MP*, 99). Maria's quotation from Sterne's *Sentimental Journey* is grimly apt: the traveler at the Paris hotel cannot free the frantic starling from its cage: to do so would collapse the entire edifice of the cage. Both the starling and the traveler mournfully agree that nothing can be done, and that the bird must be left in its cage, wildly beating its wings against the bars.

The whole day leaves all the young people feeling sad and angry, for it has accomplished nothing they wanted. Henry has refused to free Maria from her cage; Edmund is still toying with the fascinating, but for him highly unsuitable Mary Crawford; Henry teases first Maria, then Julia, then Maria, then Julia, into thinking that each is his favorite; Rushworth, the bumbling suitor, is jealous on Maria's account as well he should be; and Fanny still does not know how Edmund feels about Mary. For Fanny, "the result of the whole was to her disappointment and depression"; for Rushworth, an understandable fit of the sullens; for Julia, who had been pursuing Henry and Maria with all the fervor of Helena as she pursues Demetrius during Shakespeare's midsummer series of mistaken madnesses, nothing but futile heat and breathlessness. These wanderers in the woods all emphasize the heat and the breathless quality of the day, as though they were anxiously awaiting something unpleasant—for Maria, utter disenchantment; for Edmund and Mary, merely more gentle but inexorable quarrels signifying two people with totally different values. At times, as the couples and trios swirled around the plantation, "there was gloom on the face of each." In fact, their "spirits were in general exhausted—and to determine whether the day had afforded most pleasure or pain, might occupy the meditations of almost all" (*MP*, 100–106).

To reconstruct the flawed paradise of Sotherton is not among Austen's purposes. To reconstruct the equally flawed paradise of Mansfield Park is her purpose, but she does not pretend that the reconstruction can ever be anything but partial, for paradise is never more than partially regained. After the grim London denouement of the married Maria's elopement with Henry Crawford, and after Edmund has been forced to renounce Mary Crawford, who sees hardly anything disruptive of the social commonwealth in what Maria and Henry have done, Edmund "talked his mind into submission." He is able to do so only after "wandering about and sitting under trees with Fanny all the summer evenings" (*MP*, 462). Edmund's marriage to Fanny brings domestic satisfaction and contentment. But it shares with other grave personal compromises that adults are often forced to make, its own capacity for lifelong retrospective sorrow. On a morally ravaged estate that is not his, Edmund cannot be a green-world lover.

There have been many useful comments upon the pastoral beauties of Knightley's Donwell Abbey, that "sweet view—sweet to the eye and the mind. English verdue, English culture, English comfort, seen under a sun bright without being oppressive." But what is the heroine's connection with Knightley's green world? To the sure, the novel offers its heroine a practical, sensible, blandly autocratic green-world lover, but Emma is shut out of that sweet view, so sweet to the eye and the mind. Emma has not been to Donwell Abbey, "about a mile from Highbury," for two years. After infinitely careful planning, which typifies her exasperating chore every time she leaves the house, she finally arranges to be able to go to Knightley's strawberry-picking party. This time, she accomplished the extraordinary miracle of persuading her father to accompany her: "Under a bright mid-day sun, at almost Midsummer, Mr. Woodhouse was safely conveyed in his carriage, with one window down, to partake of this al-fresco party. . . . It was so long since Emma had been at the Abbey, that as soon as she was satisfied of her father's comfort, she was glad to leave him and look around her" (*E*, 360, 356, 9, 357). Rare trips of this kind represent the utmost extent of Emma's garden province. She had never seen the ocean and never been to London, sixteen miles away.

The unfortunate trip to Box Hill, which produced in Emma and in Frank Churchill the same kind of bad temper that Sotherton produced on its owner and its guests, took place the day after Knightley's alfresco party. "Emma had never been to Box Hill; she wished to see what every body found so well worth seeing" (*E*, 352). Apparently her abrupt new freedom—two outings in two days, and Frank Churchill's enigmatic flirting, as deliberate and as meaningless as Wickham's, Willoughby's, Crawford's, or William Elliot's—upsets Emma's sense of feminine decorum. Her conduct to Miss Bates is as despicable as Darcy's was to Elizabeth Bennet. But inexcusable as her conduct is, she is in a genuine dilemma. Several of the moderate feminists had described this feminine dilemma precisely. Women's cages may drive them crazy, make them bad mannered and sometimes even ill. But too sudden liberty in the intoxicating fresh air and grateful expanses of the countryside, or any sudden liberty of any kind, intellectual or athletic, could be dangerous both to a woman and to her community, since she so frequently lived under easily combustible pressures of the Highbury sort. Box Hill was a mere seven miles from Highbury (*E*, 521).

One of the saddest scenes that cries out for attention takes place almost a year after Miss Taylor, Emma's governess, has become Mrs. Weston. The damp July evening, with its "cruel sights" of "cold gloomy rain," wears on. Emma is once again contemplating the loss of somebody else. If Knightley marries Harriet Smith, as she fancies he may, she will first have lost her mother, then her sister, then Miss Taylor, and then Knightley, who may be a benevolent tyrant, but who shares her wit and her deep concern for her father.

Emma's renewed grief and isolation in shallow, gossipy Highbury has brought her full circle. Once again, the evening "was very long and very melancholy at Hartfield," as it had been the evening after Mrs. Weston married (*E*, 421). Once again, she sits "in mournful thought" by her father's side, grieving for yet another impending loss and a sense of moral imprisonment for which her elders and mentors refuse to accept any responsibility.

"The weather continued much the same all the following morning: and the loneliness and the same melancholy," the same "intellectual solitude," the same lack of close companions Emma's age, who could "meet her in conversation either rational or playful" still "seemed to reign at Hartfield" as had reigned there a year ago, and once again, "she had only to sit and think what she had lost."

Suddenly the weather radically improved, and as though by one of those fortuitous moments in which Austen invests an almost providential benevolence otherwise often missing in her heroines' lives:

> the wind changed into a softer quarter; the clouds were carried off, the sun appeared; it was summer again. With all the eagerness which such a transition gives, Emma resolved to be out of doors as soon as possible. Never had the exquisite sight, smell, sensation, of nature tranquil, warm and brilliant after a storm, been more attractive to

> her. She longed for the serenity they might gradually introduce; and on Mr. Perry's coming in soon after dinner, with a disengaged hour to give her father, she lost no time in hurrying into the shubbery. (*E*, 5–6, 424)

The fresh winds and the July sun are largely in Emma's imagination; for she is locked indoors with her father, until Mr. Perry, another attendant of Mr. Woodhouse's, merely *happens* to have a disengaged hour to give him. Then she is able to escape into the garden, where Knightley finds her, and all mistakes and misunderstandings are resolved. But even after Emma's marriage, she will hardly ever be able to enjoy the view of Donwell Abbey, "sweet to the eye and to the mind," for she will be almost as inescapably locked by her father's side as she was before her marriage. Knightley, of course, that sturdy squire who can walk around his estate and her father's in all weathers, will do his best to see that she gets to enjoy the exquisite sight, smell, sensation, and freedom of tranquil nature, now and then, so that she can achieve "the serenity they might gradually introduce," which she will need far more desperately than her practical green-world lover.

In *Emma*, Austen created a heroine whose feminine predicament was to be largely barred from pastoral scenes, except when she could connive with half a dozen neighbors to persuade her father that she must have a day's or an hour's liberty. In *Persuasion*, the heroine's feminine predicament is exactly the opposite. Her father and her sister, her father's surrogate son, care so little for her that she is free to come and go about the estate almost at will, and to undertake all the responsibilities that could appropriately fall to the daughter of an irresponsible squire. Yet her own particular feminine predicament is hardly any more endurable than Emma's or Fanny Price's. For although Anne can roam the countryside to ease her own intellectual solitude, as Emma and Fanny cannot, this very freedom emphasizes that she is now living a life "of declining happiness," without any function or any appropriate companionship, male or female, mature or young. "An early loss of bloom and spirits had been [the] lasting effect," and "images of youth and hope, and spring, all gone together" (*P*, 28, 85). Lady Russell has proved herself untrustworthy as a surrogate mother, and although some lingering affection for her still resides in Anne's thoughts, trust had been destroyed. Wollstonecraft had already mournfully described Anne's particular kind of predicament: "Women have seldom sufficiently serious employment to silence their feelings," especially when they allow "the selfish prudence of age to chill the ardour of youth" (*Vindication*, 75).

Austen's management of the scenes at Lyme Regis is brilliant. Once again, the weather assumes a discreet pathetic fallacy. Anne's cheeks are now pink and freshened, not only by the sea breezes and her unaccustomed opportunity to travel and to be away from those comic monsters, her father and her sister, but by the equally unaccustomed interest in her that an attractive stranger bestows upon her so markedly as to make even Frederick Wentworth look at her anew. Wentworth has temporarily been afflicted with one of Darcy's gravest faults, a disinclination to give consequence to women unless he first perceives them to be of consequence to other men. But the new scenes, the fresh air and liberty that Anne now shares with other young people, and the infectious hilarity of the young people's spirits in the evening after the day's open-air pleasures are over, enliven even Anne's nostalgic spirits. And Frederick begins to contrast her with Louisa Musgrove.

The proposal scene takes places in a city rather than in the usual pastoral setting, the garden that belongs to the heroine's father. Nevertheless, bereft of a home though both these young people are, Austen manages to invest even the Bath gardens where the proposal takes place, with benedictory pastoral feelings: "soon enough words had passed between them to decide their direction towards the comparatively quiet and retired gravel-walk, where the power of conversation would make the present hour a blessing indeed; and prepare for all the immortality which the happiest recollections of their own future lives could bestow."

These newly reconciled lovers are as unaware of time and of anything else around them as Elinor Dashwood and Edward Ferrars had been, or Elizabeth and Darcy. Once again, Austen's authorial voice invokes the authority of an experienced lover: "There they returned again into the past, more exquisitely happy, perhaps in their re-union, than when it had been first projected; more tender, more tried, more fixed in a knowledge of each other's character, truth, and attachment; more equal to act, more justified in acting."

Austen's rare and deliberate invocation of "all the immortality" for which legitimate sexual joy may prepare its providentially blessed marriage partners—so rare an event is a happy marriage in Austen's social lexicon—is quite deliberate, and quite daring, for a woman. But just as her own heroine, twenty-seven years of age, transcended destructive feminine protocols when she paraphrased Wollstonecraft, who said "many sexual prejudices . . . tend to make women more constant than men" (*Vindication*, 31), so, Anne's creator, now dying in her early forties, has also transcended Johnsonian muzzles when she wants to do a little discreet preaching. While the newly engaged couple are oblivious of "sauntering politicians, bustling house-keepers, flirting girls . . . nursery-maids and children," they "slowly paced a gradual ascent," which functions as a spatial analogy for the gradual ascent toward "immortality" (*P*, 240–241), for which a loving marriage will prepare them.

Earthly life for Austen was but a preparation for immortal life, whether one's feminine luck brings one a monster of a husband, a sea-green lover, such as the charming and highly enterprising naval captain, Frederick Wentworth—or none. Of course, fictional tradition required that Jill should get her Jack, that the battle of the sexes should end in loving kindness, despite the bizarre compensatory equations built into every marriage, and, in Austen's case, that her Christian hope and her infectious joy should triumph over her rational social cynicism. But her craft is so polished that she carefully prepares enough moral metamorphoses in her courting couples to justify their journey to the archetypal altar—one place, Austen believed, where social redemption, in preparation for eternal redemption, ought to begin.

Notes

PREFACE AND ACKNOWLEDGMENTS

1. Readers interested in examining theories of male satire might consult a few standard texts such as Frederick Kiley and J. M. Shuttleworth, *Satire: From Aesop to Buchwald*; Gilbert Highet, *The Anatomy of Satire;* John Russell and Ashley Brown, *Satire: A Critical Anthology*. Other sources that are useful, although brief, include literary handbooks, dictionaries, and glossaries of literary terms, in their latest editions. Specialists in the theories and practices of female satire need more studies on the subject than they are now likely to find on most library shelves.

2. Leroy Smith, *Jane Austen and the Drama of Woman* (New York: St. Martin's, 1983), 25.

3. See the following essays in David Monaghan's anthology, *Jane Austen in a Social Context* (Totowa, N.J.: Barnes & Noble, 1981): Nina Auerbach, "Jane Austen and Romantic Imprisonment," 23; Leroy Smith, "*Mansfield Park*, The Revolt of the 'Feminine' Woman," 144, 157; Tony Tanner, "In Between—Anne Elliot Marries a Sailor and Charlotte Heywood Goes to the Seaside," 193; David Monaghan, "Jane Austen and the Position of Women," 105, 107.

4. Mary Evans, *Jane Austen and the State* (London: Tavistock), 80–81, 53.

CHAPTER 1

1. George Macaulay Trevelyan, *History of England*, vol. 3 (Garden City, N.Y.: Doubleday, 1953), 81–91. Mary Hays, *Appeal to the Men of Great Britain*

in Behalf of Women (1798), in *The Feminist Controversy in England 1788–1810*, ed. with an introduction by Gina Luria (New York: Garland, 1974), "Introduction," 8; "A Note on the Authorship," 21–22.

2. Catherine Macaulay, *Letters on Education* (1790), in *The Feminist Controversy in England 1788–1810*, ed. with an introduction by Gina Luria (New York: Garland, 1974), "Introduction," 6.

3. Mary Hays, *Appeal to the Men of Great Britain in Behalf of Women*, "Introduction," 13.

4. Katherine M. Rogers, *Feminism in Eighteenth-Century England* (Urbana: University of Illinois Press, 1982), 218; Richard Polwhele, "The Unsex'd Females," (London: Caldwell & Davies, 1798), micropublished in "History of Women" (New Haven, Conn.: Research Publications, 1975), 6–9, 17–20.

5. Hays, *Appeal to the Men of Great Britain*, "Introduction," 12.

6. Antonia Fraser, *The Weaker Vessel* (New York: Vintage, 1984), 453.

7. Priscilla Wakefield, *Reflections on the Present Condition of the Female Sex* (1798), in *The Feminist Controversy in England 1788–1810*, ed. with an introduction by Gina Luria (New York: Garland, 1974), 2.

8. William Duff, *Letters on the Intellectual and Moral Character of Women* (1807), in *The Feminist Controversy in England 1788–1810*, ed. with an introduction by Gina Luria (New York: Garland, 1974), 274.

9. Thomas Gisborne, *An Enquiry into the Duties of the Female Sex* (1797), in *The Feminist Controversy in England 1788–1810*, ed. with an introduction by Gina Luria (New York: Garland, 1974), 58, 226–227.

10. John Bennett, *Strictures on Female Education* (1795) (New York: Source Book Press, A Division of Collectors' Editions, 1971), 107.

11. Jane West, *Letters to a Young Lady* (2nd ed., 1806), in *The Feminist Controversy in England 1788–1810*, ed. with an introduction by Gina Luria (New York: Garland, 1974), 2: 335, 264–265; 1: 70.

12. Ellen Pollak, *The Poetics of Sexual Myth: Gender and Ideology in the Verse of Swift and Pope*, *Women in Culture and Society*, ed. Catherine Stimpson (Chicago: The University of Chicago Press, 1985), 2.

13. John Locke, *An Essay Concerning Human Understanding* (1690), ed. Alexander Campbell Fraser, 2nd ed. (New York: Dover, 1959), 1: 8–9; Locke, *Two Treatises of Government*, ed. Peter Laslett, 2nd ed. (Cambridge: University of Cambridge Press, 1967), book II, sections 47, 82.

14. Mary Wollstonecraft, *A Vindication of the Rights of Woman* (1792), ed. Carol Poston (New York: W. W. Norton, 1975), 4.

15. See, for example, Katherine M. Rogers, *Feminism in Eighteenth-Century England*, 22.

16. Margaret Kirkham, *Jane Austen: Feminism and Fiction* (Totowa, N.J.: Barnes & Noble Books, 1983), 33.

17. Jane Austen, *Letters*, Index II: "Other Persons," under "Fowle, Rev. Thomas" (1) and (2), and "Fowle, Rev. Fulwar Craven," n.p.

18. Jane Aiken Hodge, *Only a Novel: The Double Life of Jane Austen*, (New York: Coward, McCann & Geoghegan, 1972), 50; James Edward Austen-Leigh, *Memoir*, ed. R. W. Chapman (Oxford: Clarendon Press, 1926), 27.

19. James Fordyce, *Sermons to Young Women*, 6th ed. (Dublin: J. Williams, 1767), 2: 9, 13.

20. John Burton, *Lectures on Female Education and Manners* (1793), 2nd ed. (New York: Source Book Press, A Division of Collectors' Editions, 1970), 1: 169.

21. Robert Polhemus, "Jane Austen's Comedy," *The Jane Austen Companion*, ed. J. David Grey, A. Walton Litz, and Brian Southam (New York: Macmillan, 1986), 61–62.

22. John Locke, *Some Thoughts Concerning Education, Vol. IX, Section 9, The Works of John Locke* (1693) (London: Tegg, W. Sharpe and Son, 1823).

23. John Gregory, *A Father's Legacy to His Daughters* (1774), in *The Feminist Controversy in England 1788–1810*, ed. with an introduction by Gina Luria (New York: Garland, 1974), 104–108, 36.

24. Hodge, *Only a Novel*, 177.

25. Elizabeth Fox Genovese, "Culture and Consciousness in the Intellectual History of European Women," *Signs: Journal of Women in Culture and Society*, 12 (Spring 1987): 538–539.

26. Maria Edgeworth, "Letter to a Gentleman from his Friend, upon the Birth of a Daughter," *Letters for Literary Ladies* (1795), in *The Feminist Controversy in England 1788–1810*, ed. with an introduction by Gina Luria (New York: Garland, 1974), 15.

27. George Saville, Marquis of Halifax, *The Lady's New-Years'-Gift or Advice to a Daughter*, 4th ed. (London: M. Gilly-Flower & B. Tooke, 1699), 31–32.

28. Hannah More, *Strictures on the Modern System of Female Education* (1799), in *The Feminist Controversy in England 1788–1810*, ed. with an introduction by Gina Luria (New York: Garland, 1974), 1: 4, 135.

29. James Boswell, *Boswell's Life of Johnson*, 2 vols., with an introduction by Sir Sydney Roberts (London: J. M. Dent, 1949), 2: 469.

30. Susan Groag Bell and Karen M. Offen, *Women, The Family, and Freedom: The Debates in Documents, vol. 1: 1750–1880* (Stanford: Stanford University Press, 1983), 33, 299.

31. Edgeworth, *Letters for Literary Ladies*, "Introduction," 5–7. See also Marilyn Butler's biographical entry in Janet Todd's *Dictionary of British and American Women*.

32. Alexander Pope, *The Rape of the Lock, Poetry and Prose of Alexander Pope*, ed. Aubrey Williams (Boston: Houghton Mifflin, 1969), Canto II, 19–32.

33. Jane Austen, *Minor Works*, table of contents, I, "Juvenilia," n.p.

34. Nina Auerbach, "O Brave New World: Evolution and Revolution in *Persuasion*," *ELH*, 39 (1) (1972): 125, 124, 126.

CHAPTER 2

1. Margaret Kirkham, "Contemporary Feminism," *The Jane Austen Companion*, ed. David Grey, A. Walton Litz, and Brian Southam (New York: Macmillan, 1986), 154–158.

2. *A Dictionary of British and American Women Writers 1660–1800*, ed. Janet Todd (Totowa, N.J.: Roman & Allenheld, 1985).

3. *Dictionary of National Biography*, 1973 ed.

4. Mary Astell, *Some Reflections upon Marriage*, 4th ed. 1700 (New York: Source Book Press, a Division of Collectors' Editions, 1970), 39–40.

5. Mary Astell, *A Serious Proposal to the Ladies for the Advancement of their Truest and Greatest Interest* (1698) (New York: Spruce Book Press, 1970), 39–40.

6. Elizabeth Hamilton, *Letters Addressed to the Daughter of a Nobleman* (1806), in *The Feminist Controversy in England 1788–1810*, ed. with an introduction by Gina Luria (New York: Garland, 1974), 1: 22.

7. Clara Reeve, *Plans of Education* (1792), in *The Feminist Controversy in England*, ed. with an introduction by Gina Luria (New York: Garland, 1974), 23, 17–19.

8. Dale Spender, *Mothers of the Novel: 100 Good Women Writers Before Jane Austen* (New York: Routledge & Kegan Paul, in association with Methuen, 1986), 64–65, 119–137.

9. Frances Burney, *Cecilia: Or Memoirs of an Heiress*, with an introduction by Judy Simons (New York: Penguin Books, 1986), xi.

10. Burney, *Cecilia*, vii–viii.

11. Katherine Rogers, *Feminism in Eighteenth-Century England*, 7–10.

12. Maria Edgeworth, *Belinda*, with an introduction by Eva Figes (London: Pandora Press: Routledge & Kegan Paul, 1986), 409.

13. Burney, *Camilla: or a Picture of Youth*, ed. with an introduction by Edward Bloom and Lillian D. Bloom (Oxford: Oxford University Press, 1983), 254–255, 456, 367.

14. Yasmine Gooneratne, *Jane Austen* (Cambridge: Cambridge University Press, 1970), 19, 7.

CHAPTER 3

1. Janet Todd, *Women's Friendship in Literature* (New York: Columbia University Press, 1980), 401.

2. Hodge, *Only a Novel*, 21–22, and family tree inside front cover.

3. Hodge, *Only a Novel*, illustrations after page 128; David Cecil, *A Portrait of Jane Austen* (New York: Hill & Wang, 1980), 54.

4. D. W. Harding, "Regulated Hatred: An Aspect of the Work of Jane Austen," *Jane Austen: A Collection of Critical Essays (Twentieth-Century Views)*, ed. Ian Watt (Englewood Cliffs, N.J.: Prentice-Hall, 1963), 166–179.

5. Annis Pratt, *Archetypal Patterns in Women's Fiction* (Bloomington: Indiana University Press, 1981), 45.

6. Hodge, *Only a Novel*, 77, 186, 194; David Waldron Smithers, "Medicine," *The Jane Austen Companion*, ed. J. David Grey, A. Walton Litz, and Brian Southam (New York: Macmillan, 1986), 305.

7. Caroline G. Heilbrun, *Toward a Recognition of Androgyny* (New York: Harper & Row, 1974), 76, 7.

CHAPTER 4

1. For a judicious study of this subject, as well as a rich bibliography, see Barbara Brandon Schnorrenberg, "Thoughts on the Education of Daughters," *Proceedings of the Consortium on Revolutionary Europe: 1750–1850*, ed. Warren Spencer (Athens: University of Georgia Press, 1983), 269–289). Professor Schnorrenberg offers a more sanguine vision of women's education than I do,

but she is describing actual improvements for all classes of women, whereas I am describing the prevalent orthodox vision with which Austen was familiar through her sermon reading and her ecclesiastical connections. Her satire on this subject in her correspondence and her fiction indicates that she saw the destructive effects of the orthodox female education often enough to disturb her.

2. Leroy Smith, *Jane Austen and the Drama of Woman*, chapter 6.

3. Fordyce, *Sermons to Young Women*, 2: 9; Bennett, *Female Education*, 19; Gisborne, *Duties of the Female Sex*, 270.

4. Ruth Kelso, *Doctrine for the Lady of the Renaissance*, with a foreword by Katherine M. Rogers (Urbana: University of Illinois Press, 1978), 25.

5. For a title by a modern author that deliberately catches the historical spirit of the post-Enlightenment feminist controversy, see Edgar J. MacDonald, *The Education of the Heart: The Correspondence of Rachel Mordecai Lazarus and Maria Edgeworth* (Chapel Hill: University of North Carolina Press, 1977), a correspondence that succinctly records the moderate feminists' ambivalence toward women's predicament.

6. Leroy Smith, *Jane Austen and the Drama of Woman*, 38.

7. Wollstonecraft, *Thoughts on the Education of Daughters* (1787), in *The Feminist Controversy in England 1788–1810*, ed. with an introduction by Gina Luria (New York: Garland, 1974), 112.

8. Joseph Litvak, "Reading Characters: Self, Society and Text in *Emma*," *PMLA*, (October 1985): 764.

CHAPTER 5

1. Robert Polhemus, "Jane Austen's Comedy," *The Jane Austen Companion*, 67.

2. William Walling, "The Glorious Anxiety of Motion: Jane Austen's *Persuasion*," *The Wordsworth Circle*, 7: 4 (1976), 336.

3. F. B. Pinion, *A Jane Austen Companion* (London: Macmillan, 1979), 48.

CHAPTER 6

1. David Monaghan, *Jane Austen: Structure and Social Vision* (New York: Harper & Row, 1980), 111.

2. Macaulay, *Letters on Education*, "Introduction," 6–7.

3. There is a discreet moment in *Pride and Prejudice* where Elizabeth just escapes catching Jane and Bingley in the act of embracing, after Bingley has finally proposed. Austen knew all there was to know about sexual attraction between the two sexes. At moments of sexual stress, both Anne Elliot and Fanny Price breathe in quick pants. The sexual yearnings of Elizabeth and Darcy are so obvious, once he has returned to Longbourn, that readers yearn with them to overcome the suspense. Julia Prewitt Brown has repeatedly described how Austen's couples who are attempting an affectionate and sexual rapprochement with each other continually seek each other out with their eyes. Austen knew quite clearly that eyes are not only the windows of the soul but the windows of sexual longings and aspirations.

The idea that there is no sexual atmosphere in Austen's novels is a phallic one, which has to do with the masculine consummation of the sex act. It fails to acknowledge the way sexual feelings and intimations are everywhere, in looks, gazes, speech, gesture, intonation, even silence, when two people are in love. See Julia Prewitt Brown, *Jane Austen's Novels* (Cambridge: Harvard University Press, *passim*).

CHAPTER 7

1. Marion Morrison, "Gardens," *The Jane Austen Companion*, 184.

2. Gisborne, *Duties of the Female Sex*, 90–91. "To dag" was a Middle English verb meaning, among other things, "To clog with dirt, bemire." The noun meant "one of the locks of wool with dirt about the hinder parts of a sheep." See *Old English Dictionary*, 3rd ed., 1947.

3. See Lawrence Stone, *The Family, Sex and Marriage in England: 1500–1800*, 444–446; Phyllis Stock, *Better than Rubies: A History of Women's Education*, 99; Josephine Kamm, *Hope Deferred: Girls' Education in English History*, 126–127; Murial Jaeger, *Before Victoria*, 167.

4. Barbara Hardy, "Properties and Possessions in Jane Austen's Novels," *Jane Austen's Achievement*, ed. Juliet McMasters, *Papers Delivered at the Bicentennial Conference of Alberta* (New York: Harper & Row, 1976), 84–85.

5. Annis Pratt, *Archetypal Patterns in Women's Fiction*, with Barbara Whitt, Andrea Lowenstein, and Mary Wyer (Bloomington: Indiana University Press, 1981), 16–17.

Bibliography

Adventurer, The. See Johnson, Samuel.

Agress, Lynne. *The Feminine Irony* (Rutherford, N.J.: Fairleigh Dickinson University Press, 1978).

Astell, Mary. *A Serious Proposal to the Ladies for the Advancement of their True and Greatest Interest* (1694) (New York: Source Book Press, A Division of Collectors' Editions, 1970).

———. *Some Reflections upon Marriage*. 4th ed. 1700 (New York: Source Book Press, A Division of Collectors' Editions, 1970).

Auerbach, Nina. *Communities of Women: An Idea in Fiction* (Cambridge: Harvard University Press, 1978).

———. "Jane Austen and Romantic Imprisonment," *Jane Austen in a Social Context*, ed. David Monaghan (London: Macmillan, 1981), 9–27.

———. "O Brave New World: Evolution and Revolution in Persuasion." *ELH*, 39 (1972): 112–128.

Austen, Caroline. *My Aunt Jane Austen: A Memoir* (London: Spottiswoode, Ballantyne, 1952).

Austen, Jane. *Jane Austen's Letters to her Sister Cassandra and Others*, ed. R. W. Chapman, 2nd ed. (London: Oxford University Press, 1952; rpt. 1969).

———. *The Novels of Jane Austen*, ed. R. W. Chapman, 3rd ed., 5 vols. (London: Oxford Univesity Press, 1932–1934).

———. *The Works of Jane Austen*. Vol. 6: *Minor Works*, ed. R. W. Chapman (London: Oxford University Press, 1954).

Austen-Leigh, James Edward. *Memoir of Jane Austen by her Nephew James Edward Austen-Leigh* (London: Oxford University Press, 1926; rpt. 1967).

Austen-Leigh, William, and Richard Arthur Austen-Leigh. *Jane Austen: Her Life and Letters, A Family Record*, 2nd ed. (New York: Russell & Russell, 1965).

Babb, Howard. *Jane Austen's Novels & the Fabric of Dialogue* (Columbus: Ohio State University Press, 1962).

Basch, Françoise. *Relative Creatures: Victorian Women in Society and the Novel* (1837–67), trans. Anthony Rudolf (London: Allen Lane, 1974).

Beer, Patricia. *Reader, I Married Him: A Study of the Women Characters of Jane Austen, Charlotte Bronte, Elizabeth Gaskell and George Eliot* (London: Macmillan, 1974).

Bell, Susan Groag, and Karen M. Offen. *Women, The Family, and Freedom: The Debate in Documents, Volume 1: 1750–1880* (Stanford: Stanford University Press, 1983).

Benkovitz, Miriam. "Some Observations on Women's Concept of Self in the 18th Century," *Woman in the 18th Century and Other Essays*, ed. Paul Fritz and Richard Morton (Toronto: Hakkert, 1976), 37–54.

Bennett, John. *Strictures on Female Education: Chiefly as it Relates to the Culture of the Heart* (New York: Source Book Press, A Division of Collectors' Editions, 1971; rpt. from Worchester, 1795).

Boswell, James. *Boswell's Life of Johnson*, 2 vols., with an introduction by Sir Sydney Roberts (London: J. M. Dent, 1949).

Brown, Julia Prewitt. *Jane Austen's Novels: Social Change and Literary Form* (Cambridge: Harvard University Press, 1979).

Burney, Frances. *Camilla: or a Picture of Youth*, ed. with an introduction by Edward A. Bloom and Lillian Bloom (New York: Oxford University Press, 1983).

———. *Cecilia: or, Memoirs of an Heiress*, with an introduction by Judy Simons (New York: Penguin-Virago Press, 1986).

———. *Evelina: or, The History of a Young Lady's Entrance into the World* (New York: W. W. Norton, 1965).

Burton, John. *Lectures on Female Education and Manners*, 2nd ed., 2 vol. (New York: Source Book Press, 1970; rpt. from London, 1793).

Butler, Marilyn. *Jane Austen and the War of Ideas* (London: Oxford University Press, 1975).

Castiglione, Baldesar. *The Book of the Courtier*, trans. by Leonard Epstein (New York: Scribner's, 1903).

Cecil, David. *A Portrait of Jane Austen* (New York: Hill & Wang, 1980).

Chapman, R. W. *Jane Austen: Facts and Problems* (London: Oxford University Press, 1948; rpt. 1970).

de Beauvoir, Simone. *The Second Sex*, ed. and trans. by H. M. Parshley (New York: Scribner's, 1953).

Dictionary of British and American Women Writers. See Todd.

Duckworth, Alistair. *The Improvement of the Estate: A Study of Jane Austen's Novels* (Baltimore: The Johns Hopkins University Press, 1971).

Duff, William. *Letters on the Intellectual and Moral Character of Women*. In *The Feminist Controversy in England 1788–1810*, ed. with an introduction by Gina Luria (New York: Garland, 1974; rpt. from Aberdeen, 1807).

Edgeworth, Maria. *Belinda*, with an introduction by Eva Figes (London: Pandora Press: Routledge & Kegal Paul, 1986).

———. *Letters for Literary Ladies.* In *The Feminist Controversy in England 1788–1810*, 2nd ed., ed. with an introduction by Gina Luria (New York: Garland, 1974; rpt. from London, 1795).

Evans, Mary. *Jane Austen and the State* (London: Tavistock, 1987).

Ferguson, Moira. *First Feminists: British Women Writers 1578–1799* (Bloomington: Indiana University Press, 1985).

Fleishman, Avrom. *A Reading of Mansfield Park: An Essay in Critical Synthesis* (Minneapolis: University of Minnesota Press, 1967).

Fordyce, James D. D. *Sermons to Young Women*, vol. 2, 6th ed. (Dublin: J. Williams, 1767).

Fraser, Antonia. *The Weaker Vessell* (New York: Vintage, 1984).

Garrod, H. W. "Jane Austen: A Depreciation," *Essays by Divers Hands: Being the Transactions of the Royal Society of Literature of the United Kingdom*, ed. Laurence Binyon, n.s. 7 (London: Humphrey Milford, 1928), 29–40.

Genovese, Elizabeth Fox. "Culture and Consciousness in the Intellectual History of European Women," *Signs: Journal of Women in Culture and Society*, 12 (Spring 1987): 529–547.

Gilbert, Sandra, and Susan Gubar. *The Mad Woman in the Attic: The Woman Writer in the Nineteenth-Century Literary Imagination* (New Haven: Yale University Press, 1979).

———. *The Norton Anthology of Literature by Women: The Tradition in English*, "Middle Ages and Renaissance [introduction]," 2–15; "The Seventeenth and Eighteenth Centuries [introduction]," 161–186 (New York: W. W. Norton, 1985).

Gisborne, Thomas M. A. *An Enquiry into the Duties of the Female Sex. In The Feminist Controversy in England 1788–1810*, ed. with an introduction by Gina Luria (New York: Garland, 1974; rpt. from London, 1797).

Gooneratne, Yasmine. *Jane Austen* (London: Cambridge University Press, 1970).

Greene, Donald. "The Myth of Limitation," *Jane Austen Today*, ed. Joel Weinsheimer (Athens: University of Georgia Press, 1975), 142–175.

Gregory, John, Dr. *A Father's Legacy to His Daughters.* In *The Feminist Controversy in England 1788–1810*, ed. with an introduction by Gina Luria (New York: Garland, 1974; rpt. from London, 1774).

Gubar, Susan. "The Female Monster in Augustan Satire," *Signs: Journal of Women in Culture and Society*, 3 (Winter 1977): 380–349.

Halifax, Marquis of [George Saville]. *The Lady's New-Year's-Gift or Advice to a Daughter*, 4th ed. (London: M. Gilly-Flower & B. Tooke, 1699).

Halperin, John. *Jane Austen: Bicentenary Essays* (London: Cambridge University Press, 1975).

———. *The Life of Jane Austen* (Baltimore: The Johns Hopkins University Press, 1984).

Hamilton, Elizabeth. *Letters Addressed to the Daughter of a Nobleman on the Formation of the Religious and the Moral Principle.* In *The Feminist Controversy in England 1788–1810*, ed. with an introduction by Gina Luria (New York: Garland, 1974; rpt. from London, 1806).

Harding, D. W. "Regulated Hatred: An Aspect of the Work of Jane Austen,"

Jane Austen: A Collection of Critical Essays (Twentieth Century Views), ed. Ian Watt (Englewood Cliffs, N.J.: Prentice-Hall, 1963), 166–179.

Hardy, Barbara. "Properties and Possessions in Jane Austen's Novels," *Jane Austen's Achievement*, ed. Juliet McMasters, *Papers Delivered at the Bicentennial Conference of Alberta* (New York: Harper & Row, 1976), 84–85.

———. *A Reading of Jane Austen* (London: Peter Owen, 1975).

Harris, Jocelyn. "Anne Elliot, the Wife of Bath and other Friends," *Jane Austen: New Perspectives: Women & Literature: New Series*, ed. Janet Todd, vol. 3 (New York: Holmes & Meier, 1983), 272–294.

Hays, Mary. *Appeal to the Men of Great Britain in Behalf of Women*. In *The Feminist Controversy in England 1788–1810*, ed. with an introduction by Gina Luria (New York: Garland, 1974; rpt. from London, 1798).

———. *Letters and Essays, Moral and Miscellaneous*. In *The Feminist Controversy in England 1788–1810*, ed. with an introduction by Gina Luria (New York: Garland, 1974; rpt. from London, 1793).

Heilbrun, Caroline G. *Toward a Recognition of Androgyny* (New York: Harper & Row, 1974).

Hodge, Jane Aiken. *Only a Novel: The Double Life of Jane Austen* (New York: Coward, McCann & Geoghegan, 1972).

Jaeger, Muriel. *Before Victoria* (London: Chatto & Windus, 1956).

Jane Austen Companion, The. See Kirkham; Morrison; Polhemus; and Smithers.

Jenkins, Elizabeth. *Jane Austen: A Biography* (London: Victor Gollancz, 1968).

Johnson, Samuel. *The Idler and The Adventurer*, ed. J. Bae, John Bullitt, and L. F. Powell (New Haven: Yale University Press, 1963).

———. *The Rambler*, II, ed. W. J. Bates and Albrecht B. Strauss, *The Yale Edition of the Works of Samuel Johnson*, vol. 4 (New Haven: Yale University Press, 1969).

Kamm, Josephine. *Hope Deferred: Girls' Education in English History* (London: Methuen, 1965).

Kelso, Ruth. *Doctrine for the Lady of the Renaissance*, with a foreword by Katherine Rogers (Urbana: University of Illinois Press, 1975).

Kirkham, Margaret. "Jane Austen and Contemporary Feminism," *The Jane Austen Companion* (New York: Macmillan, 1986), 154–159.

———. *Jane Austen: Feminism and Fiction* (Towota, N.J.: Barnes & Noble, 1983).

———. "The Austen Portraits and the Received Biography," *Jane Austen: New Perspectives: Women & Literature, New Series*, ed. Janet Todd, vol. 3 (New York: Holmes & Meier, 1983).

Laski, Marghanita. *Jane Austen* (London: Thames and Hudson, 1975).

Litvak, Joseph. "Reading Characters: Self, Society and Text in *Emma*," *PMLA* (October 1985): 763–771.

Locke, John. *An Essay Concerning Human Understanding* (1690), collated and annotated with Prolegomena, Biographical, Critical and Historical, by Alexander Campbell Fraser, 2nd ed., 2 vols. (New York: Dover, 1959).

———. *Letters on Toleration* (1689–1692), *The Works of John Locke*, vol. 6 (London: Tegg, W. Sharpe and Son, 1823; rpt. Scientia Verlag Aalen, Germany, 1963).

———. *Some Thoughts Concerning Education* (1693), *The Works of John Locke*, vol.

9 (London: printed for Tegg, W. Sharpe and Son, 1823; rpt. Scientia Verlag Aalen, Germany, 1963).

———. *Two Treatises on Government* (1690). A critical edition with an introduction and apparatus cricitus by Peter Laslett, 2nd ed. (Cambridge: University of Cambridge Press, 1967).

Macaulay, Catherine. *Letters on Education: With Observations on Religious and Metaphysical Subjects.* In *The Feminist Controversy in England 1788–1810*, ed. with an introduction by Gina Luria (New York: Garland, 1974; rpt. from London, 1790).

MacDonald, Edgar J. *The Education of the Heart: The Correspondence of Rachel Mordecai Lazarus and Maria Edgeworth* (Chapel Hill: University of North Carolina Press, 1977).

Mingay, G. E. *English Landed Society in the Eighteenth Century* (London: Routledge & Kegan Paul, 1963).

Moers, Ellen. *Literary Women* (New York: Doubleday, 1976).

Monaghan, David. "Jane Austen and the Position of Women," *Jane Austen in a Social Context*, ed. David Monaghan (Towota, N.J.: Barnes & Noble, 1981), 105–121.

———. *Jane Austen: Structure and Social Vision* (New York: Harper & Row, 1980).

More, Hannah. *Strictures on the Modern System of Female Education.* In *The Feminist Controversy in England 1788–1810*, ed. with an introduction by Gina Luria (New York: Garland, 1974; rpt. from London, 1799).

Morrison, Marion. "Gardens." *The Jane Austen Companion*, ed. David Grey, A Walton Litz, and Brian Southam (New York: Macmillan, 1986), 184–186.

Murdrick, Marvin. *Jane Austen: Irony as Defense and Discovery* (Berkeley and Los Angeles: University of California Press, 1968).

Nussbaum, Felicity A. *The Brink of All We Hate: English Satires on Women 1660–1750* (Lexington: University Press of Kentucky, 1984).

Paris, Bernard. *Character and Conflict in Jane Austen's Novels: A Psychological Approach* (Detroit, Mich.: Wayne State University Press, 1978).

Perry, Ruth. *Women, Letters and the Novel* (New York: AMS Press, 1980).

Pinion, F. B. *A Jane Austen Companion* (London: Macmillan, 1979).

Plumb, J. H. *England in the Eighteenth Century (1714–1815)*, *The Pelican History of England* (Baltimore: Penguin Books, 1966).

Polhemus, Robert. "Jane Austen's Comedy," *The Jane Austen Companion*, ed. J. David Grey, Walton Litz, and Brian Southam (New York: Macmillan, 1986), 60–71.

Pollak, Ellen. *The Poetics of Sexual Myth: Gender and Ideology in the Verse of Swift and Pope*, *Women in Culture and Society* (Chicago: University of Chicago Press, 1985).

Polwhele, Richard. "The Unsex'd Females" (London: Caldwell & Davies, 1798), micropublished in "History of Women" (New Haven, Conn.: Research Publications, Inc., 1975).

Poovey, Mary. *The Proper Lady and the Woman Writer: Ideology and Style in the Works of Mary Wollstonecraft, Mary Shelley, and Jane Austen* (Chicago: University of Chicago Press, 1985).

Pope, Alexander. *Poetry and Prose of Alexander Pope*, selected with an introduction and notes by Aubrey Williams (Boston: Houghton Mifflin, 1969).
Pratt, Annis. *Archetypal Patterns in Women's Fiction*, with Barbara White, Andrea Lowenstein, and Mary Wyer (Bloomington: Indiana University Press, 1981).
Rambler, The. See Johnson, Samuel.
Reeve, Clara. *Plans of Education*. In *The Feminist Controversy in England 1788–1810*, ed. with an introduction by Gina Luria (New York: Garland, 1974; rpt. from London, 1792).
Rogers, Katherine M. *Before Their Time: Six Women Writers of the Eighteenth Century*, ed. Katherine Rogers (New York: Unger, 1979).
———. *Feminism in Eighteenth-Century England* (Urbana: University of Illinois Press, 1982).
Saville, George. See Halifax, Marquis of.
Scott, Walter. "*Emma*," unsigned review. *Quarterly Review*, March 1815, xiv, 188–201); rpt. *Jane Austen: The Critical Heritage*, ed. B. C. Southam (London: Routledge & Kegan Paul, 1968), 58–69.
Shanley, Mary Lyndon. "Suffrage, Protective Labor Legislation and Married Woman's Property Law in England," *Signs: Journal of Women in Culture and Society*, 12 (Autumn 1968): 62–77.
Smith, Leroy. *Jane Austen and the Drama of Women* (New York: St. Martin's, 1983).
———. "*Mansfield Park:* The Revolt of the 'Feminine' Woman," *Jane Austen in a Social Context*, ed. David Monaghan (Totowa, N.J.: Barnes & Noble, 1981), 143–158.
Smithers, David Waldron. "Medicine," *The Jane Austen Companion*, ed. J. David Grey, A. Walton Litz, and Brian Southam (New York: Macmillan, 1986), 305.
Southam, B. C. *Jane Austen: The Critical Heritage* (London: Routledge & Kegan Paul, 1968).
———. *Critical Essay on Jane Austen* (London: Routledge & Kegan Paul, 1968).
Spacks, Patricia Meyer. *The Female Imagination* (New York: Knopf, 1975).
Spectator, The. Ed. Donald Bond, 5 vols. (Oxford: Oxford University Press, 1963–1965).
Spender, Dale. *Mothers of the Novel: 100 Good Women Writers Before Jane Austen* (New York: Routledge & Kegan Paul, in association with Methuen, 1986).
Stock, Phyllis. *Better Than Rubies: A History of Women's Education* (New York: Putnam, 1978).
Stone, Lawrence. *The Family, Sex and Marriage in England: 1500–1800* (New York: Harper & Row, 1977).
Sulloway, Alison G. "Emma Woodhouse and *A Vindication of the Rights of Woman*," *The Wordsworth Circle*, 7 (Autumn 1976): 320–332.
———. "Jane Austen's Mediative Voice," *Nineteenth Century Women Writers in the English Speaking World*, ed. Rhoda Nathan (Westport, Conn.: Greenwood Press, 1986).
Swift, Jonathan. *The Writings of Jonathan Swift*, ed. Robert A. Greenbert and William Bowman Piper (New York: W. W. Norton, 1973).
Tanner, Tony. "In Between—Anne Elliot Marries a Sailor and Charlotte Hey-

wood Goes to the Seaside," *Jane Austen in a Social Context*, ed. David Monaghan (Totowa, N.J.: Barnes & Noble, 1981), 180–194.

Tatler, The. Ed. with an introduction and notes by George Aitken (1898–1899), 4 vols.; rpt. *Anglistica & America* (Hildesheim: Georg Olms, 1970).

Todd, Janet. *Dictionary of British and American Women Writers 1660–1800* (Totowa, N.J.: Roman & Allanheld, 1985).

———. *Jane Austen: New Perspectives: Women & Literature: New Series*, vol. 3 (Holmes & Meier, 1983).

———. *Women's Friendship in Literature* (New York: Columbia University Press, 1980).

Trevelyan, George Macaulay. *History of England*, vol. 3 (Garden City, N.Y.: Doubleday, 1953).

Trilling, Lionel. "*Mansfield Park*," *Jane Austen: A Collection of Critical Essays*, ed. Ian Watt (Englewood Cliffs, N.J.: Prentice-Hall, 1963), 124–140.

———, ed. *Emma*, with an introduction by Lionel Trilling (Boston: Houghton Mifflin, 1957).

Wakefield, Priscilla. *Reflections on the Present Condition of the Female Sex*. In *The Feminist Controversy in England 1788–1810*, ed. with an introduction by Gina Luria (New York: Garland, 1974; rpt. from London, 1798).

Walling, William. "The Glorious Anxiety of Motion: Jane Austen's *Persuasion*," *The Wordsworth Circle*, 7: 4 (1976): 333–340.

West, Jane. *Letters to a Young Lady in Which the Duties and Character of Women are Considered*. In *The Feminist Controversy in England 1788–1810*, ed. with an introduction by Gina Luria (New York: Garland, 1974; rpt. from London, 1806).

Wollstonecraft, Mary. *Thoughts on the Education of Daughters. In The Feminist Controversy in England 1788–1810*, ed. with an introduction by Gina Luria (New York: Garland, 1974; rpt. from London, 1787).

———. *A Vindication of the Rights of Woman*, ed. Carol Poston (New York: New American Library, 1983).

———. *The Wrongs of Woman: or, Maria: A Mary Wollstonecraft Reader*, ed. Barbara Solomon and Paula Bergren (New York: New American Library, 1983).

Index